TEACHING THE
MENTALLY RETARDED CHILD

Teaching the
Mentally Retarded Child

By NATALIE PERRY

COLUMBIA UNIVERSITY PRESS

New York and London

To Walter

Foreword

In the past twelve years classes for severely retarded children have been established and they are growing in number at an ever-increasing rate. Many parents, who have hitherto preferred to keep their retarded children at home rather than send them to institutions which were overcrowded and unable to offer adequate training, are now joining together to seek more acceptable facilities.

Training programs for the severely retarded have been developed in a variety of settings: neighborhood houses, churches, club buildings, park field houses, colleges, renovated homes and school buildings, as well as in institutions built specifically for these children. The classes have been financed by state and local governments, community chests, parent organizations, private tuition, individual and group donations, or a combination of these. With such growing interest in these youngsters, questions regarding the nature of school programs are being raised by all concerned with their welfare.

The help that a teacher needs in planning and developing programs for severely retarded children may be supplied in cities by professional people to whom the teacher can turn for advice and with whom she shares responsibility for the program. In small towns the teacher must often assume major responsibility, although she may receive some guidance from others such as the staff in a public school. But the teacher in a rural community will, more than likely, have no one to help her and will probably have complete responsibility for organizing the class and developing the training program.

Teachers of the severely retarded, then, may or may not need to know how to organize a program; but once the program is under way, the role of each teacher, no matter what the setting, will probably not differ markedly from that of other teachers in the same field. The philosophy, methods, and curriculum given here can be applied by a teacher in most school situations for severely retarded children. The teacher should modify them in accordance with the amount and type of space, the variety of facilities available, and the number of children and the degree of their retardation.

Suggestions in this book should be considered tentative until better ways of helping severely retarded children are developed. It is hoped, however, that the kinds of programs and procedures found successful in the various schools with which the author has been associated will be of value to all teachers working in this new and fascinating field.

I am indebted to many people for their assistance in the preparation of this book. I wish to thank the following in particular for their reaction to the contents and for their suggestions: Egan A. Ringwall, Director, Psychological Clinic, University of Buffalo; Ray Graham, Assistant Superintendent, Illinois Department of Public Instruction; Elizabeth Boggs, President, National Association for Retarded Children; Viktor Lowenfeld, Head, Art Education Department, Pennsylvania State College; I. Ignacy Goldberg, Assistant Director, Mental Retardation Project, Columbia University; Ralph C. Preston, Professor of Education, University of Pennsylvania; Florence H. Stewart, Director, Lochland School, Geneva, New York; Betty Hilty, Supervisor, School of the Association for the Help of Retarded Children, Niagara Falls; Dorothy Ann Frye, Director, Seguin School, Berwyn, Illinois; and Anna Skiff, Health Education Associate, Medical Foundation, Boston. To the many others who looked over my outline or parts of my material, to those who raised stimulating questions and offered helpful comments, I am most grateful.

Special acknowledgement is due the staff members and parents of the Sunshine League—Erie County Chapter Association for the Help of Retarded Children, Inc., Buffalo, New York, who so willingly cooperated with me in preparing this book during the many fruitful years I worked there as school coordinator.

My thanks go to those teachers and administrators whose ideas have stimulated or supplemented my own. Over the years I have come across a great variety of methods and materials; some of these we tried out successfully with severely retarded children and subsequently I incorporated them into the development of the eclectic curriculum presented here. It is often difficult to know where an idea for a long-standing classroom practice originated, but the written sources which I have more recently read and used as references in the preparation of my book are listed at the ends of various chapters as "related reading" or in the bibliography at the end.

I also wish to express my appreciation for the fine editorial work of my two sisters, Madeline Preston and Eleanor Grahl, for the understanding secretarial help of Loretta Knowles and Pauline Inguaggiato, and, most recently, for the valuable suggestions of my husband, Walter Gruen, psychologist. I, of course, assume full responsibility for interpretation and content.

Thanks are also due Robert L. Smith who generously donated his time, and whose expert photography enriches the meaning of the text.

NATALIE PERRY

Brookline, Massachusetts
May, 1960

Contents

Illustrations

TEACHING THE

MENTALLY RETARDED CHILD

I. Home-School Relationships

A good home-school relationship is essential for the optimal development of the severely retarded child as well as for the development of an adequate training program. Parents often need support from the teacher to gain confidence while learning to cope with the unique problems confronted in helping their retarded child to develop to his fullest. As the parents come to feel that they are competent to help in all phases of their child's growth, and to understand that the teacher has an interest in their efforts, they will be ready for the teacher to discuss with them what the long-term goals for their child are and how the special program of the child's class is designed to meet those goals.

Parents need more interpretation in understanding school goals for the retardate than they do in understanding the more commonly accepted educational goals for the average school child. It is not surprising that parents think of "book learning" in connection with school goals, and find it difficult to accept the idea that learning to tie a bow, for example, is a more realistic school goal for a severely retarded child.

THE SCHOOL'S RELATIONSHIP WITH INDIVIDUAL FAMILIES

Learning from the severely retarded child's parents about his development and current behavior at home will contribute to the teacher's understanding of her pupil and will aid her in working with him.

The severely retarded child is even more in need than the

average child of consistency in home-school guidance of his growth and development, because he has exceptional difficulty in carrying over learning from one situation, the school, to another situation, the home. He needs the continuity of cooperative effort between teacher and parents to help him establish consistent patterns of behavior.

The Teacher's Role

A teacher may have had little experience in working with parents and will be most fortunate if she has a more experienced person who can advise her, such as a school social worker, school psychologist, visiting teacher, parent-education counselor, experienced supervisor for trainable classes, or understanding principal. Any one of these people could be helpful in interpreting a group of parents to the teacher, in planning with her for parent conferences, in counseling with the parents on various problems, in referring parents to other agencies for help, and in developing an active interest on the part of parents, as individuals and as a group, in the operation of the trainable program.

Whether or not there are trained workers to help with home-school relationships, the wise teacher will plan to have some contacts with individual parents. Parents feel it is the teacher who can tell them best about the progress of the child in school, and they like to tell the teacher of his achievements at home. A teacher will generally see the parents alone, but at times she may wish to ask the parents if a certain professional member of the school staff may join the conference.

Initial Contacts with Parents: The time at which the teacher herself will first talk with the parents depends upon how much responsibility the teacher is given in determining the course of the training program. In a large public program, the teacher may not meet the parents until the first day of school, since previous contacts with parents and child may have been made by a psychologist or other staff member before assigning the child to the teacher's class.

Some teachers learn a great deal about a child from information given to them or to other staff members by parents either verbally or on required forms. (See Appendix A, p. 237 for an example of one such form.) The parents' written permission is necessary to obtain information from hospitals and doctors who have studied the child. Reports from or interviews with these sources are valuable in order that the school staff know as much as possible about each child. Recent psychological and medical examinations should be required of all school entrants. Sometimes even these are inadequate because of a child's special problems. The parents may therefore be required to have the child studied completely in a clinic which provides diagnosis with a team approach, including psychiatric and neurological examinations.

All reports about the child are, of course, confidential. Every teacher should realize that information about the child and his family, including the teacher's own observations, is for no one except for the teacher or other professional staff member helping her with the child. There have been many unfortunate situations where teachers have acted unprofessionally in mentioning such private matters to other people. Untrained volunteers and office personnel who type or keep records or come into contact with the parents also need to be impressed with the confidentiality of information they acquire. The teacher, if submitting reports to be typed, can omit names and fill them in later herself. The teacher should talk to all people planning to help at school about the strictly confidential nature of what they observe about particular children or their families.

When outside agencies or individuals ask for confidential information in conversation, perhaps on the telephone, the teacher should act according to the policies of the school. In many schools, information is only given upon written request, with the written permission of the parents.

Reports from other agencies, even if they are recent, may not give an adequate behavior picture of a child for determining his placement in class. Perhaps a report on adjustment to a previous situation which was much too difficult, described him as being ill-adapted to any group activities. The same child might respond better in a program and environment more suited to his individual needs. Sometimes hyperactive children can only benefit from being in a school where extraneous materials are kept out of sight, and when class periods are very short and geared to their special needs. For such reasons it is most helpful for the school to see the child, preferably with other children as well as alone, before placing him in a trainable group. Consideration must be given to the feasibility of grouping the children somewhat homogeneously in order to develop an effective training program.

When plans are being made to enroll a child, it is wise to include both mother and father in preliminary conferences. Each may contribute different information and insight about the child. A school case worker can assist the teacher greatly by being included in these initial interviews as well as at some future conferences. It is advisable to find out the parents' own evaluation of the child and what they consider important for him to learn. This may provide the teacher with some cues as to where to start in helping the parents understand the school goals and the role of the school in training. If the parents' aspirations are too high and their plans unrealistic, their goals for the child in the near future and for his later life can come closer together as parents and teachers talk things over.

The principles which apply to these early conferences are to be the bases for later conferences, though they will vary somewhat as parent and teacher become better acquainted and mutual confidence is established.

Parents' Preliminary Observations: When parents considering enrollment of their child observe a trainable class in session and see the children who are already enrolled, the teacher should see the parents after class, or some trained person should be on hand during or after the parents' visit to answer their questions and interpret what was observed. In the beginning it is common for parents to feel that their child is much more like the average child than the children already in the group, and may have reservations about his placement in it. Although the child might be happiest and able to function best in that particular group, his parents may need to be persuaded to accept plans to place the child in the class recommended for him.

Preliminary Contact with the Child: Before the child is introduced into the group, he should come with a parent for a visit with the teacher so that he can get acquainted with her and she can learn more about the child's developmental level and how he learns. This is an opportunity for the teacher, by observation, to gain some impression of the relationship between the child and parent—parental overprotection, shame, rejection, warmth, perfectionism, or defensiveness; and child overdependence, self-confidence, exhibitionism, or hostility. The teacher can understand more of parent and child as she observes them together from time to time.

The First Parent-Teacher Conferences

After the child is enrolled in school, the mother or father usually like to have opportunities to talk to the teacher about the child. Although this can be done informally, it should not be in a room with the child or when the teacher is with her class. Even if retarded children may not seem to understand the words of a conversation, they may sense a certain feeling from tone of voice or manner of behavior, or they may understand more than one would expect, and thereby become anxious. The teacher can suggest a conference time or, for short talks, may confer by telephone or letter. She may use the latter methods to inform the parents about relatively small matters which she feels are of immediate importance; but extreme care should be taken to avoid misunderstandings which might arise from poorly expressed communications with particularly sensitive parents.

Since parents will want reports concerning their child's adjustment to the new school, they should be encouraged to discuss this with the teacher soon after the child is enrolled. After about a month or two, when the child has made an initial adjustment so that the teacher has a clearer impression of how he usually functions in various class situations, a conference should be scheduled. New parents frequently approach these conferences with misgivings, since they are concerned that their child, as in the past, may not be making much progress. The teacher should clearly point out the purpose of these conferences: (1) to give the teacher the opportunity to learn more about the child from those who know him best; (2) to give the parent a picture of the child and his activities at school; and (3) to encourage the parent to participate in planning the kinds of learning experiences the child should be having currently and in the very near future.

Planning the Conference: The teacher should plan her conferences carefully, going over her records on the child's school behavior for the period to be studied, summarizing the general picture he presents and noting progress—minimal though this may be in the first few months—and problems concerning his adjustment and growth. She may need to review for herself the material in the child's record file from hospitals and specialists, so that she has a clear understanding of his handicaps and potentialities. She will review what she knows of his home background and the attitudes of his parents. With this background material on the child, the teacher can plan the tentative school goals to be discussed with the parent. Before the conference the teacher may want to talk over her plans with her supervisor.

For the first conferences, the teacher should plan to emphasize the child's positive qualities and de-emphasize the child's problems, until the parents feel comfortable in the conference situation. In planning what to discuss, the teacher should also keep in mind the length of the conference. If possible, an hour should be allowed. It is good practice to inform the parent concerning the amount of time scheduled for the conference.

During an individual interview, the parents should be invited to contribute their suggestions. The teacher may explore with them what the child does at home and what their attitudes are toward his home accomplishments. As she learns more about the parents' evaluations of the child and what the parents think significant in the child's accomplishments, the teacher begins at a more realistic level to help the parents understand what she is trying to do for the child.

At this conference, if the parents are ready, or at a later one the teacher and parents can review specific school goals for a certain period of time, such as a semester. In the following conferences the parents and teacher can again discuss these goals, in light of the progress which has been made. The parents have, then, tangible evidence that the school is interested in the child and capable of helping him. After noting achievements this far, goals for the next period can be planned on the basis of his progress, and on the additional knowledge acquired by teacher and parents about his needs and abilities.

When talking about goals or progress with parents, it is necessary to be specific and concrete if effective communication is to take place. For example, it is advisable to report: "Johnny can get the toe of his rubber on his shoe now," rather than "Johnny is doing more for himself." The teacher should also explain goals or kinds of progress in such terms that parents will be able to recognize their value. Instead of saying merely, "He can alternate beads now," explain, "He can string a whole lace of big and little beads, alternating sizes. This shows that he is able to concentrate and that he distinguishes size." Rather than talking about bead-stringing, however, the teacher may wish to discuss self-care skills or domestic skills that the parents can observe at home and in which they can expect or watch for improvement.

Making Referrals: The teacher will not have answers to all a parent's questions. She should feel free to say to parents before giving an answer to something they have asked, that she would like to think it over or talk about it (in general terms) with someone who has more knowledge about the particular problem under discussion; or she can advise the parents where they could seek further information about it. She can later ask the principal, case worker, or other trained adviser for further information, or for advice to give the parents as to where to go for the information they seek.

Even though it may be desirable for the social worker or principal to refer the parents to specific agencies, the teacher should know the resources in her community upon which the school could call to aid parents with specific problems. Most cities and some towns have a community planning organization such as a Council of Social Agencies or Welfare Council from which a teacher may obtain information regarding the kind of help each of the many recognized agencies in the community is prepared to give. Such problems as the following should not be handled by the teacher, but by a case worker or a community agency: severe behavior problems, inter-family problems, financial problems, medical problems, the problem of institutionalization. The person referring the parents will want to prepare them, so that they will expect only the service that the agency has to offer. For example, parents would be disappointed if they went to a child guidance clinic with the hope that their child would become brighter, when the main help given them might be in their adjustment to the problem of having a retarded child.

Continuing Contacts with Parents

Throughout the school year the teacher will continue to make contacts with parents, new and old, and encourage them to make contacts with her. Parents may have various matters they wish to talk over with the teacher and will expect to hear from time to time how the child is getting along in school.

Written Reporting by the Teacher: To improve her future contacts with parents and the plans for their child, a teacher will find it advisable to write up not only her own reports on the child but also the results of each parent conference.

Presenting written reports on the child to his parents has the advantage of reaching both parents more readily, but the disadvantages are of misinterpretations and of fostering possibly unhappy comparisons by mothers and fathers of the different children in the class, rather than helping the parents appreciate the progress their own child has made. There is probably less chance of misinterpretation if the teacher talks from a written report or from notes but encourages verbal reactions from the parents and tries to make sure the parents understand the material covered as they discuss it together. Brief notes of one or two sentences describing some new achievement of a child can be sent home with the child from time to time. Such notes keep the parents in touch with the child's school activities and assure them of the teacher's interest.

The Parents' Contributions: After parents and teachers have communicated often enough so that the parents know the goals of the school and are not defensive if the teacher asks about the parents' goals for the child, the teacher may be able to encourage the parents to work toward some of the same goals that the school believes are important for the child. Some parents would even be willing to keep records relating to certain areas of particular importance for their child on which the school was also recording in detail—perhaps some problem of behavior. Toilet-training and such habits are best established with close cooperation and careful record-keeping on the part of both home and school.

In many cases a teacher can do more harm than good if she is over-eager for information from parents about the child's behavior at home. Many a father and mother feel, because their child achieves so little and behaves differently from most children, that they have done a poor job as parents, and do not like to talk about problems their child has or difficulties they have with him. A teacher must proceed very slowly and with sensitivity in helping parents to understand the value to the child of this type of cooperative exchange of information.

Even if the parents relate problems about their child freely to the teacher, it is inadvisable for a teacher to give helpful advice as to how to deal with the youngster at home unless specifically requested. One needs to have a broad background of experience and a very wide knowledge of the child and his home; certainly, a teacher should offer her suggestions only very humbly when she considers the parents' many years of living with and planning for the child. Unless her suggestions are constructive and accepted as suggestions rather than criticism, they will not be helpful to anyone.

Parent Observations at School: Parents will be better able to visualize their child's continuing needs and the goals of the school program if they have the opportunity to observe their child in his school situation from time to time. How a parent interprets what he sees in school will, of course, depend upon how he feels about his child and the school. Many parents may not have known retarded children other than their own and may feel that the other children in the class behave very differently from their own. These parents might profit from informal contacts with some of the children at P.T.A. picnics and school parties, where they come to see the children as individuals and notice that they behave in many respects on the level of their own youngster, though in some ways they may function better and in others, less well.

A child will naturally behave differently if he knows his parents are at the school or if he sees them in the classroom. A little pane of one-way vision glass can be placed in a schoolroom door. If the teacher wishes, this pane can be kept covered, so that observations take place only when arranged. If a small pane of plain glass is already in the classroom door, a piece of tinted cellophane, doubled, can give a one-way vision effect, if the hall is very dark, and the classroom light.

When a parent has to observe from within the classroom, she can sit in an inconspicuous corner or behind a screen with large perforations, where she can pretend to be assisting the teacher by writing. The child will know she is there, but may ignore her after a while if the parent understands she is to be as unobstrusive as possible.

Any time parents observe at school, they should be prepared to remain long enough to talk with the teacher or other staff member after observing. From such visits parents may begin to realize the difficulties that a severely retarded child has in being taught with a school group rather than individually, although from a social standpoint group training is usually the better situation for him. Most parents will come to appreciate the amount of stimulation and encouragement that is being given their child in order to have him benefit from the learning experiences to which he is exposed. After a school visit, parents may be better able to understand the teacher's answers to their questions as to why their child is not going into a more advanced class, or why he is not learning to read and write.

Interpreting the Child's Rate of Progress to Parents: Although a teacher may begin to feel she is communicating and interpreting successfully to certain parents, and the parents seem pleased with the progress of the child, she should not be surprised or discouraged if she finds these parents later feeling dissatisfied with the school program for the child. At first a child may make progress quite noticeable to the parents, who then begin to feel the child is over the big hurdle of starting to learn. They may expect, at the end of a year, changes in class activities corresponding to changes similar to those between kindergarten and first grade.

The teacher may continually need to point out that severely retarded children will stay much longer at one level of development, playing the same kinds of games and working with the same kinds of materials over a much longer period of time than the average child. Although the parent may think of his six-year-old as being at least ready for kindergarten work, the retarded six-year-old will be ready to participate in only some of the kinds of activities and respond to only some of the types of equipment in the usual nursery school. After being in school a number of years, he may still be enjoying and benefiting from play with big blocks, dolls, and such activities usually considered for much younger children. Naturally the teacher will include a greater variety of activities, especially little school jobs, crafts and self-care skills which young children do not ordinarily have in school; but she will continue to use materials familiar to the child that she knows are of interest and value to him and on his level of ability even when the parents feel that the child should have outgrown such materials and should be bored with them. Often parents are feeling their child must at least be ready for writing and reading books, when in fact he is not yet capable of drawing a circle, naming colors, or listening with interest to a story. The teacher needs to interpret again and again the needs of the child and the goals of the program.

The Child's Contribution: A child himself, with encouragement from the teacher, can contribute to the parents' knowledge of his school program. This may not always, however, be a happy experience for everyone. If a child takes home work he has done himself, it may be too imperfect to please the parents, and other children in the family may ignore or laugh at his efforts. On the other hand, a parent, when he sees what the child has begun to learn, may put pressure on him to do it again at home and may confuse or worry him by teaching him in a way that he does not understand or for which he is not ready. It is highly desirable to wait until the parents become well acquainted with the school's goals and activities before sending the child home with tangible examples of his work.

A retarded child may, however, be his own report card. He may not be communicative concerning his school activities, but he will often give cues as to what he is learning by his behavior. It might be expected that he will show that the school is salutary for him by his emotional tone and general behavior when he returns from school. A child who arrives at home in good spirits, or with greater interest in his home, is no doubt learning at school some important things about living.

Carry-Over of Specific Training: If parents become interested in carrying over into the home what their child is learning in school, the teacher can discuss certain self-help skills and habits which can be taught at home and at school simultaneously— traveling to and from school alone being a good example. There will be other learning activities, such as bow-tying, which the teacher will feel would better be taught entirely at school. Otherwise, the child may be confused instead of helped because of variations in school and home teaching methods. There will even be instances where the teacher will wish to discourage rather than encourage the duplication at home of some of the toys used by the child in school. Reasons for such decisions will have to be given to the parents who wish to help at home.

In regard to the value of carry-over, then, the main point is to have the parents understand the specific kinds of toys, materials, and methods that can probably be used successfully at home, and the skills and habits, attitudes and concepts the child is developing at school which, with encouragement, may show some carry-over into the home.

PARTICIPATION IN THE SCHOOL BY GROUPS OF PARENTS

Besides helping their own child at home, parents who are sincerely interested in furthering the training process of their retarded child may best contribute to this end by participating with other parents in the activities and interests of the school or class as a whole. Often a parent gains a great deal of understanding about the school through his contact not only with the staff, but also with another parent or group of parents.

Enlisting Parent Participation

A new teacher who does not know most of the school parents will find that one capable and friendly parent representative cooperating with her can help her establish a working relationship with the parent group. The parent representative can find out the special abilities and interests of other parents, information that will be valuable in encouraging parent participation. Although participation at first may be only in small ways, even this small contribution will lead the parents to a greater understanding of what the school is trying to accomplish. A wide range of helpful activities offered to the parents has a good chance of attracting a high percentage of them. Beginning activities might include: shopping or borrowing something for school use, making cookies for a school party, making smocks or curtains for school, repairing and painting furniture and equipment, making a form board or other small piece of equipment, accompanying a class on a trip, showing or taking movies of children's activities, or soliciting certain kinds of outside volunteer help. Later, as parents with special talents and understanding become well acquainted with the program and children, they may be asked to show other parents around the school, write about school activities under the direction of the school staff, play a musical instrument or demonstrate some other skill before the class, or, if a registered nurse, assist the doctor in giving inoculations. (It is inadvisable, however, to have a parent participate in the class in which her own child is a member.)

Through activities like these, the parents become more closely associated with the school and gain a knowledge of the training program. They also become acquainted with each other and are therefore ready to participate in parent meetings.

Group Programs

With assistance from someone experienced in group work, an especially good program for parent participation can be planned. Parents become more interested and contribute more toward improved parent-school relationships when they formulate a program under their own leadership. There will be much accomplished and learned if parents themselves can be encouraged to take the responsibility for their activities even though the school staff should probably advise, and be ready to render assistance when called upon.

Participating in group activities with parents of other retarded children definitely benefits the individual parent. Besides giving him a feeling that he is helping his child, he gains for himself a new circle of friends drawn together to work on a common problem. In this group, perhaps for the first time, he does not feel isolated with his special problem of having a retarded child, and he is continually reassured by contacts with the other parents. As he talks more freely with them, he gradually perceives his own situation in better perspective, and he, his retarded child, and the rest of the family will all benefit.

At the beginning of the school program in the fall, the school staff may arrange a meeting with the parents at which teachers describe the program and activities, and parents have an opportunity to get acquainted with other parents and the staff. If this meeting is successful, parents may want a similar one from time to time.

Parent-Teacher Associations: With or without a suggestion from the staff, parents may want to start a parents' group— perhaps a P.T.A.—with scheduled meetings in which parents raise questions about the school, plan activities to help the school, and learn the goals of the school program. The P.T.A. may arrange for the showing of films about mental retardation at its meetings and invite speakers (including the teachers) to talk about various aspects of the field of mental retardation. Small study groups of parents may be formed to study particular problems. The school P.T.A. may wish to affiliate with the National P.T.A. This is often salutary for these parents, who gain recognition from such membership and who soon learn that they have some interests in common with parents who do not have a retarded child.

Discussion Groups: Through participation in P.T.A., a parent may develop insight into his child and the school program. He may also gain insight into his own feelings about his child and how to help him by regularly attending a small discussion group. Such discussion groups, which usually meet weekly over a specified period of time, may be especially therapeutic for parents concerned about some of the problems they are facing or anticipating with their retarded child: toilet-training, the cerebral palsied child, discipline, sex education of the adolescent, or planning for the older retardate. These discussions are led most effectively by a psychologist, social worker, doctor, or group worker who understands the problems of the parents. The purpose of such meetings is often not to acquire specific information but to air feelings about having a retarded child and to learn how to handle these feelings in order to live more comfortably with him.

Organizations for the Retarded: In many communities, the parents interested in programs for their retarded children often join with parents of other retardates to form organizations for the retarded, some of which have very broad purposes. An example of the many fine organizations is the Association for the Help of Retarded Children, with its local chapters throughout New York State. It works for the betterment of retarded children, encouraging action along such lines as: public understanding of the problem, public school classes for mentally retarded children, community recreational programs, improved legislation, proper institutional care, increased and coordinated services from public and community supported agencies, and provisions for professional training of needed personnel. Such local organizations for the retarded often are affiliated with the National Association for Retarded Children, which works along lines similar to the A.H.R.C. It also gives considerable attention to research. The N.A.R.C. and the most effective local groups include professionals and other citizens interested in the field, as well as parents.

Parents who join organizations like these derive satisfactions from a sense of belonging to and working toward something much bigger than themselves and their own retarded children. At the same time, a parent's functioning in such a group often contributes to his own understanding of the goals for severely retarded children. The parent learns not only from specialists and other parents but also from reading the association's publications or other literature recommended by the association or housed in its library.

Home-School Misunderstandings

Even when there has been considerable communication between home and school, and where the school staff has been interpreting to parents frequently, parental aspirations may continue to be far above the possibility of achievement of the severely retarded children.

Occasional misunderstandings between parents and staff inevitably arise. For just such eventualities, the teacher needs interested professional advisers, preferably in the form of a professional advisory council, to review the school's goals and interpret them to the parents' organization or, if there is none, to the parents themselves. At the same time, there should be a parents' council which would act as a sounding board for parents' irritations and could discuss any problems with the school staff and advisory committee before an unnecessary explosion occurs. School committees composed of parents, professionals (including staff representation), and laymen have also been very successful in ironing out seemingly irreconcilable conflicts or misunderstandings.

There will always be unresolved conflicts, because there will always be parents who cannot quite accept the kind of program the school staff feels is the best that can be offered their children. Some of these parents will withdraw their youngsters. Others will continue to send them to school, but will express feelings of resentment and antagonism toward the school and its staff.

A teacher need not feel too overwhelmed by attacks upon the school or upon herself personally, if she is doing what she and the other authorities in the field believe is best. She will realize that parents of an average child are not always pleased with his accomplishments and naturally hope that it is the school, rather than the parents or child, which may be responsible for the discrepancy between the parents' picture of what the child should have learned to do and what he is actually doing. Teachers of retarded children will attempt to maintain their objectivity and at the same time will keep trying to interpret to the parents the school goals for the severely retarded. Whether to resolve a sudden conflict or to work on long-term goals, it is of great importance to bring parents and others interested in the retarded child together—the parents to provide the dynamic quality so necessary for progress, and the professionals and other interested citizens to lend strength, special knowledge, stability and perspective to the parents' efforts.

RELATED READING

Dittmann, Laura L. *The Mentally Retarded Child at Home: A Manual for Parents.* Washington, D.C.: Children's Bureau Publication No. 374. U.S. Government Printing Office, 1958.

Gabbard, Hazel F. *Working With Parents.* Bulletin No. 7. Washington, D.C.: U.S. Government Printing Office, U.S. Department of Health, Education, and Welfare, 1949.

Gabbard, Hazel F., and Gertrude M. Lewis. *Reporting Pupil Progress to Parents.* Education Brief, No. 34. Washington, D.C.: U.S. Government Printing Office, U.S. Department of Health, Education, and Welfare, 1956.

MacDonald, J. Clifford. *Role of the Parent.* New York: National Association for Retarded Children, Inc., 386 Park Avenue South, 1956.

Scarborough, Willie H. *A Letter to Parents.* New York: National Association for Retarded Children, Inc., 386 Park Avenue South, 1954.

Stacey, Chalmers L., and Manfred F. DeMartino (editors). "Counseling with Parents," *Counseling and Psychotherapy with the Mentally Retarded.* Glencoe, Illinois: The Free Press and the Falcon's Wing Press, 1957. Chapter IX, pp. 380–460.

Symposium: "Counseling the Mentally Retarded and Their Parents," *Journal of Clinical Psychology.* Monograph Supplement No. 9 (April, 1953), pp. 1–26. (Reprints distributed by the Association for the Help of Retarded Children, Inc., 200 Fourth Avenue, New York.)

II. The Trainable Child and His Teacher

WHO HE IS

The term "trainable child" in present usage refers to a severely retarded child whose rate of intellectual development is markedly low (usually including the group with an intelligence quotient ranging from 50 down to 35 or 30). When four years old chronologically, he is, in many ways, similar to an average child of one or two years of age. Although he continues to mature intellectually, he will not be unlike a child of three to six years in many aspects of his development when he is twelve years old.

The trainable child, even when confronted with the learning tasks of a younger child of the same mental age, is not able to learn all those tasks, and what he does learn he may grasp at a much slower rate and frequently in a qualitatively different way. He shows little imagination and deals with concrete rather than abstract kinds of knowledge. His capacity to understand academic subjects is limited to simple rote learning and he has difficulty transferring this learning to everyday situations. Few trainable children are able to fit into our present society to the extent of supporting themselves and living independently, but most can make known their wants, learn to care for themselves, be of use at home and, with supervision, get along with their neighbors in the community.

Until recent years the trainable child was excluded from

most public schools, but now classes are being established especially for him. He is usually identified in kindergarten or first grade because of his poor adjustment or inability to learn in class, and he is then referred to the school psychologist for evaluation. Often a psychiatrist also will see a child who tests very low. The diagnosis of the latter may be of special significance. In organizing a class for trainable children it is advisable to try to select only the child whose diagnosis indicates that his primary handicap is a mental retardation at the trainable level.

Needs of the Trainable Child

A trainable child has the same basic needs as all children: love, a sense of belonging, a sense of worth, a chance to express himself, an opportunity to realize his capacities. These children, probably more than most children, need the help of the teacher to find ways of meeting these needs.

Trainable children are often burdened with many handicaps in addition to (or as a result of) their mental retardation. Though there are many exceptions, they are apt to have motor responses which are awkward and uncoordinated, nervous systems which do not react quickly to stimuli, and weak physical constitutions lacking in normal resistance to infection. Many have physical handicaps such as epilepsy and loss of hearing or vision. Even when their sensory acuity is normal, trainable children may have specific perceptual problems. A proportionately large number of these children, as compared with the normal population, are distractible, hyperactive, and excitable.

A trainable child may often feel insecure because of his handicap, and his lack of understanding of his environment and of the people in it. He does not feel he belongs and this feeling is heightened by his not being readily accepted in our society. For an extended period he can neither communicate his wants adequately nor gain satisfactions from achievement because he does not achieve what others would recognize as important at his age. In order to help him derive these satisfactions, his interest in people and things needs to be stimulated. He has to be helped to talk; he has to be shown with much patience how to do the many things other children learn easily. His mother often is too busy or too tired to give him all the help he should have. He needs a person whose main function is to teach him things which will make life easier and more enjoyable for him.

A trainable child will need more help than most of us do to maintain himself in the community. A great deal of his happiness depends upon his good relationships with other people. It is very important, then, that he develop cooperative habits and attitudes. He needs to be with other children who are near his size and developmental level so that he can have friends and learn to get along with them. The teacher's job is to provide experiences which will help him in his emotional, social, physical, and mental development so that he will fit better into the pattern of life around him.

Potentialities of the Trainable Child

Just as any child is different from every other, so trainable children are different from each other. One cannot say specifically what a given trainable child will be able to achieve. Perhaps he will function at a very immature level, even in his own home. Or he may be exceptionally capable and responsible, functioning almost normally in certain aspects of his life. Most trainable children have potentialities for learning self-care and adjusting socially to the family and neighborhood. Some can learn to perform productive tasks in a sheltered environment at home or in a special school or workshop. With guidance, most are capable of partial self-direction. A number of older trainable boys and girls may be able to contribute to their own support. They may be employed at very simple jobs not requiring much speed, alertness, or independent judgment.

Most severely retarded are capable of great loyalty and devotion to those who are interested in them, for it is people rather than ideas or things that matter to them. The general friendliness of these children and their willingness to serve others are potentials that should not be ignored.

School Goals for the Trainable Child

Goals for trainable children can be grouped into three rather overlapping categories: (1) self-care, (2) socialization, and (3) expression. Self-care includes motor development, health, safety, and such skills as eating, tying shoes, and personal grooming. Socialization includes understanding and appreciating one's environment and interacting effectively with other people. Socializing activities would include following directons, playing group games, working on projects, learning perceptual skills, and making trips in the community. By "expression" we mean use of language, music, or any creative art through which a child can derive inner satisfaction. As with people of normal intelligence, expressing oneself through these media can be wholesome outlets to tensions and to aggressive feelings.

The purpose of emphasizing these three goals is to develop in the child a pattern of behavior which will make him as independent as possible. A mentally retarded boy or girl who can take care of his personal needs, who can participate acceptably in family or neighborhood work or play, and who has developed emotional stability, will be contributing indirectly as well as directly to the functioning of his home and community. To the degree that he can achieve some level of independence, he reduces his own frustration level. At the same time he enables his parents to spend more of their time and energy on other family and community responsibilities.

THE TEACHER OF THE TRAINABLE CHILD

It would be advisable for a teacher of the trainable child to have prepared herself for this work by study in these areas in particular: education, psychology, early childhood education, education of exceptional children, education of trainable children. The latter should include such course material as the teaching of arts, crafts, music, and recreation designed for the trainable; the interpretation of tests and measurements as applied to severely retarded children; the stimulation of language development in the trainable; occupational training for the severely mentally retarded; and social problems of the trainable.

Some colleges which train teachers for the educable mentally retarded are now relating course material to the teaching of trainable children, but few colleges as yet have courses specifically oriented to the problems of the very severely retarded. A student planning to work with these children, therefore, when taking courses in related fields, such as early childhood education and the education of the mentally handicapped, will need to try to apply what she can to the severely retarded. When studying the education of the mentally handicapped in general, a student should not develop unrealistic goals and methods for working with the trainable. She should be constantly aware of the differences between the trainable and the less severely retarded—the "educable" mentally handicapped.

Of the courses in the education of exceptional children, those emphasizing the teaching of subject matter (to higher level children) will be of less value in contrast to those which provide a rich understanding of the retarded child and of human behavior in general. Other subjects of value to the teacher of the trainable might include introductory courses in domestic science, group work, health and hygiene, physiology, anthropology, and genetics and eugenics.

The student, in addition to her course work, should have supervised experience with children in a nursery school or kindergarten, and in some other setting such as a group work agency, camp, residential school, or a home situation. It is very important, especially because of insufficient course material, that the student also receive in-service training in a good school for severely retarded children, since in this field it is necessary to observe well-trained, experienced teachers. Through working with them, through regular and frequent staff conferences, and through study of written materials concerning the children, the new teacher can gain an understanding of the trainable child and knowledge of how to approach and work with him.

State requirements for teachers of public school classes for the trainable vary. According to a survey reported by Samuel

Kirk (*Public School Provisions for Severely Retarded Children,* Albany: 1957), "State regulations reflect the emerging but yet unstructured program of teacher education." Information concerning requirements can be obtained from each state.

The same characteristics of a good teacher for average young children are needed for an effective teacher of the severely retarded. Emotional maturity, warmth, interest in working with the children and objectivity toward their problems are especially important aspects of the personality of the teacher of trainable children. A teacher of the trainable also needs to be inventive and original in making plans for helping each child.

When a teacher works with the same trainable children over a period of years, as is frequently the case, she has an opportunity to study each child, to know him well, and to build a good relationship with him. She may receive more than the usual amount of love and respect from her pupils because of their greater dependence. In turn, some of the younger children will need much mothering from the teacher. Even the older boys and girls, who often feel insecure and rejected, seek overt demonstrations of affection from the teacher: physical contact, the giving of presents, or performance of services for them which they could do themselves. A sensitive teacher will recognize how a child may be feeling and give needed reassurance, but will also keep in mind the goal of future happiness for each child: independence and adjustment to society. She must maintain her objective, professional role of educator in her relationships with both the pupil and his parents. She will work with the parents, not as case worker or family friend, but as their child's teacher who is trying to bring about a mutual understanding of common goals for him at home and school.

Grouping the Children for Classes

If the teacher is to determine the group into which a child should be placed, she will need to obtain information about the child. Some type of blank (see sample in Appendix, p. 237) for gathering information is helpful in evaluating the developmental level of the child.

Depending upon the school facilities and the staff available, certain criteria for admission into the class will need to be established. These criteria would necessarily include, in addition to the psychological and psychiatric evaluations, a report from a physician stating that the child is physically able to participate in the school program. It is also necessary that a child be emotionally and socially able to participate in the class program without requiring the undivided attention of the teacher and without endangering himself or others. Although reports from clinics, professional people who know the child, and schools he has previously attended may suggest how the child will behave in class, a trial period in the class is usually necessary before the teacher can really know whether the child can adjust to his new group situation. Another criteria for admission which may need to be included is that the child be toilet-trained.

In setting up classes for the trainable, the children need to be grouped according to developmental level, with social and emotional maturity being of primary importance. Intellectual ability is not a primary consideration in grouping these children. Much of the perceptual training is done individually, and other intellectual learning, such as language development, can be geared somewhat to each child's level even in group activities. The mental age range of a group of trainable children with a chronological age span of several years will not be as great as that in the usual public school class.

Some authorities suggest having special classes for youngsters who are particularly hyperactive and excitable, because they may learn better in situations adapted to their particular needs. This may not be feasible or even desirable for trainable level children with such behavior problems. No matter how carefully a teacher might plan the environment and teaching methods for a class of emotionally unstable children, each member would react to every other member and the results might be less effective than having them learn in a mixed group. There are advantages to having different types of children in a trainable class. The passive ones have a calming effect on the excitable children, while the latter may stimulate the others to speech and action. In teaching children on the trainable level, it may be more effective in a mixed class to work with a problem child for a short part of the day while the other members work or play on their own, than it is to try to set up a separate class for the emotionally less stable children.

It is possible to make successful groupings of trainable children with four or five years' difference in their chronological ages, such as five to nine, or thirteen to eighteen. Each child has to be studied carefully to see whether, emotionally or socially, he belongs in the more or less advanced group. Also, the child's size has to be considered. For example, a large, immature youngster might be a hazard to a young group and would therefore have to be placed in the advanced group because of his size.

Certain activities prove very successful when two classes of different maturity levels are combined. Two or three groups could well combine for singing games, lunch periods, special film showings, certain outdoor periods and some phonograph listening. One advantage of combining classes is that the younger benefit from emulating the older, while the older develop feelings of their own worth and attitudes of responsibility toward those less capable. Another advantage of combining groups is that it may add to the quality of the program. One teacher may be freed to accompany games on the piano while the other teacher directs the groups; or one teacher can supervise some of the older pupils' serving of lunch while the other supervises the children's eating.

But, generally speaking, it seems better to keep the groups separate. The more children there are together, the more distracted and excited they become and the less opportunity they may have for learning experiences.

Size of the Group: The size of a group depends on the developmental level of the children, the length of time they have been in school, the experience of the teacher, the amount of assistance she has, the physical set-up and the policy established by the school authorities. In public schools, for example, the number of children may range from five to fifteen, often with no assistance for the teacher.

It would seem that in a beginning class a teacher without assistance might work well with no more than six young, immature trainable children, with six to eight children in an intermediate class, and with seven to nine in an advanced class of older children. If the teacher has a full- or part-time assistant, she could have a somewhat larger class. If the teacher is inexperienced and the children in the group are young or particularly difficult, it is better to start with a very few youngsters, only gradually enrolling additional ones.

Parents ordinarily should not be asked to assist in class. Other volunteers who are dependable, emotionally stable, and willing to follow explicit directions can be of great help if they come frequently and regularly and are given orientation and close supervision.

Planning the School Program for the Trainable Child

In order to reach long-range goals for each child, it is necessary to plan periodically for the individual as well as for the class as a whole. The teacher of trainable children will find many problems connected with planning. She will be confronted with extreme ,individual differences and special handicaps among the children in her class. She may find the group behavior quite unpredictable, depending upon which children are present or absent. It is hard for her to know just what her particular children will be able to understand and what skills they can master and how to present effectively what she hopes the children can learn. No matter how difficult planning may be, achieving long-range goals without regular planning is almost impossible.

After the child's records have been studied, the teacher has a general idea of the prognosis for the child and the long-term future goals over the school years. Then semester and yearly goals will need to be charted: the skills and habits to be learned, and general activities and equipment to be used in developing these skills and habits. Finally, more specific activities for shorter periods of time can be planned. These monthly or bimonthly plans will be helpful in carrying out the yearly plans.

As the weeks go by, the plans will have to be revised—extending the time periods for some learning experiences, deleting other activities, reviewing more often than was planned. A teacher will be frustrated unless she uses her plans flexibly as general guides whether they be yearly or daily ones.

The following is a very abbreviated example of the kind of short-term planning which a teacher might do for a particular class of nine- to ten-year-olds on developmental levels of around three and a half to four and a half years, who have been in school a year or two. This sketch lists a few group activities which a teacher might particularly wish to emphasize and coordinate in the program. She would also include many other learning experiences as the plans developed and she observed the responses of the children. The teacher would tie in auditory and visual aids (stories, songs, pictures, films) to the firsthand experiences given in the outline.

In addition to the group plans listed, it is understood that there would be individual plans for each child. For example, the October plans might include emphasis on the color "orange" for a few children who might not yet know this. The teacher might plan for another more advanced child to learn how the pumpkin, attached by its stem, grows on the vine, whereas she would not plan to develop this concept with all the group at this time.

September to October

Orientation, adjustment of the new children to group.

Review of last year's skills, habits, knowledge, concepts.

Familiar activities and games to help children become better organized and work and play independently, thus freeing teacher to work with new children.

October to November

Trips to farm to pick out pumpkins for jack-o'-lanterns, to get corn stalks, to see pigs eat corn.

Visual Discrimination: big, middle-sized, and little pumpkins, the geometric shapes of features of various jack-o'-lanterns, and of the pumpkin.

Making jack-o'-lanterns from pumpkins.

Making jack-o'-lanterns and corn from clay and other art media.

Talking about corn: its color, use as food, the kernels, stalks.

Talking about pigs: their size, the noise they make, the food they eat.

Decorating room for Halloween with pumpkins, corn stalks, and jack-o'-lanterns.

November

Thanksgiving foods, including pumpkin and corn (language, sense training: smell, taste, color, shape).

Trips to farm to see and bring back samples of produce.

Self-expression centering around these foods.

December

Holiday plans: making gifts and decorating the room; having a party for parents.

January and February

Snow activities: making snow balls, sliding on sleds or snow coaster, making snow men, throwing snow at each other or at other targets.

Winter weather: talking about snow, cold, kind of wraps.

Simplified table-setting: tea parties in doll corner, colors of dishes.

The postman: his functions, playing postman.

Craft activities centering around Valentine's Day.

Setting table for Valentine's party: spoons, napkins, cups, and maybe knives (to cut cupcakes in half).

March and April

Continuation of table-setting practice.

Review of corn, planting of kernels in little pots.

Weather: rain replacing snow, wraps changing from winter ones.

Spring: talking about eggs, hens, chicks; visiting farm to see these, taking dried corn to feed them; collecting eggs to take to school.

Boiling and decorating eggs, putting them in baskets.

Postman: sending invitation to another class or to a few guests to attend luncheon party.

Luncheon party: boiling eggs, making prepared gelatin, serving bread and butter, milk.

Table-setting for party, including various tableware pieces and dishes.

May

Transplanting of corn.

Visits to farm: seeing spring corn or other plants coming up, chicks growing bigger; seeing baby animals, learning names.

Seeing plants started which were seen in fall as produce.

Composing letter to farmer thanking him for visits; presenting letter to postman.

Table-setting: outdoor picnic at a table.

Reviewing of skills, habits, concepts and knowledge developed during the year.

Independent work and play while teacher evaluates each child's achievement (such as table-setting).

Termination party (using table-setting abilities again).

By following such a planned program, the teacher will be reviewing learning experiences frequently and doing so in an interesting variety of ways so that skills will be better established and clear concepts will be developed. As the teacher looks over her plans, she can easily see if she is tying in a new learning experience introduced at the beginning of the year with its development and review each month.

Daily schedules for the class, as well as monthly plans, are important. Many of the best teachers may not have elaborate schedules written down for each day, but a good teacher will have a general outline for the daily periods, and a good idea of what she plans to do on a certain day during each of the periods. She will want to have a clear understanding of how she will introduce a new activity, stimulate the children in reviewing an old activity needing more repetition, make use of some material brought in the previous day by a child, or expand some new interest of the group. She may be facing a new behavior problem or the introduction of a new child into the group.

Daily, just as monthly plans, may not be carried through as outlined. Teachers will wisely have other ideas in mind should the class not respond to planned activities, and she will be ready for suddenly appearing critical incidents. However, it would be expected that most days the teacher would be able to use her plans, at least in part. (See Appendix B, pp. 242–45, for sample schedules.)

Transportation

One big problem in planning a program and making schedules is the irregular attendance of these children. They are more apt to be sick than the average child. Unless there are arrangements for school bus transportation, the children are usually brought to school by their mothers. With the best of intentions, a mother's many responsibilities may interfere with her getting her child to school regularly. More dependable transportation such as a school bus is of great help to trainable children, because they especially need to attend school regularly. Since they learn slowly and forget easily, they should have the routine and repetition which comes with regular attendance.

Whenever possible, the older boys and girls should be taught to use public transportation. (See Chapter IV for a description of learning to travel alone.) When all the children come in a school bus, the school should cooperate with the bus drivers in every way to help the children learn acceptable, safe travel behavior. In some cases, depending upon the number and developmental level of the children, it may be necessary for an extra adult to accompany the children, or for older children to supervise younger ones. Class discussions can help the older boys and girls conform to acceptable standards during their bus rides. The bus driver should keep the teacher informed about minor difficulties so that she can work out these problems before more serious ones develop.

Physical Set-Up for the School

Classes for trainable children have been conducted successfully in a great variety of settings, each of which may have drawbacks depending upon the developmental level of the group, the teacher-pupil ratio, and other factors. Public places such as churches or neighborhood houses may offer large rooms and extra facilities such as gym or woodshop, but they may lack storage space for all the school things which must be put away at the end of each day. Most public school classrooms have no facilities for practicing domestic and outdoor work, no place to isolate or work individually with a trainable child, no washroom where he can go unsupervised, and often a lack of facilities for meetings or conferences.

A renovated home makes a fine place for older boys and girls to learn domestic tasks and yard care, especially if there is access to the kitchen and utility room. Usually there are rooms for small groups or for individual work. Disadvantages frequently include a lack of large rooms, and the problems of financing and of meeting fire, zoning, health, and safety requirements of city authorities and insurance companies.

Minimum requirements for a school with classes for trainable children would be:

1. Building meeting general educational, city, and insurance standards for health, light, heat, and fire prevention, taking account of physically handicapped.

2. Easily accessible, enclosed playground facilities (especially important, since some of the children cannot be left out alone to play).

3. Space available for resting cots, since the children tire easily.

4. Adequate closet space and cupboards with doors that hook because of the need for a great variety of training materials to be stored out of sight.

5. Lockers and ample space in the classroom or in an enclosed hall for teaching dressing skills.

6. A large room for recreation and rhythms, without too many exits.

7. Bathrooms adjoining classrooms, one with a shower or tub.

8. A small room containing nothing within child's reach, for testing, speech, or isolation purposes. (Materials can be taken into the room as needed.) If necessary a good-sized playhouse without a roof may be built for this purpose.

9. An office for filing case records, telephoning, conferences with parents and visitors.

10. For observation, small high panes of glass in solid door. (If the teacher wishes it to be one-way at times, she can attach several layers of green cellophane to the pane and turn out hall lights so visitors cannot be seen.)

11. A good-sized kitchen with sink for washing clothes and rags.

12. School windows high, or with blinds, so children are not distracted by external stimulation.

13. Sound-proofing as an aid to lowering nervous tension of some of the youngsters.

14. School classrooms large enough for sitting or moving about without crowding, but avoiding large, empty areas which encourage running, wandering and asocial behavior. Partitions can break up a large room so that there will be prescribed sections for different activities.

General Principles Relating to the Teaching of the Trainable Child

While each severely retarded child is different, there seem to be some principles generally applicable to his training. I mention some of these in case the teacher should find them appropriate in working with various children in her group:

1. Trainable children more readily learn even in the beginning steps of an activity by being shown and guided, rather than by being given elaborate preparatory verbal instructions.

One method of teaching in the regular classroom is to begin with the teacher's explanation, followed by answers of the children to the teacher's questions and, finally, performance by the children, aided by the teacher's questions or suggestions from time to time. A trainable child, especially a young one, learns very little in this way. Instead, the teacher and the child would begin with the *doing* of a task, the teacher giving much assistance at first but expecting active participation by the child. Gradually the child will do more and more until he can do the job alone. It is valuable to have the teacher talk about the task during the activity and to encourage the children to talk about it afterwards.

Thus the trainable child develops knowledge and concepts, attitudes and appreciations. Instead of telling him that he must wash his hands before lunch every day and expecting him to do so because he is told, it is more effective to go with the child at the proper time and help him wash. At the same time the teacher can talk about what is happening, helping the child to focus attention on the activity and gain concepts relating to it. She may point out to the child that one always washes before eating. Later, the activity can be acted out in the song: "This Is the Way We Wash Our Hands," followed by: "This Is the Way We Eat Our Lunch," reinforcing the establishment of the sequence. Finally the child may be able to answer the question, "What must we do before we eat?" In this way, through habit training first, the child develops concepts—in this case, a health rule.

The way the older children learn safety rules is not by discussion. Although a little verbal preparation about safety rules before entering a woodshop may be helpful, the children will actually learn the rules by going with the teacher to the woodshop where they will each have a turn being shown by the teacher how to hold the saw and walk with it, and where to put hands and body when using the saw. As each child uses the saw, he will see that it cuts wood, and at this time the teacher can point out that it can also cut fingers and remind him to keep his free hand out of the way, letting the vise hold the wood. Later the class may be able to formulate the safety rules that operate in the woodshop.

Although the immediate objectives of the school curriculum will therefore be learning skills and habits, this does not mean that the development of knowledge and concepts, of attitudes and appreciations is not considered important. These are also major aspects of the curriculum. It is because the trainable child has difficulty in their mastery that we need to use the most effective way of developing them—through the teaching of skills and habits.

2. The severely retarded child, in contrast to the average child, seems to learn little incidentally, as compared to what he can learn through direct teaching. If he does not know how to use his handkerchief, it will be important for the teacher or parent, and probably both, to try to teach him. The teacher can seldom take for granted that such a child will "pick up" some skill or concept.

What has been said does not mean that the acquisition of skills and habits through direct teaching is all that is included in the child's school day any more than it means that the curriculum does not include developing concepts and appreciations. Some school activities (such as self-expression) may not include direct teaching, and others (such as resting and lunching) will not be primarily for the learning of skills.

3. In planning what a particular trainable child needs to learn, one should consider not only the child's mental age, but also his general developmental level. Growth in all developmental areas is not necessarily consistent in one child, so the teacher should note what her trainable child has just learned in one area and then encourage and stimulate him to take the next step in that particular area. She can get a good idea of what this next step should be by knowing the usual sequence in development for the average child and seeing where her trainable child is in this sequence.

Watch for signs of learning readiness. As with all children, a teacher observes her pupil to see when he is ready to learn. Otherwise, if he is exposed to a certain learning situation before he is ready, or if a readiness is not recognized when it appears, the child may become resistant to the activity when it is presented later. A teacher can see signs of readiness in many situations, one of which is play. She need not feel a failure at being unable to teach a fifteen-year-old boy how to kick a football if she has discovered that in free play period he chooses to pull a child in a wagon—the play of a four- or five-year-old; for football is an advance in development beyond wagon-play and there are probably intermediate steps which this boy needs to take first.

4. When possible, a child should see a need for the skill he is learning. One can increase motivation by arranging situations that will make the child feel the importance of being able to do a particular thing, and then foster in him the realization that it is something he can learn. As he attempts to learn it, recognition and success will help him see the goals more clearly. He will gain skills, habits, and concepts through the introduction of daily life experiences on a concrete level where the skills are often obvious. Other things will be learned only through extra drill and by means of games where the need is not so evident.

5. Much of what he can learn must be taught through specially devised techniques which make learning easier and more enjoyable for him. Skills will have to be separated into their component parts and each part taught thoroughly before the next step is introduced. It is advisable to set up a definite procedure for an activity and see that it is followed, step by step, each time. Being consistent in the method of teaching the activity will add to the effectiveness of the teaching.

6. The children seem to learn best when taught one thing at a time. If a child has learned to count five objects, he should then be taught to count six, but not seven until he has learned six. If he is learning to say the word "butter" when shown butter, he should not also be expected to learn the new concept "yellow" at the same time.

7. A severely retarded child needs much repetition and drill if he is to learn. Many short practice sessions that are repeated

at frequent intervals over a long period of time help the child to absorb and retain what he is learning. After the teacher is sure a learned response is very well established, she can go on to teaching something else, but she should remember to give plenty of opportunities for the practice of the response that has been learned so well, or the child will certainly forget it. (Of course, a teacher would not spend time teaching him something that he would not use at least occasionally.)

8. Even though practice and drill are essential for severely retarded children, frequent repetition with no slight variation in procedure may be of negative value. It encourages perseveration. Such rigid, repetitive behavior is often extreme in some trainable children. If perseverative behavior increases, the children will have greater trouble adjusting to life where changes, at least minor ones, occur almost constantly. Also, if there is little variation in drill work, a child may become accustomed to responding without thinking. In habit formation, response without too much thought may be effective; yet sometimes even here it is probably wise to shift the arrangement of materials or the location for the performance of the routine behavior. For example, the child may learn to brush his hair sitting down at a table before a mirror, but he can also learn to do this standing up and even without a mirror.

Exact repetition, though it may be advisable for habit training, is less likely to be effective where thought or insight is involved such as in counting objects. A child may learn to count colored beads on an abacus, but should also count colored jelly beans that are not fastened to a wire. Later he can count objects in other situations. Although slight changes in materials and situations are wise, the procedure and techniques of the counting should remain the same. The objects should be arranged in a row and the child will count the first, then the second, and so on. When he finally reaches the stage where he can count children, he will, for a long time, begin with the first in the row and count from left to right. Only after counting objects has been thoroughly established can some changes be introduced such as an informal arrangement of the children rather than the structured row. Slight changes are of great value in counteracting perseverative responses.

9. A child can only learn if he attends to what is being taught. With a teacher's providing the best motivation, she is sometimes unable to hold even the older trainable pupils' attention on anything but the most concrete material, which requires less intellectual effort. A very skilled teacher of the trainable, when relating a familiar, favorite story, can hold the attention of her class; but trainable children do not easily become absorbed in verbal material. A trainable child is usually much more interested in tangible objects—especially his classmate beside him whom he may hug or hit, smile or spit at. If he is not at the stage where he has begun to relate to his peers, he may try to get his teacher's special attention by talking to or smiling at her, or by being mischievous. If he is not yet at the level of being aware of people, he may become absorbed in his own body. Brain-injured children and other severely retarded children are especially attracted to moving objects such as cars seen through the windows, or the teacher's earrings, glistening objects such as sunbeams or eyeglasses, patterns or designs such as wallpaper or the egg-crate appearance of some fluorescent lights, and sounds, even if distant. We say that a child is "inattentive"; he may be attentive, but to something other than the lesson.

What can be done about "inattention"? Here are some suggestions for attracting, holding, or regaining a trainable child's attention, assuming the teacher has carefully planned her material to be challenging, but not too difficult, for the developmental level of most members of the class:

a) Active periods should be alternated with quiet periods to give the children a change which will increase their interest and give them an opportunity to relax. Relaxation, of course, can mean active physical play, after the children have been working quietly at their tables. Even when sitting quietly in the classroom, children can be stimulated to observe carefully, think, and answer questions about objects or pictures.

b) Distractions can be removed from the room so the children will be able to concentrate better. The teacher can wear gay clothes, but not striking prints and shiny jewelry. She may draw the blinds to exclude outside stimuli. She can close windows where traffic goes by, and open windows overlooking a more quiet area. She may arrange seating so that the excitable children cannot touch each other. She can limit the use of pictures, decorations, and displays of the children's work to the rooms and halls where activities do not require close attention, or she may use screens (sturdy, stable ones) to surround her group when it is together in a small area. Visual distractions can thus be kept to a minimum. Doors, if opaque, can hide interesting materials in the cupboards. Curtains can cover mirrors and picture displays which are not in use. The teacher usually will see that the children have nothing in their hands during a discussion session because they can scarcely resist playing with what they hold. In a "show and tell" period, the children can keep their objects under their chairs until each one's turn comes, or on top of a cupboard, if necessary.

c) The teacher can sit close to the children where she can see them all, look directly at those whose eyes are wandering, and touch a child to redirect his attention. It is surprising to learn that some teachers of trainable children conduct their music classes by sitting at the piano with their backs to the children.

The teacher, if she watches the children closely, will know if they are attending. It is easy for a teacher to become absorbed in what she is trying to teach and forget to watch the children. For example, when the child is learning to cut, a teacher may concentrate so intently on guiding the child's hand to keep the scissors on the line, that she does not notice the child's wandering attention.

d) During a demonstration, discussion, or story period, the teacher can use certain kinds of stimuli which help to hold the children's attention: (1) *Visual:* her own gestures and facial expressions, exaggerated and frequently changed; her movement from place to place or from sitting to standing; displaying of pictures or objects (one at a time). (2) *Auditory:* the teacher's own dramatic tones or changes of volume and pitch in her voice; her speed of talking; exaggerated emphasis; use of especially interesting words or vocal sounds, like a realistic-sounding bark of a dog; her singing of a song, clapping her hands, or using a rhythm instrument for a special sound effect. (3) *Other stimuli:* opportunities for the children to smell, touch, handle something shown, or to do or show something themselves. The children learn best by doing.

e) The children can be personally included in stories and discussions to focus their attention. Their names can be used. ("This little boy had red socks just like our Bobby's.") The teacher can also refer to the children's families at home.

f) Certain motivations can be used, if carefully selected, to help the children attend better. For some types of learning activities, there may be enough satisfaction and motivation to hold a child's attention if there is simply a task to be completed. Although an adult would expect a child to become bored using the same materials over and over, some retarded children may not only like, but also need, a good deal of repetition in perceptual motor tasks. Moreover, some motivations may be too emotionally charged for excitable children, distracting them from the task at hand.

g) Certain toys can help very distractible children to focus their attention on the current learning situation. The children need well defined limits to the number of ways to work with the materials, the amount of work to be done and the size of the working area. An inset puzzle has this type of definite structure. There is only one way to do it correctly—one place for each puzzle piece. There is an obvious end to the task and there is a limited area in which to work. In contrast, a box of cubes is a less structured material (though it can be made more so by telling the child to fit the cubes in the box). There are few limits as to how the cubes can be used, no well defined goal, no recognizable self-correction, and no clearly defined limitation of space. Beads and pegs can be used in well structured activities. These may help a distractible child to concentrate when trying to work independently without close supervision.

When structured materials are used, the task required by them should be varied from time to time and their difficulty increased. (For instance, there are great varieties of sizes, shapes, and colors of beads. If kept in many separate boxes according to bead type, different kinds of perceptual learning can take place in the use of them, as well as growth in concentration and independence. Besides merely stringing beads, a child can sort them by color into different boxes, match all the same ones on a string, alternate types, and count and string a given number of one and then another type).

Usually it is a waste of the teacher's time to give a whole class something as structured as form boards. Such activities have their place with a few children when the teacher is concentrating on teaching some other activity, perhaps a new one, to another child or to a small group of children.

As the reader can see at this point, the teacher who is best prepared for her group, by having a variety of props in the cupboards, in her pockets, or in her head, may have a physically tiring but more emotionally satisfying day, for the children will wander less, fuss less, and be more responsive.

h) If it sounds too strenuous, there is one last suggestion which is easier and sometimes more effective for teachers to use to gain complete attention: Stop the activities and remain perfectly quiet and relaxed, waiting.

In chapters following are lists of activities which represent examples of the kinds of experiences that seem appropriate for severely retarded children, arranged according to different levels of ability: Beginner, Intermediate, and Advanced.

Beginner, as it is used here, does not necessarily refer to a young child or to a pupil who has just started school for the first time. It refers to a child at the Beginner level of functioning in regard to the school program, or to certain school activities. Not only may there be an older pupil needing Beginner activities, but there also may be a young child who has never attended school before and yet is considered ready for Advanced activities in language, music, or some other phase of his development.

A teacher may wonder what level of activities is suitable for her class. Probably no one level will be, because some of the children will be more advanced than others and because each child's level of performance will differ depending upon the type of activity. If a child is particularly uncoordinated, he may need physical and craft activities on the Beginner level. He may, however, be relatively articulate and understand spoken language well enough to be ready for Advanced language activities. Although he may sing well and have a rather highly developed rhythmic sense and be able to benefit most from such activities on the Advanced level, his poor coordination may make it advisable for him to have body rhythms at the Beginner level. In other phases of his development, he may be at the Intermediate level.

Some children who in the past have been meeting constant failure, will benefit from work on a simple level, not because they lack the ability to do harder work, but because they are in need for the time being of a great many successes. A teacher may also find that a child who usually functions at an Intermediate level in most activities may function only at a Beginner level on a particular day. This may be due to emotional, social, or physical disturbances which have occurred even before the child arrived at school. The teacher will have to adjust her plans, so that she will present her pupil with simple enough activities to prevent frustration and help him feel comfortable on a trying day.

The children will also differ in the time it takes to progress from one level to another. An older but inexperienced pupil may progress fairly rapidly from the Beginner to the Intermediate level in a number of activities. Other pupils with less ability to grasp new situations may progress very slowly, regardless of their age.

It is not surprising, then, for a teacher to find that in any one type of learning situation, the level of activities she will need to plan for the children in her class may range from Beginner to Advanced. She may, for example, have a child who cannot say a word, and several children who are ready for Advanced speech. Because all members of one class are not on the same developmental level, and because a member may function at different levels in different activities, the lists have first been grouped according to the type of activity before being divided according to ability levels. This arrangement will help the teacher find activities suitable for each child in her class for any period of the day.

Often a teacher may not know the level of activity which would be appropriate for a child, especially a new child. She should try an activity, preferably a simple one, and if it is too easy or too difficult for the child, she can select other experiences on a more appropriate level.

The inexperienced teacher may feel overwhelmed at having to plan a program for individual members of the class who are at various stages of maturity. In the long run, it is less difficult than working with a trainable class in which all members are given the same work. In the latter situation, some children may become very upset because the activity is beyond their abilities, and others may engage in unplanned and distracting behavior out of sheer boredom.

In most situations, a teacher can work with each child at his own activity level, even when presenting similar materials to all. For example, all children may be encouraged to use the jungle gym. The Beginner will be guided in climbing to the first rung and then in walking along it, going no higher. The Advanced acrobat can be stimulated to climb to the top and slide down the pole. In craft work, the novice may need special aids which the Advanced pupil can do without. The teacher will find such aids described for each new type of activity.

There cannot, of course, be hard and fast lines drawn between the three different levels of activities. One level gradually approaches the next, and they may overlap. Throughout the book, activities introduced in a listing at one level are often also appropriate for children at a more advanced level. They have not been included in the more advanced lists, however, in order to avoid tiresome repetition. Not only activities, but also books, songs, and other educational materials may be suitable for both Beginner and Intermediate and even for the Advanced.

Where appropriate, the activities on one level have been arranged according to difficulty, with the simplest ones presented first. What is easy for one child may not prove so easy for another. The teacher will find that her own judgment of suitability of an activity may not coincide with the lists here. In spite of the hazards in making these artificial levels, it is felt that most teachers can find them helpful if they use them as guide lines only.

No list of activities relating to social and emotional development has been included. A moment's deliberation will reveal that these characteristics are already incorporated in most of the school program and would be of slight benefit to the children if introduced as isolated activities. Often activities have been included because of their superior social and emotional values. In the text, social goals and emotional factors related to the school activities are indicated before various activities are described.

RELATED READING

Cruikshank, William M., and G. Orville Johnson. *Education of Exceptional Children and Youth.* Englewood Cliffs, New Jersey: Prentice-Hall, Inc., 1958. Chapter VI, pp. 227–62.

Cruikshank, William M., and Norris G. Haring. *Assistants for Teachers of Exceptional Children.* Syracuse: Syracuse University Press, 1957.

Gesell, Arnold, and Catherine Amatruda. *Developmental Diagnosis.* New York: Harper & Brothers, 1954.

Gingeland, David R. "Some Observations in Evaluating the Progress of Severely Retarded Children in a School Program," *American Journal of Mental Deficiency,* LXII (July, 1957), 35–38.

Goldberg, I. Ignacy, and William M. Cruikshank. "The Trainable but Noneducable: Whose Responsibility?" *National Education Association Journal*, XLII (December, 1958), 622–23.

Goldstein, Herbert. *Report Number Two on Study Projects for Trainable Mentally Handicapped Children*. Springfield, Illinois: Office of the Superintendent, January 1, 1956.

Guenther, Richard J. *Michigan Demonstration Research Project for the Severely Mentally Retarded: Final Report*. Lansing, Michigan: Department of Public Instruction, 1956.

Heffernan, Helen (editor). *Guiding the Young Child*. Committee of the California School Supervisors Association. Boston: D. C. Heath and Company, 1951.

Hirsch, Ernest A. "The Adaptive Significance of Commonly Described Behavior of the Mentally Retarded," *American Journal of Mental Deficiency*, LXIII (January, 1959), 639–46.

Hudson, Margaret. "Some Theoretical Aspects to Curriculum Building for the Severely Retarded Child," *American Journal of Mental Deficiency*, LX (October, 1955), 270–77.

Ilg, Frances L., and Louise Bates Ames. *Child Behavior*. New York: Dell Publishing Company, 1956.

Jacob, Walter. *New Hope for the Retarded Child*. New York: Public Affairs Committee, Inc., 22 East 38 Street, 1954.

Jewish Hospital of Brooklyn. "All Day Institute on Mongolism," *Quarterly Review of Pediatrics* (May, August, November, 1953). (Reprints distributed by the Association for the Help of Retarded Children, Inc., 200 Fourth Avenue, New York.)

Kirk, Samuel A. *Public School Provisions for Severely Retarded Children: A Survey of Practices in the United States*. Albany: Inter-Departmental Health Resources Board, 1957.

Kirk, Samuel A., Merle Karnes, and Winifred Kirk. *You and Your Retarded Child*. New York: The Macmillan Company, 1955.

Lewis, Richard S., Alfred A. Strauss, and Laura E. Lehtinen. *The Other Child*. New York: Grune and Stratton, 1951.

Martin, Bertha W. *Teaching Extremely Retarded Children*. Kent, Ohio: Kent State University, 1955, pp. 4–15.

Masland, Richard L., Seymour B. Sarason, and Thomas Gladwin. *Mental Subnormality*. New York: Basic Books, Inc., 1958, pp. 311–58.

McCaw, William Ralph. *Non-Institutionalized Training of Re-

tarded Children in Ontario. Toronto: The Ryerson Press, 1956.

Michael-Smith, Harold. *The Mentally Retarded Patient*. Philadelphia: J. B. Lippincott Company, 1956.

National Association for Retarded Children. *Some Thoughts on Planning Day Schools for Retarded Children*. New York: National Association for Retarded Children, Inc., 386 Park Avenue South, May, 1958.

Ottawa Department of National Health and Welfare, Mental Health Division. *The Backward Child*. Ottawa, Canada: Edmond Cloutier, 1955, pp. 5–33.

Rosenzweig, Louis E. "Report of a School Program for Trainable Mentally Retarded Children, October 1951–June 1952," *American Journal of Mental Deficiency*, LIX (October, 1954), 181–205.

Ruoff, Amy E. *A Plan for Teachers of Trainable Mentally Handicapped Children*. Abington, Montgomery County, Pennsylvania: Abington Township Schools, 1957.

Sarason, Seymour B. *Psychological Problems in Mental Deficiency*. New York: Harper & Brothers, 1953.

Sarason, Seymour B., and Thomas Gladwin. "Psychological and Cultural Problems in Mental Subnormality: A Review of Research," *American Journal of Mental Deficiency*, LXII (May, 1958), 1115–1270.

School of Education, University Extension, University of Kansas. *Curriculum and Methods for the Trainable Retarded*. Lawrence, Kansas (June 4–14), 1958.

Strauss, Alfred A., and Laura E. Lehtinen. *Psychopathology and Education of the Brain-Injured Child*, Vol. I: *Fundamentals and Treatment*. New York: Grune and Stratton, 1951.

Thorpe, Louis P. *Child Psychology and Development*. New York: The Ronald Press Company, 1955.

Wolinsky, Gloria F. "Theoretical and Practical Aspects of a Teacher Education Program for Teachers of 'The Trainable Child'," *American Journal of Mental Deficiency*, LXIII (May, 1959), 948–53.

Woods Schools Publications. Pamphlets include *The Adolescent Exceptional Child*. Child Research Clinic, the Woods Schools, Langhorne, Pennsylvania.

JOURNALS

These three journals usually contain many good articles pertaining to the severely retarded.

American Journal of Mental Deficiency. The American Association on Mental Deficiency, 372–74 Broadway, Albany, New York.

Exceptional Children. Council for Exceptional Children, 1201 Sixteenth Street, N.W., Washington 6, D.C.

Training School Bulletin. The Training School, Vineland, New Jersey.

Annotated bibliographies can also be found in:

Children Limited. The National Association for Retarded Children, 386 Park Avenue South, New York.

Psychological Abstracts. The American Psychological Association, 1333 Sixteenth Street, N.W., Washington 6, D.C.

Research projects being conducted under grants from the U.S. Office of Education are reported yearly in:

Cooperative Research Projects. Issued by the U.S. Department of Health, Education, and Welfare, Office of Education, Washington, D.C.

III. Physical Development

Most of the trainable children's school activities will involve bodily movement. Gross-muscle training is provided through body rhythms in music class and in active domestic or yard work as well as in play. Control of the small muscles develops during self-care routines, art and craft work, job activities and so on. This section on physical activities will discuss only the development of large-muscle skills primarily in play activities. Additional suggestions for physical exercises and body rhythms are included in Chapter V.

The purposes of large-muscle activities are to increase the pleasure and satisfaction derived from active work and play, and to develop muscular coordination, courage and persistence derived from individual or group games and use of playground equipment. Engaging in simple water activities or learning the fundamentals of swimming, if they are carefully and sympathetically taught, are especially helpful to a child who is lacking in good physical coordination or self-confidence. Body rhythms and certain physical exercises which may improve the children's posture and carriage may help the children to be accepted better by other people. Physical activity also provides socially acceptable outlets for inner tensions and drives, enabling the child to adjust better to the present and to be more adeqately prepared for the future.

Facilities of a good school program for physical development should include an enclosed playground and an indoor playroom (for inclement weather) small enough to discourage asocial children from indulging in such behavior as continual and disorganized running about. A small playground makes supervision of the whole group more effective. The playground should be adequate enough, however, to permit solitude for a child when he needs it and to allow for safe play with a variety of equipment. It should have an area for group games and sports. (Older boys and girls might need an additional area outside the small playground. A small swimming pool for beginning learners which has adequate life guard protection is to be highly recommended.

Equipment for physical activity should be safe, not requiring judgment on the part of a child, as does a large seesaw; and it should be such that it needs no more supervision than is regularly provided. (Ice skates in most situations would not be practical.) The best kind of equipment is that readily used by more than one child at a time, in order that social intercourse may be encouraged. A swinging boat is preferable to an ordinary swing, for example; a wagon, to a toy tractor.

Few of the activities listed in this chapter and in other parts of this book are highly competitive. Stress on individual competition would appear to be undesirable for very retarded children for several reasons. In many competitive games, only one among many players can be the winner, so there are far more children suffering failure than achieving success. This can be especially damaging to children who have encountered failure so often. Also, if importance comes to be attached to winning, a severely retarded child may be disturbed in many situations, since he will usually be the loser when competing with normal people in the home and neighborhood.

A teacher who emphasizes winning over other children as the goal of an activity may hinder the development of motivations that could be of significant value to a retarded child all his life: the fun of working and playing with others, the knowledge of having contributed to the realization of a common goal, the satisfaction that comes from helping another. Group competition, because it involves teamwork and cooperation, seems to be a more salutary incentive than individual competition. Children keeping score for their team in kickball will learn about the meaning of winning and losing, but emphasis is on the fun of playing together.

One kind of competition with incentive value to a retarded child is that of comparing his present accomplishment with his past record. The teacher can encourage this by pointing out to a child: "You never climbed the jungle gym before, and today you did. You are learning new things all the time." Other than this variety, the less emphasis the school places upon competition, the happier a severely retarded child can be and, in the long run, the better he can function in society.

PHYSICAL ACTIVITIES

A. Gross-Muscle Activity with or on Equipment

I. BEGINNER

Lift and move large blocks and cartons.
Push or pull cars, wagon, doll buggy.
Climb in and out of wagon.
Climb in and out of swinging boat.
Climb on and off tricycle, spring-steel horse, small merry-go-round.
Jounce when seated on horse, and on large inflated truck or airplane tube.
Step on and off and also jounce on jumping board—a plank suspended by cinder blocks at either end.
Climb to first rung of jungle gym and, by stepping sidewise, climb around jungle gym; climb up and down play practice-steps, holding onto rails; climb up low slide.
Slide down low slide.

II. INTERMEDIATE

Walk along jumping board, up inclined plane.
Ride, standing up, on back of tricycle.
Climb in and out of snow coaster. (Obtainable commercially. Resembles a large saucer, bigger than garbage can lid. Rider

can hold straps at edge on each side. Rope is attached for pulling. Can be used on ice or any kind of snow. Since the unpainted aluminum kind are especially slippery when wet, oil cloth can be taped inside, with reverse side up, so that child can step in and sit down or get out without slipping.)

Pull another child in wagon or snow coaster, holding handle with both hands. (Using two arms is better exercise.)

Pedal tricycle.

Steer wagon when riding in it and being pushed.

Roll in barrel when being pushed.

Pump when swinging in boat. Push boat when others are in it.

Bounce and rock with another child in large inflated truck or airplane tube.

Climb up ladders, on jungle gym, up steps of high slide, on top of barrel and through barrel (when it is stationary, on its standard).

Walk between rungs of ladder placed flat on ground, walk along rungs on jungle gym, walk between two lines on floor.

Ascend to top of jungle gym and climb around it.

Hang from bar of jungle gym, from parallel bars, from horizontal bar.

Step over and jump over a rope.

Jump off steps and jumping board; jump from height of 12 inches off end of inclined plane.

Slide down high slide.

With support from adult, use roller skates. (Training skates are easier to get on, and move more slowly. Upon the occurrence of the inevitable fall, get up by crawling to a fence or other support, kneeling in an erect position, then placing one foot in regular standing position, and finally pulling oneself up while holding onto fence.)

III. ADVANCED

Propel and steer wagon and scooter.

Jump and skip rope; jump across space between two lines on floor.

Turn the jump rope.

Crawl up inclined plane.

Walk on line on floor.

Play "Follow the Leader" on outdoor equipment—horizontal bars, parallel bars, ladders, jungle gym, inclined plane, barrel, in a variety of ways: hang, climb, crawl, walk, balance, jump, swing.

Roller skate, perferably on a coarse pavement, to minimize speed.

B. Games Using Gross Muscles

I. INTERMEDIATE

Clown: Do somersaults, roll over, jump up, fall down on mat or grass.

Dog and Bone: One player sneaks up behind "dog," a blindfolded player, and tries to snatch his "bone," a blackboard eraser or other object. As soon as the "dog" hears someone creeping up, he gives chase.

Duck, Duck, Goosie: Player who is "It" walks around the outside of circle of children, saying "Duck" as he taps each one on the head. When "It" says, "Goosie," child just tapped chases one who is "It." "It" dashes around circle and is safe if he reaches "Goosie's" place before being caught.

Simple Tag: But who does not know how to play this?

II. ADVANCED

Wheelbarrow: One player takes legs of another, who walks on hands. Have wheelbarrow relay races in pairs.

Follow the Leader: Do stunts on mat, imitating leader.

Stepping Stones: Step or jump (to music) from "stone" to "stone" (circles marked on floor, or large pieces of stiff paper), until music stops. Player not on "stone" must sit in center of circle until next time music stops, when someone else will be "out."

Snake Game: One player runs, pulling rope around outside of circle of seated players who try to grab it. One who catches rope then has turn to run with it.

Ring Toss or Horse Shoe Pitching (using rubber horse shoes):

Use one stake, so players really aim. Keep score with tallies (see p. 153).

Who Is Leader: Players sit in circle. "It" leaves room. Teacher then selects someone to be leader and makes certain all players know who is leader and realize they must watch him. Leader starts clapping, which is signal for "It" to appear, and other players do likewise. As leader shifts to different action, other players also do so as rapidly as possible. "It" must guess who is leader.

Hide and Seek.

C. Ball Play and Ball Games

I. BEGINNER

Punch inflated doll, bat balloon.

Kick big beach ball anywhere, or to teacher, taking turns with other children while they stand or sit in a row.

Roll 6" or 8" ball, or inflated automobile tube, to teacher. (Children sit on floor in row, with legs apart for ball play; stand, or sit in chairs for play with tube.)

Catch ball or tube when rolled (or kicked) by another child.

II. INTERMEDIATE

Hit punching bag.

Kick volley ball.

Catch beach ball, volley ball, or smaller ball when teacher throws it. (Children stand or sit in chairs in row.)

Roll ball back and forth. (Children sit in parallel lines.)

Bounce 6" or 8" ball to teacher and catch it when teacher bounces it back.

Bounce and catch ball alone.

Throw crocheted ball, stuffed oilcloth ball, or bean bag into wastebasket or cardboard carton open at top and front, or into holes in a cardboard or wooden target board.

Roll ball or deck tennis ring into "goal cage" (carton open at bottom and front).

Play bowling game.

Bowling: Children sit in two lines facing each other. Duckpins are lined up between. Players roll ball to knock pins down. Team scores are kept. (Best players sit at end of lines, farthest from pins.)

Variation of Bowling Game: Children sit to one side. One player after another steps up to bowl, trying to knock down duckpins. Three chances allowed. Each player sets up pins for next player. (Note: In games of this sort, teacher should vary position of starting line, depending upon individual child's ability.)

III. ADVANCED

Hit punching bag rhythmically, alternating hands.

Bounce balls in unison. Each pupil bounces a ball in time with rhythm of musical accompaniment, such as: "Bounce, bounce, catch."

Play ball games.

Musical Ball: Players form big circle. Ball is thrown from player to player around the circle. Player holding ball when music stops sits on stool in center of circle, changing places with player already sitting there. To avoid confusion when the two players change places, person having ball when music stops waits in his place, holding ball. Player in center goes to him and takes ball, thus finding correct place to stand.

Kick Ball: Form two small teams facing each other in small enclosed place. Kick ball back and forth trying to make goal by having ball touch wall or fence behind opponents.

Volleyball: Play simplified version, using small court.

Base Kick Ball: Similar to simplified baseball. Use less than four bases to begin with. Have catcher, kicker, pitcher and fielders. Pitcher rolls ball to kicker (who should learn to kick with instep of foot).

Badminton: Hit bird back and forth over net.

Basketball: Shoot for baskets. Use larger ring than standard size if necessary in order that players can meet with some success.

Croquet: Have wickets set close together if game is too difficult. Players must always keep mallet between legs when hitting ball.

Keep Away: One team throws ball to teammates while other team guards opponents and tries to intercept ball. When ball is intercepted, second team tries to keep it. Teacher will have to play a very active part to keep game going well. She should call frequent rest periods so everyone is active while game is in operation.

Baseball: Play on small diamond, which is enclosed. A soft rubber ball, six inches in diameter or larger, can be used at first. Wide board, shaped and taped at one end for better gripping, will help poor players to hit ball.

Pin Ball: Choose teams. Players on one team throw the ball down the court from player to player until close enough to knock over opponents' tenpin with ball. Opponents try to intercept ball as it is passed, and to guard its pin. Team knocking pin down scores one point. First team making five points is winner.

D. Water Play and Swimming

I. BEGINNER

To become accustomed to the water:

Sit by plastic wading pool and splash water with hand.

Sit on edge of larger pool and kick water.

Sit in plastic pool, along with other children, playing with toys (buckets, boats, watering can made of plastic or rubber).

Permit own body to be doused with water—at first only gently sprinkled by teacher.

Stand in water, splashing it with hands.

Walk in larger, deeper pool, pushing toys.

Run into fine hose spray; permit hose spray near face.

Play "Ring-a-Rosy," squatting in water up to neck for "Fall down!"

Play "Row, Row, Row Your Boat," rocking with partner while seated in water.

II. INTERMEDIATE

Holding onto teacher, put face in water.

Play "Ring-a-Rosy," going under water for "Fall down!"

Kick when held in prone position.
Kick holding onto edge of pool in prone position.
Make arms go in crawl-like fashion when crouching in water.
When head and back held, float on back.
When held, float in prone position, face in water.
Play walking races in water up to waist.
Jump up and down in water holding hands with friends.
Jump into shallow water from sitting position on edge of dock
   or pool.

III. ADVANCED

Play tag in water.
Float in prone position without being held; face float with kick.
Face float with crawl arm stroke.
Back float without being held.
Jump into water from standing position.
Duck, expelling breath. After rising to surface, inhale through
   mouth. Do several times continuously.
Play game of retrieving something from bottom of pool.
Throw and catch ball, playing in water with friends.
Tread water.
Participate in swimming races, using arms or legs or both,
   as instructor designates. (Handicaps can be given superior
   swimmers.)
Participate in endurance tests, seeing who can float, hold breath
   or tread water the longest.
Learn the complete crawl and other strokes when ready.

RELATED READING

Benoit, E. Paul. "More Fun for Institutionalized Retarded Chil-
   dren," *American Journal of Mental Deficiency*, LVIII (July, 1953),
   93–107. (Reprints obtainable from the National Association for
   Retarded Children, Inc., 386 Park Avenue South, New York.)
Fait, Hollis F., and Harriet J. Kupferer. "A Study of Two Motor
   Achievement Tests and Its Implications in Planning Physical Edu-

cation Activities for the Mentally Retarded," *American Journal of Mental Deficiency,* LX (April, 1956), 729–32.

McCartney, Louise Dawley. "Program of Motor Therapy for Young Mentally Deficient Children of the Non-Familial Type," *Training School Bulletin,* LIII, No. 4 (June, 1956).

National Association for Retarded Children, Inc. *Swimming for the Mentally Retarded.* (Prepared in cooperation with Richard L. Brown, Director of Water Safety, American National Red Cross.) New York: National Association for Retarded Children, Inc. 386 Park Avenue South, New York.

Sember, Andrew T. "A Critique of Summer Recreational and Craft Activities for Mentally Retarded Children," *Training School Bulletin,* LIV (November, 1957), 37–40, 44.

IV. Self-Care

Most families and teachers appreciate the value of having a trainable child learn self-care, since assisting a child in his eating, dressing, or bathroom chores is time-consuming. Though some people may gain emotional satisfaction from doing everything for a retarded child, society does not appreciate unnecessary helplessness. An overprotective parent will realize eventually that his grown child's being a constant burden is not making either of them happy.

A retarded child needs a chance to grow up. As he learns to care for his own physical needs, he begins to gain a sense of personal worth and a feeling that he can direct his own life to some extent. Through teaching him self-care skills, we aid in his growth toward emotional maturity and social adjustment.

If a retardate learns to care for himself, he can gain recognition from his family and others who appreciate his attempts, and thus be able to get along more happily in home and community. The effect of self-care ability on a retarded adult's emotional well-being cannot be overemphasized. The learning of self-care skills is an area in which, with practice, he can meet with the success he so badly needs.

It is much easier to do something for a trainable child than it is to teach him to do it himself. A great deal of patience is required on the part of the teacher during the training process while she learns how much can be expected of her pupil. And it is a triumph for both of them when even a small skill is mastered.

TEACHING SELF-CARE SKILLS

The methods used in teaching a child self-care are of utmost importance to avoid his feeling worthless because of too many failures. Here are some general principles for helping him learn to dress, feed, wash, and toilet himself:

1. Know your child. Find out from his record and from his parents just what his level of development is and how he learns best.

2. See that the learning experience is a pleasant one. There are many ways to do this. One way is through a teacher's enthusiastic attitude, which has a wonderful effect upon trainable children.

3. Teach each skill the simplest way and in stages, one step at a time. Analyze each skill, breaking it down into very small steps. Try out different techniques with the children, studying their effectiveness. Teach the easiest part first.

4. Give the child ample time and opportunity to work on a new task.

5. Be consistent. If a child is expected to put his boots on one day, he should do so every day. (Make allowances, however, for days when he is not quite himself.)

6. There should be realistic motivation, whenever possible. (The child should button his wraps so he will be ready to go outdoors to play, rather than button two pieces of cloth together to please the teacher.)

7. Give encouragement and praise for real effort. Retarded children seem to need more adult approval than do other children.

8. Don't expect perfection. Mistakes and accidents are common when a child is learning. Perhaps he will have a tumble because he is trying to walk with two feet in one pant leg, or will spill the juice when serving himself, because he tries a quick method—from pitcher directly to mouth. Although mishaps like these cannot be ignored, they need not cause dismay. Neither does a teacher need to be too concerned if a child shows no progress in a self-care activity within a reasonable length of

time. Drop the training for a while to avoid further frustration on the part of both teacher and pupil. Don't worry about such failure; there will be many things these children will not be able to learn in spite of the best efforts of the teacher and the child's desire to please.

9. Be flexible. If one method or technique does not work after an adequate trial, analyze the problem carefully. You may discover the source of the child's difficulty and a new approach may bring success.

The next few pages give suggestions for helping a child master some of the skills involved in one particular area of self-care: dressing. To develop the necessary skills and habits in other areas of self-care, the teacher of the trainable will want to give attention to details in a similar fashion.

Detailed Suggestions for Training in Dressing Skills

Putting on and taking off wraps are important activities in most everyone's day. As the children learn to take off their outer garments when entering school and to dress for out-of-doors, they learn general dressing skills which should, with parent cooperation, be carried over into the home.

Putting Away Wraps: Almost every child can be expected to take some responsibility for hanging up his own wraps and putting his overshoes in their place. To help the children learn to put wraps away independently, without conflict, each child can be assigned a hook or locker with his name or other personalized identification on it. Two hooks can be given to those with motor difficulty, or to those with extremely bulky wraps.

If the children have no lockers, hats which will not hang up can be put in home-made personal locker boxes. In bad weather, the teacher can chalk off and label places on the floor under the children's hooks, for each child's overshoes. Additional help in identifying ownership of wraps can be provided by requesting that parents label every outdoor garment their children wear to school.

Removing and Putting on Clothing: A child has to learn

many steps when getting into and out of his wraps, especially his winter ones. Some of those steps are much harder than others. The child should not be expected to learn how to do everything at once. When it comes to the more difficult garments, he will take only partial responsibility at first. Each child will need to be watched to see that he is not becoming frustrated by having to take too big a step forward, or by having to work too long at any one process. If, for example, a child is learning to button his coat, he should not necessarily be expected to do them all. The teacher can button two of the buttons first, and then tell the child to work on the last one. If after a week or so of buttoning this button the task becomes less difficult, the child may be left with two buttons to manage and later, three.

Zippers may present a problem. If encouraged to handle his zippers alone, the child's attempts may end in his getting the zipper stuck. When a child manipulates things with yanks and jerks, the teacher may want to give help immediately. Any teacher of small children can probably remember the day when she had to forget all else and give her undivided attention to one child, wiggly and frantic, who seemed permanently zipped in his coat.

While some children have trouble with the actual manipulation of their garments, others struggle more with orientation (back and front, right and left, inside and outside, top and bottom). If a child has not learned the way a garment should be put on from its appearance, cues may be given that will help him. Artificial cues, such as a bit of colored cloth in the back or in one sleeve may be used to avoid a child's becoming frustrated before the teacher has time to direct her attention to him. Natural cues inherent in the garment itself, such as its shape, are better. When the teacher has time and the child appears ready to learn, she can explain to him how the back of a slip-on sweater is higher than the front. She will show him how to lay the front down on a table, and to face the table and put his arms and head into the sweater. The teacher might try to find time to lay out the garment the same way each time, so the child can learn how it looks and, eventually, how to lay it out himself. In getting hats on frontward, a mirror is helpful to some children.

General cues that would apply to a whole category of wraps seem more worth teaching than cues applying to one particular article of clothing belonging to one child at a particular time. If a child has learned from the shape of the shoe which foot to put it on, he has learned much more than if he has learned that his buckle shoes should be worn always with the buckles on the outside where they will not catch on each other. If he can learn the secret of putting on any shoe or any coat correctly, life will be much easier for him.

When the children go outdoors in the winter, wraps may have to be donned and removed several times during the school day. The youngster with poor manipulative ability may have had little time to do much else than get dressed and undressed if he has to do all he possibly can by himself. He may miss the fun of playing with the group in the snow. At these times such a child can be given a head start in the dressing process, or sometimes all his garments, such as boots and snowpants, need not be removed when he arrives at school. When the time comes to go home and some youngsters just cannot face the long procedure of getting wraps on again, the teacher may give extra help to prevent discouragement. On such days, the schedule might even be rearranged so that the children can have their outdoor period upon arrival at school when they are dressed for outdoors, instead of in mid-morning. However, this may not be possible if it is too cold early in the day to enjoy being out.

Hints to Parents: To encourage all the children in learning to help themselves with their wraps, the following additional suggestions might be made to parents in writing:

1. Place wide, strong loops in coat, cap, sweater, and snow pants so that they will stay on hooks even when bumped.

2. Label all outdoor garments.

3. Boots and rubbers should not fit so snuggly that they are too hard to get on and off.

4. In snowy or sloppy weather, boots rather than rubbers should be worn so that the child will not have to change his shoes and socks in school or get his pant legs wet.

5. Boots without a gusset or with no opening down the front are a struggle for child and adult.

6. Tie shoes tightly so they do not come off when the child pulls off his boots. An older child can be taught to tie double knots in his shoelaces after the bow is made.

7. Rubbers and boots should be marked with India ink, since adhesive tape wears off.

8. For a small child, sew a long tape connecting his two mittens so that one can be thrust through each sleeve of his coat to keep them from getting lost.

9. Suspender snaps attached to cuffs of coat may prevent loss of a mitten for some children, but serve merely as toys for other children.

10. Older children should have pockets big enough to contain their gloves when gloves are dry.

11. Each child should have a cap that he can, if possible, fasten alone.

12. The cap should be of such a shape and size that it will not slip down over his eyes.

13. In cool weather and for rough play outdoors, girls should have slacks—ones which they can quickly pull up and down themselves. Most easily managed are those that are large enough but with no zippers to catch and no suspenders to be buttoned, and which have only two fairly large buttons on the side.

14. Trousers should be loose enough at the waist so the boy can snap, button, or hook them.

15. Boys who cannot do fastenings should have suspenders and loose enough pants so they simply have to be slipped down.

16. Temperature and other weather conditions necessitate changes in the amount of outer clothing the child needs. Children should not be bundled up every day. A child does not require a heavy scarf and sweater and snow pants and a coat on a warm winter day. Here, as in most situations, common sense is the best guide.

SELF-CARE ACTIVITIES

A. Dressing and Undressing

I. BEGINNER

Pull mittens off; put in pockets.
Pull hat off; hang on hook or put on shelf.
Zip coat down; take coat off (given help with unbuttoning stiff buttons).
Hang up coat by big, stiff loop.
Take toes of boots or rubbers off, heel removed by teacher.
Get wraps.
Put hat on.
Put out arm or leg in preparation for adult's help in dressing him.
Put arm in coat if adult holds coat and guides arm toward correct sleeve.
Zip coat if started in track.
Put toes in rubbers or boots, if adult indicates correct one for each foot.
Remove shoes at rest period if laces loosened.

II. INTERMEDIATE

Untie or unsnap hat.
Unbutton coat and sweater.
Take off slip-on sweater if helped pulling first sleeve off.
Take rubbers or boots off.
Take off snow pants.
Hang clothes neatly on hook.
Put away wraps independently.
Put hat on right-side to, if marked, or with some distinction in appearance between front and back.
Put coat or coat-sweater on with arm in right sleeve.
Put on slip-on sweater if laid out on table correctly.
Get snow pants on if laid out on floor.

Untie and remove shoes at rest period.

Put clothes on in appropriate order (e.g., scarf before coat).

Learn to snap, buckle, button, and zip.

Begin to learn to tie bow.

Since shoelaces are difficult for children first learning to tie bows it is well to use special boards made for practicing. Use a board 18″ x 8″ x 1″. Thumbtack two starched sashes about 3″ wide—such as a yellow one 2-¼′ long and a red one 2′ long—one on each side of board. Make a knot near the end of the yellow sash to aid in manipulation. Place board so that red sash is on the child's right. Proceed as follows:

1. Right hand pull red sash all the way across board toward upper left-hand corner.
2. Left hand take hold of yellow sash by knot and put it over and then under red sash.
3. Right hand pull yellow sash while left hand pulls red sash.
4. With both hands make small loop in red sash near point where sashes cross.
5. Hold loop tightly between thumb and index finger of left hand.
6. Right hand take hold of yellow sash near point where sashes cross, and pull tightly around left thumbnail and then behind loop.
7. Right index finger push yellow sash against left thumb until left thumb is pushed out of hole and yellow loop has followed it through hole.
8. Left fingers pinch yellow loop tightly and right fingers pinch red loop tightly.
9. Both hands pull.

Until the child learns to pull the bow tight, it may be necessary for an adult to tighten it for him so that he will not be discouraged by having his own become loose just after he has tied it.

Button large buttons in large holes—own coat or manikin's and other children's smocks.

Recognize different kinds of clothing. (Point to garment teacher names; if speech is adequate, name garments that teacher points to.)

Learn to lace own shoe. With a two-colored lace, practice lacing shoe which is attached to a board. Each hole can be colored inside and out to indicate in which hole to insert corresponding lace. After pulling lace through hole, be sure to drop it on that side of shoe before picking up other lace.

Put on shoes by loosening laces first and taking care not to break down counters. Try using shoehorn.

III. ADVANCED

Turn clothes right side out before hanging up.

Hang clothes on hanger.

Get all wraps on correctly.

Snap, button, buckle, and zip all wraps.

Don head scarf, knotting under chin. If square, fold correctly.

Arrange neck scarf and hat neatly before mirror; turn down coat collar.

Button up when particularly cold; open coat when warm, and leave gloves off when warm.

Recognize which clothing is appropriate to certain kinds of weather. (Point to picture of garment when teacher describes certain weather conditions. Also, tell when certain garments should be worn.)

B. Washroom Activities and Personal Grooming

I. BEGINNER

Keep dry by using toilet at scheduled periods and/or communicating need at other times.

Pull pants up and down.

Boys stand to urinate.

Flush toilet.

Wash and dry hands with little help but, if necessary, with reminders as to order of procedure.

Wipe nose when reminded.

II. INTERMEDIATE

Care for self independently at toilet.

Wash with little superivsion. Push up sleeves, insert stopper, run water properly, soap hands, rinse hands, remove stopper, wipe hands.

Wash and dry face when necessary, using mirror to see when clean.

Wipe nose when necessary without reminder; blow nose.

Cover mouth when coughing or sneezing.

Brush teeth and care for toothbrush. (Special practice periods may be needed.)

III. ADVANCED

Toileting done with dispatch. Clothing carefully arranged (shirt in).

Washing procedure, including rinsing of bowl, done with dispatch and no supervision.

Grooming requiring specific practice periods:

Hair: Brush and comb, clean out brush, wash brush and comb; part hair, make pin curls, put in bobby pins, barrettes, braid hair.

Nails: Scrub, clean, file.

Shoes: Wipe off, shine, clean and polish.

Cosmetics: Older girls learn to apply and remove.

Care at menstrual periods for older girls.

C. Eating and Drinking

I. BEGINNER

Eat only edible things.

Eat only when sitting down at table.

Eat only food set before one or passed to one.

Eat and drink without much spilling.

Feed self with spoon.

Wipe mouth when asked.

Stay in seat until all are finished or until most are excused.

II. INTERMEDIATE

Wait until all are seated and served before starting to eat.
Keep chair close to table; keep crumbs on table. (On occasions
when careless about crumbs, sweep up floor after meal time.)
Spoon food neatly.
Keep sandwich together.
Take only one cookie when plate is passed.
Wipe fingers and mouth when finished.
Keep napkin in lap.

III. ADVANCED

Eat in usual order—dessert last.
Eat at reasonable speed.
Take serving plate from left, help self, pass on to right (or vice
versa).
Talk only when no food in mouth.
Take small-sized bites.
Chew and sip unobtrusively.
Wipe fingers and mouth effectively when necessary.
Spread with knife.

D. Using Transportation Facilities

I. BEGINNER

Travel with the class in a car when going on an excursion:
Stand on sidewalk until driver is ready.
Wait until car door is opened.
Wait until invited to get in.
Sit where told, and stay sitting, relatively quiet.
Keep fingers and hands away from car door, never opening.
Talk or sing quietly, not making sudden or loud noises.

II. INTERMEDIATE

Act out riding in cars.
Take bus trips with the class:
Line up by the door of the bus.
Pay fare.

Walk to a rear seat.

Talk quietly.

Act out taking bus trips.

III. ADVANCED

Take trips on public transportation with the class. Discuss, before and after, acceptable behavior:

Identify the number or name of the appropriate bus for particular destination.

Identify entrance door.

Use hand rails.

Know bus fare, have money ready, use transfers.

Give special consideration to others (offering seats to others).

Don't talk to driver while bus is in operation.

Move back in bus away from entrance door and bus driver.

Stand, holding on, when bus is crowded.

Know where and when to get off; recognize needed street names such as those near the school and near one's home.

Ring for stop.

Use in an acceptable manner such facilities as escalators, elevators, and revolving doors, showing consideration for others.

Discuss behavior in public places, including not talking to strangers other than policemen.

Discuss what to do if lost, or if strangers are annoying.

If advisable, travel to and from school independently (parent-teacher cooperation and guidance needed for this).

RELATED READING

Chamberlain, Naomi H., and Dorothy H. Moss. *The Three R's for the Retarded: A Program for Training the Retarded at Home.* New York: National Association for Retarded Children, 386 Park Avenue South (1954), pp. 22–29.

Des Moines Department of Public Instruction. *Recommendations for the Establishment of and Programming for Trainable Classes in Public and Private Iowa Schools.* Des Moines: Department of Public Instruction, 1958.

v. Self-Expression

Severely retarded children can and do express themselves and grow in their creative ability when given adequate opportunity and stimulation. This may come as a surprise to teachers who have become discouraged after trying "free expression" periods during which the children became uncontrolled or where the results of the children's activities showed little progress. Since many trainable children often have little imagination and have tended to imitate others instead of carrying through original ideas, it has commonly been accepted that teachers should emphasize direct teaching of skills, giving relatively little attention to helping the children develop their own effective means of expression. This chapter will suggest ways for teachers to provide experiences which trainable children can respond to spontaneously.

WHY CREATIVE ACTIVITIES?

Babies express themselves freely in random movements of arms and legs, in babbling, crying, and later in facial expressions and laughter. Young trainable children will express themselves similarly. Their vocalizing, random motions, and later their gesturing, scribbling, pounding of clay, or dumping of blocks should be regarded as the beginnings of self-expression. It is difficult for teachers to accept such behavior as valuable to the child because it persists so long; but one needs to recall how much more slowly the trainable child develops in comparison with the average child. Whereas an average child of two is beginning to scribble, a trainable child may not reach that stage until he is four or over, and he will probably be scribbling many years after the ordinary child of three or four has emerged from the scribble stage. Since the quality of the trainable child's scribbling will usually change gradually from mere random motions to a more controlled form of scribbling, the teacher can feel that the child not only is expressing himself, but also is developing his forms of self-expression, however slowly.

Through certain kinds of stimulation, the teacher may be able to increase the speed of the child's development, but she needs to be careful not to inhibit his spontaneity. Trainable children will function better and more happily if they can preserve some of the satisfaction which derives from the early spontaneous but uncontrolled behavior out of which develop later forms of expression such as music, dancing, drama, language, drawing.

Opportunities to express himself and special attention to his mental health need to be given the trainable because he is constantly frustrated in adapting to a world so little understood by him and peopled by those so much more competent. He needs guidance in developing ways to deal with his emotions and to use them constructively. A parent feels more strongly compelled to suppress aggressive behavior in a retarded youngster than in the average child because society seems particularly intolerant and fearful of the display of such feelings on the part of the retardate. In a good school program, the child will be shown and given encouragement to direct his hostility and aggressiveness into channels satisfying to him but not dangerous or too upsetting to others. He needs time, a variety of media, and the teacher's understanding stimulation to find ways by which he can express himself for his own greatest comfort. He gains self-confidence and feelings of independence as he learns that there are occasions in school when he does just what he feels like doing, within the limits of the physical and peer-group environment.

Besides the great value to the emotional well-being of the

child and his future happiness, there are further reasons why self-expression activities are important to include in the school curriculum. They can contribute to the child's intellectual growth by helping him become more aware of himself and his environment. For example, as he draws a picture of himself, he becomes more aware of what he is like, how he feels, and what he is doing. Through his desire to express himself in his drawing, he will observe more closely and will be reviewing his knowledge as he draws. The teacher can stimulate the child to develop greater understanding by recalling for him a variety of experiences to which he can respond creatively. It should be emphasized that it is important to encourage, not the child's accurate portrayal of his environment, but rather his expression of what he actually experiences, especially his feelings about what happens to him. His knowledge of this environment will grow as he reacts to it in a variety of ways.

Through the child's creative work the teacher can gain insight into what the child does not understand about himself and his environment. This will suggest aspects needing further development through various class activities. An older group could take sketch books they have made to the zoo. After observing and talking about the animals, they could draw pictures of them. From the pictures, the teacher may be able to discover what might be of value to emphasize on observing the animals during the boys' and girls' next trip to the zoo.

The trainable child, through creative activities, develops his perceptual abilities. As he scribbles, handles lumps of clay, plays with blocks, lets sand run through his hands, or splashes in water, he gains greater kinaesthetic and tactual awareness. As he paints or draws he responds to color and form, thus growing in visual awareness.

Although some educators feel that children with poor visual perception need a good deal of stencil and tracing work and picture-copying, it is possible that even these children will learn as well or better through the more highly motivated activities of self-expression. For example, a child who draws on his own initiative may make a great effort to observe or recall the perception of the subject he is trying to portray, and may do his utmost to represent it as he observes or perceives it. If such conscious effort in representation is made, perceptual growth may take place relatively rapidly, whereas slower perceptual growth is likely to take place in stencil work where there may be little conscious attention to the form that is being filled in.

For developing a child's hand-eye coordination and manual dexterity, self-expressive activities may be even more effective than the educational toys and other activities developed primarily for this purpose. Making his hands and fingers do as he wishes—poking holes in a particular arrangement in a ball of clay, making the paint brush produce the effect he wants, or putting on a dress-up costume to assume the role one wants to —these may provide greater motivation for developing manual skill than doing as the teacher or an educational toy suggests.

Self-expressive activities help a child develop socially. Greater awareness of himself and his environment helps the trainable to understand and relate to other people, those on whom he will be dependent all his life. Also, creative activities can be used to communicate with other people. Communication through an art medium can be important for the trainable child, whose oral language is generally limited and who usually lacks the ability to express himself in writing. Self-expression activities may help a child socially in still another way: after developing creative responses to art media, he may be able to carry over this spontaneity to his relationships with other people, thereby increasing their effectiveness.

An older girl, Rose, who seldom had play companions at home, found drawing and clay-modeling an interesting way to entertain herself and also an effective means of communication. She drew pictures of situations important to her and presented them to her friends at school. One day a teacher hurt her foot by stumbling down the stairs. This made a great impression on Rose, who saw it happen. She drew many pictures of this. On one paper she made two drawings representing time sequence. In the first, the teacher, supporting herself with a cane, was being helped down the stairs by another teacher. In the next, the disabled teacher was trying to get into the car of the other teacher, already at the wheel. These two drawings were presented to a third teacher to whom Rose wished to communicate the story of the accident. Since her speaking vocabulary was limited to that of a two- or three-year-old, a graphic form of communication meant a great deal to this girl.

How to Guide the Child Toward Self-Expression

Besides his intellectual limitations in creative ability, the trainable child probably has not had much experience in expressing himself due to his lack of self-confidence and the small amount of satisfaction derived from his creative attempts, often depreciated by others. He undoubtedly needs special guidance in learning adequate methods of self-expression.

The teacher will probably need to use many strong suggestions to help a trainable child become more fully aware of what he experiences and how to express himself about these experiences in various media. He can gain ideas about what to create by being encouraged to recall and talk about what he understands and has experienced, especially that which has emotional appeal.

One day a grandmotherly teacher's aide finally submitted to the pleas of the children to take her turn at jumping rope with them. That day Janis, who usually had no ideas of what to draw, portrayed the new rope-jumper—a favorite of hers.

Children who continually do a cramped, inhibited type of work, such as breaking off tiny bits of clay, may be guided toward working with bigger pieces and making bigger things. Finger painting or painting with large brushes on big sheets of paper would be of more help to these children than crayons or small blocks. Perseverative children can be shown new ways of working and thinking by suggestive questions and different kinds of materials. If a trainable child of ten or over is still not portraying recognizable objects in his drawings, it does not mean that he will not eventually do so without being made to copy the teacher's work or to follow standardized directions.

A group of older boys and girls experienced a rainy day. With stimulation from the teacher, they talked about how the rain looked, what they do when it starts to rain, and what they wear in the rain.

One pupil was a hyperactive, disorganized girl of 13, new in school, whose drawings had previously appeared to be undifferentiated scribbles. When making her picture of the rain, she hastily scribbled very intently, bearing down heavily, while exclaiming, "It's raining hard!"

Another member of the class, Debbie, whose pictures had not shown recognizable form up to this point, showed originality in portraying the raindrops by covering her paper with dots.

Kurt, whose paintings and drawings were always geometric shapes, usually unintelligible, heard Debbie making her raindrops, and did likewise; but he then demonstrated initiative by turning his thick crayon sidewise to gray the whole scene.

Short horizontal lines represented rain for one pupil, short vertical lines, for another. Houses, figures, and rain apparel were included in some of the pictures. Each picture was different. These pupils' portrayals of rain show that trainable children can express themselves by drawing if given encouragement and stimulation. Each of the drawings, no matter how crude, had meaning to the boy or girl who made it, and served the purpose of true art—self-expression.

In the list of Self-Expression Activities, pp. 81–88, are some simple things that a trainable child might want to create, though he might need stimulation. In making an apple of clay, for example, the child would probably need to have satisfying experiences, such as cutting up and eating apples, while talking about their shape and color. After the class has been discussing and singing about Thanksgiving foods—perhaps apples in particular—and has seen, smelled, handled, and tasted a variety of actual fruits and vegetables, the child may feel stimulated to make an apple if colored clay or dough is presented for class use.

Actual experience immediately preceding the use of a creative medium is a form of stimulation especially effective with retarded children. Lowenfeld, in his book *Creative and Mental Growth,* describes (p. 93) how he activated the passive knowledge of average children by discussing with them and then giving them experiences in the classroom, such as biting into hard candy and then suggesting they draw "eating candy." Without direction the children all included teeth in their representations that day.

Many self-expressive activities for trainables could be stimulated in this way by giving the children actual experiences just before they have an opportunity to recreate them in art media.

One morning the pianist for a class of eight trainable children, most of them 11 years old, played a piece familiar to them and asked them what they could do to the music. "Arms go up, down," answered one girl. All the children together then stretched their arms up and then lowered them, accompanied by the piano. After this, David was given a turn alone while the class sang the song about David swinging. Before he did so, the teacher told him to see how high he could stretch and then asked him what he was doing, and how he was doing it. The teacher made him even more conscious of his arms by pulling them up even higher and asking him to see if he could keep them that high. After David had "swung," he was again asked what he had been doing and just how he did it, whereupon he was invited to a table to draw his experience. When seated, David was reminded to review the experience verbally, so that it would be uppermost in his mind as he picked up his crayon to draw.

Each child in turn was given the same experience as David, with similar stimulation. Some distractible children, when they sat down to draw, needed more questioning and reviewing than David, and even an opportunity to re-enact the experience. Three of the children with better attention than David participated together in the "swinging." Afterwards, while drawing their experiences, they were seated at different tables so that they would not be influenced by each other.

When they were finished, each child was immediately asked about his picture. All except one of the pictures portrayed arms, even though some children had not been known to put arms on figures before. Most of the arms extended out at the side, but in two drawings the arms were extended upward, and, in most of the drawings, were longer than usual. One child had drawn a recognizable human form, though crude, for the first time.

After having such firsthand, kinaesthetic experiences, older trainable boys and girls also can represent themselves in various activities rather than continually drawing stereotypes—airplanes, flowers, trees, or houses.

When a child is especially delighted, he may be highly motivated and need to have the opportunity immediately to express these feelings in some creative medium. The teacher may encourage the children's portrayal of positive feelings by suggestive questions such as, "What do you love to do?" or by referring to situations or people the child likes, such as, "It is snowing," or "You are going shopping with your mother." When a child is upset, he may need help in expressing these feelings in a similar way. A rag doll "baby" may be scolded and beaten. A "daddy" modeled from clay may be decapitated. Or a fear may be diminished after it is painted:

Hank was very much afraid of thunderstorms. The rain storm from Grofe's "Grand Canyon Suite" was played on the phonograph and the attention of the children was directed to parts of the music sounding like the rain, wind or thunder. After talking about the music, the children were encouraged to paint a thunderstorm. Hank selected black and dark blue to paint the storm, adding vivid red for lightning. This whole experience of hearing the record of the storm and painting it was repeated to help Hank, whose fear lessened considerably after a number of these experiences of "painting out" his fear.

Rose, who frequently used art as a form of communication, also expressed her feelings through her art work. Once, just before the class had begun their painting period, she had been scolded for tampering with the phonograph when the teachers were absent. In art period she then painted herself playing the phonograph. (Since then the boys and girls have had the opportunity to learn on a less delicate instrument how to operate a record-player carefully.)

Self-Expression Through Dramatic Play

In other activities, such as dramatics, many trainable children show little imagination, but this is not true of all of them. You may find children with imaginary playmates. One mongoloid boy in the author's experience had a "wife" who was to be included at the lunch table; another scolded herself and when asked about this said her "Daddy" was talking. Other trainable children have excitedly and spontaneously depicted the exploits of cowboys or "bad guys" and "good guys" with no encouragement in school. Many trainable children, especially the older ones, play "house," "barber," and other such games.

Some trainable children, and often the younger or less mature ones, cannot imagine the simplest situation. One group could not portray giving a cat milk, without having the actual dish in hand, and then did not realize that it had to be placed on the floor so the "cat"—another child—could drink from it. Trainable children will require much stimulation to begin imagining situations. They may benefit from guidance in recalling their experiences, and from the presence of realistic, concrete objects to use as props.

Although many of these children need encouragement and suggestions to grasp the idea of pretending, they do not often benefit from imitating a teacher's portrayal, which may be meaningless to them. The value of make-believe to the child comes from portraying behavior as he himself has seen and understood it, or as he would like it to be.

Rehearsing for even very simple dramatic productions has not been included in the list of activities, because spontaneity and true self-expression, to bring about greater understanding of oneself and one's environment, are often sacrificed in productions directed toward audience acceptance.

Also, these children's individual performances for an audience are not encouraged in school. Trainable children may act cute when they are small, but few of them will be capable of providing quality entertainment to an adult audience later. In order to gain legitimate recognition, the severely retarded child should be trained, not in dramatic presentations leading to exhibitionism, but in language development through which he can communicate with other people, and in work activities through which he can serve other people.

When the trainable child participates in dramatic play, or any creative activity, the teacher should constantly ask herself, not "What kind of finished product can I help him make?" but "What is the child getting out of this activity?"

Charles had been diagnosed, when younger, by the best hospitals and clinics as deaf, emotionally disturbed, or mentally retarded, or a combination of these. For a while he had been taught as a deaf child. At the age of seven, upon recommendation of a clinic which had newly studied his case, he was placed in a school for trainable children. He was reported to be functioning in many ways like a trainable child, and rated on intelligence tests as border-line between educable and trainable. He had previously attended nursery schools, but he was so shy and inhibited that he would not even talk to his teacher in his new class. When given paint or crayons he merely scribbled and would not play with clay. He was the only child in class who never wanted to take a drawing or painting home. His mother said he had been encouraged to use creative media at home, but that he probably compared his drawings with the superior ones of his younger sister and so showed no interest in drawing or clay work.

In school Charles was permitted to carry around and encouraged to play freely with his teddy bear and, later, a toy frog which he brought from home. In free play period they were his companions in his "house," in which he played the role of mother. He talked freely to his toy pets, and, much later, began to include the teacher, who had gradually begun to let him know she was interested in his play. Later still, as he found his play was accepted and he could enjoy it unselfconsciously, he began to include another child or two in his play. In school at this time he was still speaking to no one except his teacher and classmates, and to them only when no one else was present. For a long time he talked to them only in the free play period, when he always played "house."

In music class, where other older children and other adults, such as the music teacher, were included, he did not participate in rhythmic activities at first. After a while, he was willing to have his teddy bear act out "The Bear Went Over the Mountain," or his frog jump to appropriate music. He used these animals over an extended period of time to do what he was too selfconscious to do himself.

It was primarily the frog and an attachment to one of his class-mates which stimulated Charles to express himself in an art media other than dramatic play. His friend Paul had a toy frog too, and Paul placed his own frog on the table beside the terrarium where the real frog was. Charles would do the same with his frog. Once when Paul drew a picture of his frog, Charles did too—copying the *idea* of drawing his frog from Paul, but not Paul's *portrayal*.

Charles also became interested in three live turtles. His favorite song became the turtle song, and he would ask for it and act it out himself—not needing the frog or bear any more to perform for him. His picture of the turtle, "Red Spot," with three worms which the children had fed him was stimulated by his interest in the class pets and his experience in feeding them. At this point he was able to tell his teacher about his picture, motivated as he was by his satisfaction with his drawing. He began to use clay, as well as crayons and paints, to portray the turtles.

Finally, as time went on, some of Charles's growing freedom in expressing himself in a variety of ways carried over into the home. Although he still would not sing in school with the large group of older and younger children, his mother reported he sang school songs to himself at home. His reluctance for about two years to take pictures home was ignored by both home and school, but his mother was delighted to find that, one day, he brought a picture home of his own accord.

After two years Charles was comfortable enough with people so that he wanted to accompany Paul to the speech teacher. Here he received some help in talking more freely. If he had not left the school, the speech teacher could have begun working directly on improving his speech sounds, which were more infantile than one would expect of a boy of his mental age (the result, possibly, of some fluctuating loss of hearing).

The child guidance clinic where he was taken periodically found him to be much improved socially and emotionally on each of his visits and attributed it in some part to the kind of school atmosphere, teacher, and program which he was being given. The opportunity for Charles to express himself freely in one area—dramatics—and the gradual, gentle stimulation of other types of expression helped him develop a variety of media for expression, so that he became a happier, freer boy. He showed growing self-confidence in a variety of ways: in his "showing off" at times, in his ability to run errands and deliver verbal messages, in his actually speaking to strangers, in his speaking up for what he wanted.

After two years in the trainable class, Charles might have adjusted to an educable class if there had been a suitable one for him. At the end of his third year, he had grown enough in self-confidence to convince the clinic, the school, and his parents that he should try an educable class. Even though the children were his superiors mentally, physically, and chronologically, he was able at this point to make a satisfactory adjustment to the class.

SELF-EXPRESSION ACTIVITIES

Water Play: Given a large basin of water, a Beginner will have a fine time squeezing sponges, pushing objects in the water, and chasing soapsuds. He will, however, need considerable supervision and also a smock that has waterproof material sewn inside the front of the smock. An Intermediate may like to blow soap bubbles, give the rubber doll a bath, or sail his boats. More satisfactory than the large basin, when the weather is warm, would be the wading pool.

Sand or Sawdust Play: An outdoor sandbox containing a small amount of damp sand and some rubber or plastic shovels and pails is fun for the Beginner. Dry sand or sawdust needs more supervision, since it more readily flies into eyes and hair. Hats with brims and with ties under the chin reduce such sandbox hazards.

The Intermediate may want a sprinkling can, so that he can mix a little water with his sand. Utensils for "cooking" and large trucks (rubber or plastic) are often popular. If there can be no sandbox outdoors, a sand table or sawdust table might possibly be installed in a suitable room. Sawdust is easier to sweep up but it is slippery. A locked cover on an indoor sandbox would prevent its use at unsupervised moments. A more Advanced group may use a sand table or sawdust table in making a town or city of blocks or cardboard boxes.

Modeling: A Beginner can be given dough or plasticene (warmed, if necessary, to make it very pliable). Since he is apt to put the clay in his mouth, each child's clay may be kept in a separate plastic bag with his name on it. The Beginner may pound, pat, poke, pinch, squeeze, break, pull, roll, or throw his clay down on the table. Later, after many experiences with it, he may start making a number of shapes that look alike.

If, after a number of exposures, some children still do nothing at all with their clay, the teacher may be able to stimulate their interest by calling attention to other children. Perhaps a child will only start if the teacher is sitting beside him, playing with a piece of clay. She may even need to put her hand on his to get him started.

Some children need many reassurances that they can wash their hands afterwards before they will touch clay. Perhaps a child will need a stick or knife to poke and cut the clay before feeling comfortable about putting his fingers in it. More Advanced pupils may use sticks to make designs, decorations or features of a face.

Gradually, as a child develops, he will begin to make original, crude objects and may talk about them—perhaps a snowman, a candle holder, a jack-o'-lantern, a decorated egg, or the school turtle. He may want to model something when he is playing at cooking and eating: a birthday cake, a hot dog, a hamburger, fruit or cookies which he can pass to his friends; also, utensils for cooking or dishes from which to eat.

Self-hardening clay, which can be painted with tempera when dry, and later shellacked, will be good for making objects that are to be saved for a time, or taken home. Colored dough (one part flour, three parts salt, with vegetable coloring) will also harden, and is much cheaper. Plasticene is more easily kept off the floor than the self-hardening clay, which might better be used outdoors with inexperienced children. After self-hardening clay has become hard, it can be softened if not painted by being put back in the jar and left to soak in water.

The Advanced modeler makes plans, expresses more ideas and executes his plans better than the Intermediate. He may portray himself or another person in a variety of activities: swimming, holding a baby or other valued object, sitting on a stone or stool, sleeping in a bed, or kicking a ball. Or he may relive firsthand experiences with an animal he knows by creating it of clay. If he enjoys modeling, he may make something at home and bring it to school to show his classmates and teacher.

Blocks and Boxes: A Beginner will often dump blocks back and forth from pail to pot or arrange them in the box. He may put them in rows or in a pile. If different sized sets of blocks are given him from time to time, he may vary his activities. If he has large floor blocks, he can spread them out and walk on them, or pile them up.

An Intermediate may build a train, a bed and chair for his doll, a street for a toy car, a garage, or a fence for toy animals. He may want to build a house, a store, or furniture from large blocks or cardboard cartons. A large, flat piece of cardboard is fun to have as a roof.

Even Advanced boys and girls often like to make stores, a post office, or a library from the large blocks. They will use small blocks for houses in miniature cities.

Construction Toys: Both Intermediates and Advanced pupils will have fun creating vehicles, buildings, or designs with Tinkertoys, Blockraft, Snap Blocks, or other construction toys. (See Appendix E, "Selected Educational Materials," for sources of some of these.) The more Advanced pupils can make shelters and even towns (adding toy people, cars, planes, and animals) from Lincoln Logs or Minibrix. Long boards may represent bridges or railroad tracks.

Finger Painting: A Beginner in finger painting would be happy using fluffy white soap flakes on a smooth, bright piece of linoleum. An Intermediate can enjoy the regular finger paint, using fingers, palms, and whole hands as he wishes. Not only will he make designs, but he may portray such situations as: snow, rain, wind, running fast, spinning like a top, the grassy park, the lake, or taking a bath. An Advanced finger painter may represent many other situations or feelings, and make more delicate or complicated original designs.

Finger painting is messy and the teacher will need to plan this period carefully. An extra volunteer may be a necessity. A sink with running water should be available near by. The children should use smocks which extend to the knees. Dress sleeves ought not to be exposed. Smocks can be worn with the opening in the back, rather than the front. The child should sit high enough so his arms are horizontal to the table top. If a child is very reluctant to touch the paint because he does not want to get his fingers messy, he can be given a piece of cardboard with notched edges to use instead of his fingers until he gets accustomed to working with the paint. A kind of finger paint which saves the teacher's time is that which comes in powdered form and can be sprinkled on the wet paper quickly.

Drawing with Crayons: When a Beginner is given a thick, dark crayon and a large piece of newsprint he may show no interest, making a few light marks while hardly looking, or he may scribble a few seconds before losing interest. Gradually his interest may grow. He may want a second paper after finishing with one, and will like a different colored crayon.

The Intermediate can select his own crayon—a dark one, however, so that he can easily see the lines he makes—and can draw on newsprint of various shapes to stimulate different kinds of drawing. His scribbles will eventually assume some design— a scribble in one spot balancing another, a repetition of certain types of scribbles, a kind of scribble that appears repeatedly from one picture to another, scribbles that show more control. He may enjoy making his designs on his placemat for lunchtime, or decorating eggs, pumpkins, valentines, or snowmen cutouts. Gradually an Intermediate may begin naming the pictures he makes. The teacher will not ask him, "What is that?" but encourage the child to "tell about" his pictures sometimes. He then may give some other description of what he did or how he felt, not being impelled by this kind of question from the teacher to label it as a representation of something. Later on, the child may plan to represent something before he draws, and his pictures may represent recognizable objects.

A child needing special stimulation may respond to a topic of special interest to him and close to his experience, such as one of these: my family, my doll, my birthday, marching in music class, our turtle, my house, the grassy park, spinning like a top, rain.

An Advanced pupil may draw things, feelings, and people from home and school environment, and activities close to his own experience, such as music activities or domestic tasks. At this stage he can probably do well with an ordinary-sized dark crayon and, when finished drawing, can color in his outlines with crayons of other colors if he wishes. In addition to the children's ideas, the teacher may suggest topics such as the wind, fire, snow; or topics to stimulate awareness of body parts—brushing my teeth, drinking my milk, blowing my nose, eating my breakfast, looking for a coin I lost, playing ball, at the dentist, watching television, reaching for an apple, picking flowers, swimming, getting a ring for my finger, I am tired; topics with special emotional appeal—my party, my doll, my pet, my birthday present, my friend, my new clothes.

An Advanced pupil may be stimulated to draw an activity immediately after experiencing it: blowing up balloons, eating chewy candy, stretching his arms overhead, skipping or galloping, reaching for a high balloon, jumping over a rope, pulling each other while holding hands. After having interesting experiences recalled to him, an Advanced pupil may be able to respond through drawing, relating himself in his drawings to his environment: dusting the schoolroom, his room at home, at the doctor's or dentist's office, playing with others on the playground, coming to school with the things he brought, climbing the jungle gym.

A pupil in the Advanced stage may plan his drawing, and then draw recognizable representations of people, animals, and objects: the flower he is growing, the gold fish, the cat that is visiting school, his juice and crackers, a place-setting, teachers and children in his class, his family and friends, saying "Goodbye" to mother, shaking hands with friends. Gradually he may include several related things in one picture or several pictures, so that a story is told: visiting the zoo, going shopping, what he did today. He may also continue to draw designs at times. These may be of various colors and can be used to decorate napkins or place mats. He may draw on his own initative at home and bring his drawings to school to show the class. The Advanced group may even be able to work on a mural together.

Water-Color Painting: Before a child starts to paint, certain preparations need to be made, either by the teacher, when the child is inexperienced, or by the child himself. Paints can be prepared by the teacher ahead of time. Inexpensive paint, such as Alabastine, a powder paint, is adequate for the immature child, but it does crack and rub off when dry. Tempera paint is better if paintings are to be preserved and, if liquid starch is mixed with it, it will go farther. Paints should be mixed so the color is rich and the paint not too runny. Use large pieces of newsprint and large, long-handled brushes, and have sponges or rags on hand. Children should wear smocks. If children paint while standing at a low table, their arms can move freely. Most children will sit down unless the chairs are moved out of the way. A youngster who tends to move about may be provided with a chair to help him concentrate.

The Beginner can be given plain water in a small can with a wide base, for "painting" on dark wrapping paper or colored construction paper placed on table or floor. After some success in this activity, he can be given a little paint of one color to use on wrapping paper or newsprint.

The Intermediate can select, from among the colors the teacher has mixed, the paint he wants. There should be one paint brush for each container of different colored paint, so that it will not be necessary to wash off the brush when changing color. A small milk carton with the top cut off is satisfactory as a paint container. The depth of the paint should not be more than half the length of the brush bristles. The child will need to wipe his brush on the side of the paint container to prevent dripping and undesired soaking of paper. The Intermediate needs to learn to paint only on the paper, and to ask for fresh sheets when necessary. He will experiment with painting for some time, painting designs and forms as he develops.

For children who have limited ideas of form and little enthusiasm for painting, the teacher might stimulate them with suggestions of what they might paint: jack-o'-lanterns, colored eggs, rain, valentines, balloons, flowers, snow, playing with a big colored ball.

After considerable experience with painting of one color, the

Intermediate may be ready to try more than one color, in sequence. Still later, he can be given two colors at once, each with its own separate brush.

Painters should take as much responsibility as they can for cleaning up after painting. A teacher's aide is helpful on painting day to provide additional supervision while the children wash up and clean off the tables before smocks are removed. If the paintings are not too wet, space can be easily found by hanging them with spring clothespins on a wire stretched across the room, high above heads.

The Advanced painter may be able to handle two or three colors, using one brush, a can of water for rinsing, and a cloth for wiping his brush after it is rinsed. He will have his own ideas of what he wants to paint, but sometimes the teacher may give topical suggestions reflecting the pupil's interests and experiences, which may be particularly well expressed in paint: a sunny day, fire, picking flowers, the man who sells balloons, the trees in the autumn, splashing or swimming in the lake, gold fish in the aquarium, a new dress (or sweater and pants).

Advanced pupils may enjoy making a mural, depicting some common experience. They can each use separate sheets of paper, which will then be connected into one long strip, or the paper can be in one strip before they start to paint, depending upon how effectively the children function together.

Collages: Intermediates and Advanced pupils may like to select and arrange various shapes of colored or metallic bits of paper on sheets or on long strips of paper. Various other materials, such as string, drinking straws, milk bottle tops, corrugated paper, buttons and bits of colored cloth of different textures can be arranged in a similar fashion. Paste, rubber cement, or transparent tape can hold them in place. More able pupils can use staples if they desire. The Advanced pupils may work on a large collage together.

Dramatic, Dress-up, and Doll-House Play: Some Beginners have fun putting on veils, funny hats, and old skirts. A large mirror will add to their interests. They like to carry old purses and suitcases, packing and unpacking them. They may dress as mother or father, imitating some of the activities seen at home. Some youngsters will take a doll in a wagon or buggy, put it to bed, sit it up to eat, or give it a bottle.

Intermediates may play more in a group. In playing "house," different children may assume the different roles of mother and father. They may cook and have a tea party which includes several children. One child may launder, another may take care of the baby. Barber, doctor, dentist, or policeman (with large vehicles and the baby buggy as "traffic") are subjects popular for play-acting. The Intermediates usually love parades, for which they dress up and carry horns, flags, and drums.

For some Intermediates who want to play dollhouse, colorful, sturdy boxes, open at the top and with sides about three inches high can be provided. In such "rooms" the small furniture and bendable dolls will move about with ease, and their activities can be readily observed.

Advanced pupils may plan and dress up for Halloween or impromptu plays. They may want to make hats, aprons, horns, capes, or flags for a holiday parade. Sometimes they will be interested in dramatizing acceptable behavior in common social situations. Self-conscious pupils can use hand puppets to talk, sing, or dance for them. Pupils may act the part of family members or others in their environment, especially those members who present problems to particular pupils. The functions of community workers can be acted out with some degree of reality by Advanced boys and girls. A teacher may suggest problem situations which might occur or may have occurred in the daily life of a retardate who goes to and from school and perhaps other places alone: what does a girl do, for example, if a strange boy starts teasing her? Play-acting may clarify such problems and suggest solutions.

RELATED READING

Heffernan, Helen (editor). *Guiding the Young Child*. Committee of the California School Supervisors Association. Boston: D. C. Heath and Company, 1951. Chapter XI.

Lowenfeld, Viktor. *Creative and Mental Growth*. New York: The Macmillan Company, 1952.

—— *The Meaning of Creative Arts for Exceptional Children*. (Originally presented as paper at the 36th Annual Convention of the International Council for Exceptional Children in Kansas City, Missouri, on April 12, 1958.)

—— *Your Child and His Art*. New York: The Macmillan Company, 1955.

Schaeffer-Simmern, Henry. *The Unfolding of Artistic Activity*. Berkeley and Los Angeles: University of California Press, 1948.

Stacey, Chalmers L., and Manfred F. DeMartino (editors). "Psychodrama," *Counseling and Psychotherapy with the Mentally Retarded*. Glencoe, Illinois: The Free Press and the Falcon's Wing Press, 1957. Chapter VI, pp. 277–93.

VI. Music

In the school program for the trainable child, music serves as a means to an end, rather than as an art to be perfected to give pleasure to oneself and others. Because bodily rhythms and vocalizing (crying and laughing) are natural forms of expression for any human being, and because primitive responses to music require less conscious intellectual effort than other forms of expression such as drawing, music is employed in all aspects of the program to help retarded children develop to their fullest potential.

IMPORTANCE OF MUSIC TO THE TRAINABLE CHILD

Although music is effective in teaching any child, it is of particular value in a training program for retarded children. Because most of the children are fond of music, they respond to it and can focus their attention on musical activities. A child who seems unaware of his surroundings may start rocking when music is played and, through the stimulation provided by the teacher he may gradually begin to notice the music and become aware of how he can respond to it. Eventually, with encouragement, he may respond not only by rocking but by clapping, jumping, or beating a drum.

The teacher can make many learning experiences more pleasant and effective by associating them with music. Trainable children may show little interest in understanding numbers, but they will enjoy the drill on meaningful counting when it is part of a singing game. In one such game, the players form a circle with one player in the center. The children sing, "One in the circle, sing a song . . . 'til another comes along." Another child then joins the one in the center. After the group counts the two children, they sing, "Two in the circle . . ." etc. One child after another is added to the group in the middle of the circle and the group is counted each time.

Older pupils may not like physical exercises but may enjoy doing them to music. A child who is afraid of a new activity, or has an aversion to working with certain materials such as paste or sandpaper, may be helped to try it if a song accompanies the activity.

Whatever a trainable child is learning can be emphasized, and past experiences can be reviewed, by the use of music. Whether he is learning about big and little, left and right, or about a train he saw, he may learn more and remember better if he sings about it.

Because of its effects upon the emotions, music can help to create within the child a mood or attitude conducive to better functioning and learning. Soft, slow music may calm an excitable child or quiet a noisy group. A brain-injured child may be running wildly back and forth, getting more and more excited and disorganized, but may settle down to march in a circle with other children if appropriate music is played.

Stirring music may stimulate an unresponsive child into active participation with the group; and gay music may change the mood of a temporarily unhappy youngster. A child who is angry can express his hostile feelings through music by pounding a drum, crashing the cymbals, or stamping his feet, and as a result may later feel ready for other more constructive activities.

The children need physical exercise which they must get indoors in bad weather. The volume of noise and closer contact with other children in play activities and in disorganized running about in limited space may confuse and excite a trainable child unduly. In music class, however, body rhythms can give the youngsters satisfying outlets for their energy without causing bedlam in the schoolroom.

Because music is something most children like to hear, it may help them to develop better auditory perception and memory. The trainable child learns to recognize certain tunes and rhythms he likes. He learns to discriminate between loud and soft, or fast and slow, through the teacher's associating these words with musical activities. As a child becomes more accustomed to listening and responding to a variety of sounds, he will be preparing to discriminate between the many complicated combinations of sounds which make up human speech. As he beats the triangle and then the drum, he will notice the difference between these contrasting sounds. Still later, he will make distinctions between sounds or words that are not so extremely different. Auditory training through musical activities, therefore, can help the retarded child to comprehend the sounds of language.

Singing helps some children with their speech. Since they never seem to tire of old songs, it gives them a pleasurable reason for trying to make various sounds and to practice them without boredom. It also gives additional exercise to the lips, tongue, and other speech mechanisms; and the rhythm of the music is helpful in developing rhythmic speech and better articulation. For example, a new word incorrectly pronounced by the children can be taught by singing it with them on each note of the scale to rhythmic piano accompaniment. The children always enjoy this and the accompaniment helps them get the correct accent and number of syllables in the word, if the pianist is careful to play the rhythm correctly. A beginning talker gains practice in verbalizing if, after hearing a word accompany his musical activities, he starts joining in with it— "Pound, pound, pound," or "Jump, jump, jump."

Music activities can be used to promote the social development of a retarded child. They help to develop a child's awareness of others and can bring about a feeling of organization within the group. When a child who has never participated begins to clap or sway with the others, he is taking a step toward socialization. Since nearly every child enjoys the music class, even a child who tends to isolate himself may participate with others in musical activities, thus finding out that doing things with others can be fun. Later, he may take part in singing games and then in activities where success depends upon the contribution of the entire group. The rhythm band is a good example of group musical activities. The children have different instruments, but they may learn that no one instrument or person is more important than the other. A timid child gains confidence from knowing the group needs him. In music class a child may learn that he cannot always do what he wants, but that he needs to wait his turn, or sing the songs and participate in the activities that other children want. He learns that he is more readily accepted if he is cooperative.

SELECTING MUSIC APPROPRIATE FOR THE TRAINABLE CHILD

Since music can serve so many purposes, the teacher will want to select the music carefully to meet the special needs of the school program. It is not at all easy to find just the right music for these children. In selecting a piece of music for the retarded, one usually needs to go over it at least three times, each time keeping in mind one of the aspects of the selection: the melody, the rhythm, or the language.

What is suitable music for trainable children? The following criteria are helpful:

1. *Simple*. It is advisable to have the melody usually not longer than 12 measures, with repetitious phrases and a very limited range of notes. The rhythmic patterns should be short and repetitious; and the words and sentences of any song should be few in number and often repeated. The words ought to be fairly easy to pronounce and the sentences short. The accompaniment should be simple.

2. *Familiar or natural-sounding*. The melody should be singable, the rhythmic patterns such that children respond naturally with motions. The notes should be of ordinary length—neither very short, nor with long holds that the children cannot sing. The vocabulary and sentence forms ought to be those in common usage and arranged in a natural way of speaking, the

musical emphasis coinciding with the customarily stressed syllables in the words. It is best if the phrasing of the music corresponds naturally with the phrasing of the words as spoken.

3. *Clear.* The rhythm should have prominent beats emphasized a little more than ordinarily, as the piano can do so well. It is important for the singer to use a clear tone and to articulate distinctly, and for phonograph records to have good sound reproduction.

4. *Slow in tempo.* The children need to have time to sing the words, beat the rhythm, or respond to the meaning of the words. Directions on phonograph records for doing something to music need to be given very slowly, with pauses for children to get ready to respond. A piece for one rhythmic activity needs to be repeated long enough for the children to have time to act, and there should be a long interval before the next piece so they can sit down and get ready to listen to the next part of the record. A speed regulator on a phonograph is especially helpful for singing games or dances.

5. *Interesting and stimulating in melody, rhythm, and language* (unless used for quiet relaxation), but not too exciting, as syncopated rhythms might be. It would be well to have a variety of short songs or pieces on one phonograph record if it is being used for listening only, so the children's attention will not wander.

6. *Educational.* The melodies often can be based on folk tunes which have stood the test of time, or upon melodies of famous composers. The lyrics can be educational, giving information, suggesting ideas or attitudes and reviewing experiences.

7. *Meeting a wide range of needs.* The members of the class will vary considerably in language and musical ability. It is advisable to use some songs which contain parts consisting of only a few simple notes with very simple words, but also more difficult parts which will be of interest to those more advanced in speech. The least mature children will have a chance to participate by singing the very simple sections, while the others will enjoy singing the more difficult words. The same principle can be applied in selecting pieces for rhythm band use.

8. *Directed to those who are listening.* When purchasing

records, the audience must be kept in mind. Some phonograph records such as those directed to "Baby," would not appeal to a trainable youngster of eight or nine.

SUGGESTIONS FOR GUIDING MUSIC ACTIVITIES

A few hints of special importance to the teacher of trainable children in guiding music experiences are given below. Many other suggestions applicable to all children can be found in the introductory material found in the books listed in Appendix F, p. 264.

1. It is especially helpful to have a piano for accompanying body rhythms and for rhythm band because it can emphasize the beat so well. It is very important for the pianist to play rhythmically. While playing, she must also be able to watch the children, to accompany them at a suitable tempo, and to hold their attention. (The class should sit to one side of the piano.) If there is an accompanist, he must be one who can follow the teacher's directions quickly and exactly. If a piano is unavailable, sometimes a drum accompanied by singing, or certain phonograph records, may be substituted. While a phonograph is being played, it is good practice to keep it closed and if necessary, high enough so that it cannot be reached. Otherwise the intriguing spinning of the records may distract some children from attending the music.

2. At times throughout the school day, an observant teacher may stimulate a child's awareness of rhythm when he starts swaying or clapping spontaneously, by singing or playing an accompaniment on the piano. In music class the teacher can first watch the young child as he does a body rhythm, so she can play in time to his spontaneous rhythm, rather than expect him to conform to her tempo.

3. Children should become familiar with a musical selection before being expected to respond to it in a specified way. The music can be played while the children listen and later rock or clap. After several days or even weeks, when the music has become familiar, the children will be ready to learn the appropriate body rhythm, game, or song.

4. Some trainable children may respond naturally when they hear music, but most need help when learning a variety of body rhythms appropriate to the music being played. One trainable child may learn a body rhythm simply by observing the teacher or another child doing it well. Another child may need to be shown *how* to observe what the teacher is doing. He does not notice that the teacher is walking on her toes unless she calls his attention to her feet and raises her heels while he is looking. He does not extend his arms unless he sees her in the process of raising hers. She may then walk in front of him, facing him with her arms extended, so that he will do likewise.

If a child does not seem to learn from observing, and yet seems developmentally ready to learn a body rhythm, the teacher might give him physical assistance in assuming the appropriate position. To show him how to tiptoe, she may support him under his arms, raise him on his toes and help him walk in this position. For "airplane," she may raise his arms and support them in the extended position, removing her support momentarily until he gets the idea of keeping them extended himself. At first, for the difficult "Duck Walk," a child may need to be supported under his arm pits while he tries to walk in a squatting position. Then he can make attempts by himself.

Results can be achieved with other children through the use of verbal directions. For a child who is clapping fast in an uncontrolled way, a teacher may say, "Make a big clap"; she may say, "Try to touch the ceiling with your hands," to give him the idea of raising his arms straight over his head. A child's own verbalization may help him to attend better and use his body with greater control. He can sing, "Step, step" as he is walking to music. When he is to play a bell at a certain time, he may find it helpful if he sings all the words, starting to play the bell on the cue words, "Ding, dong." In a rhythm band piece, he may be able to play as directed if he says, "Beat, rest, rest," and so on.

5. A teacher of a beginning group of trainable youngsters may have difficulty introducing singing games. She could enlist the assistance of some volunteers or more mature trainable boys

and girls to help hold the children's hands. They can also carry on the singing when the teacher has to give verbal directions. For Beginners, the most successful games are those in which all the players—except perhaps the one who is "It"—are seated.

When a youngster drops out of a game, he may disrupt it and distract the other children. If a game is chosen where all the children hold hands, this child is less likely to become a problem. When the teacher is confronted with the problem of a child too shy, negative, over-active, or playful to stand up and join hands, she may be able to start him in the game by giving him the privilege of sitting in the middle of the circle.

MUSIC ACTIVITIES *

A. Finger Plays and Action Games (while seated)

I. BEGINNER

Pound fists together or on chair or floor, while singing about hammering.
Roll clay and sing about rolling.
While teacher sings, play pat-a-cake, rock baby, wash face.

II. INTERMEDIATE

Sing and play game "Did You Ever See a Lassie?"
Sing and play "Eensie Weensie Spider." Substitute wiggling of fingers for the usual, more difficult finger activity of representing spider.

III. ADVANCED

Sing and play "Follow the Leader."

B. Body Rhythms

I. BEGINNER

Rock back and forth or sideways in chair.
Clap hands.

* For songs and music to accompany activities suggested here, see Appendix F, pp. 259–64.

Walk in large circle, following others around room.

Run freely.

Jump with both feet.

Sway sideways.

Roll on floor.

Spin like a top while standing or sitting.

Walk with arms extended sideward, keeping them steady, like an airplane.

Walk like a show horse: Raise knees high in front, while taking short steps. (Teacher helps, if necessary, by walking backwards in front of child and extending her hand over each of his knees. Child tries to touch her hand with first one knee, then the other.) Same activity may be used for walking in deep snow.

Tiptoe. Get idea from watching teacher's heels as she raises them from the floor.

See-saw. Rock back and forth, holding hands with partner and facing him, feet arranged so that right foot of one partner is outside and his left foot is between the feet of his partner.

Run on hands and feet, like a dog.

II. INTERMEDIATE

March in a large circle.

Swing arms straight over head and back to sides rhythmically.

Gallop. May be facilitated if teacher takes both hands of learner and slides sideways with him in gallop time. It may be helpful if the teacher says, "Put one foot forward," before the music starts.

Tramp.

Crawl slowly like a turtle.

Take slow, heavy strides like a giant.

Simulate leaves or snowflakes falling: Stretch arms high above head. Have them descend forward slowly to the floor, without legs bending if possible. Fingers are wiggled at same time.

Walk slowly on all fours, legs straight, simulating a bear.

Run, arms extended at sides and moving up and down like a bird.

Imitate an elephant: Walk slowly in bent position, swaying sideways, arms straight and hands together like elephant's trunk.

Walk like a duck in squatting position, hands on hips, elbows extended.

Hop on one foot. If necessary, hold onto furniture for support at first. After hopping on one foot, change to other for a while.

Skip. To learn, hold onto teacher around waist in skating fashion, while teacher demonstrates how first one, then the other foot is extended in front while other foot is hopping. "Put one foot forward, then the other."

Jump slowly with both feet, like a rabbit or frog.

Simulate ascending jungle gym or steps of slide: Raise knees high while standing in place, arms reaching up alternately.

III. ADVANCED

Act out swimming: Rotate arms in crawl fashion; stepping motions with feet.

Slide sideways, either holding partner's hands while facing him, or moving sideways, single file, around circle.

Sway like trees in the wind, bending to side, arms extended.

Leap.

Combine several actions: Run and leap, walk and run, etc.

Do exercises to music such as deep knee bend; stretching of arms up, out, down.

Listen to music and then do original dance to it. Or, after showing teacher the kind of original dance desired, do it when teacher plays appropriate music for it.

C. Body Rhythms or Motions Emphasizing Auditory Perception

I. INTERMEDIATE

Do body rhythms in time with music.

Do body rhythm indicated by a familiar musical selection.

Walk to music, then tiptoe when music becomes quieter.

Clap loudly when music is played loudly, clap softly when music is soft.

Walk to music, then run or gallop when music changes speed or rhythm becomes fast, then walk again as music indicates.

When spinning as a top, fall down on last chord of music.

Bounce balls to music, saying: "Bounce and catch, and bounce and catch."

Be a jack-in-the-box: From a squatting position, jump up on chord. Also, make a toy jack-in-the-box pop up on chord.

Be Jack-Be-Nimble: Jump over a very short candle or block, at end of song, or when chord and word "Jump" is sung.

Play game of Pass the Pumpkin:

Pass the Pumpkin (or egg, depending upon the season): Children form circle and sit down. One child sits inside circle. Children pass pumpkin around circle while music plays. Child in center goes to one holding pumpkin when music stops, takes other child's place at same time he takes pumpkin from him. Child who had pumpkin sits inside circle.

II. ADVANCED

Musical Chairs (or Going to Jerusalem): In this popular old game, some children may be too frustrated when they are "out." They can be the ones who take the chairs off the end of the row of chairs after the music stops each time. Then they may sit by the piano, keeping time to the music with relatively quiet instruments (thin sticks or tiny rattles) which will not drown out the effect of the piano's stopping if they forget to stop.

Bounce balls to music: "Bounce, catch, hold" (3/4 time); "Bounce, bounce, bounce, hold" (4/4 time); "Bounce and bounce and bounce and hold" (6/8 time).

Do body rhythms appropriate to drum beat or to one musical piece that is played at different speeds or volumes: Run; walk; skip or gallop; tiptoe; stamp; clap hands loudly or softly; jump or hop.

Keeping time to the music, do a combination of rhythms appropriate to the music: Tiptoe and jump, run and leap, skip and whirl, push and pull (with partner).

D. Singing Games

I. BEGINNER

Jump with other children on jumping board while teacher sings
slow, rhythmic song such as "Get on Board, Li'l Children"
or "Jump, John Doe."

Play with children on equipment while teacher sings appropriate song, such as "Here we go round the jungle gym," to
"Mulberry Bush."

Walk to own name while other children sing the name, repeating
it up the musical scale. Each child has a turn.

Roll ball while song is sung.

Play game indicated by words of each of these singing game songs
and other very simple ones:

Row Your Boat: Rock forward and backward with partner,
while seated on the floor facing him. Also, row like a racing
crew, several children sitting one behind the other with hands
on each other's shoulders. Rock back and forth.

See-saw: Sway back and forth with partner.

Train: While all children walk, taking very small steps around
the room, hold onto shoulder or waist of child in front.

II. INTERMEDIATE

Play more difficult singing games, following directions given in
song books.

Halloween Game: Form circle, with pumpkin in center. To
the tune of "Mulberry Bush" sing "Now we get ready for Halloween . . . and make a Jack-o'-Lantern." A player will enter
the circle and act out "This is the way we cut off the top to
make a Jack-o'-Lantern." Another child will then act out remaining verses.

III. ADVANCED

Play singing games already listed, and more difficult ones such
as "Looby Loo," "Hokie Pokie," and "Paw Paw Patch."

E. Play-Acting

I. INTERMEDIATE

Act out songs appropriate for play-acting, such as those describing community workers, animals, or school and home activities.

F. Rhythm Instrument Activities

I. BEGINNER

Play freely with various sound-making toys.
Starting and stopping:
  Keep instrument quiet until told to play.
  Play only when music begins and stop when music stops.
  Keep instrument quiet even though music is playing.
  Play instrument only when directed.
In group, play instrument different from those of other children, so that sound of own instrument can be heard. When proficient, play same instrument as other children.
Beating rhythmically:
  Pound clay or pegs into board rhythmically. Teacher sings in time to child's beats.
  Clap hands in own rhythm. Teacher sings or plays accompaniment.
Listen to and watch others beat time to music.
Join teacher in beating time to a song.
Join other child who is keeping time to music.

II. INTERMEDIATE

Starting and stopping:
  Instrument should be forfeited temporarily if played when it should be silent.
  Near end of song play instrument, where words and music indicate it, without direction from teacher.
  Play instrument during song when directed by teacher; stop when directed.
  Play instrument with one group of children and remain quiet while other group plays, then play again as in "Jingle Bells"

when one group simulates horses' hoofs with clappers and sticks during verse of song, while others play bells only during chorus.

Beating in time:

Listen to music, then clap in time. Later, when music is familiar, beat instrument in time.

Beat in time to piece at medium speed, then to one at faster tempo, then to one at slower tempo.

Handling instruments:

Hold instruments as teacher demonstrates, to get most effective sound from them.

Use instruments only for band play. Instrument is removed if not used in acceptable fashion.

III. ADVANCED

Starting and stopping:

Start playing after an introduction.

In band number, start playing from melody and rhythm cues for a particular instrument.

Lead band, indicating when different instruments come in.

Beat only on accented beats.

Play only one beat where music indicates, as a cymbal crash in Haydn's *Surprise Symphony* and in "Pop Goes the Weasel."

Beating time:

Change tempo with tempo change in music.

March and beat time.

Dance and play instrument in time (individually).

Volume:

Beat softly or loudly, depending upon teacher's direction or upon piano or words of song.

Handling instruments:

Experiment with different effects produced by playing instrument.

Learn from teacher different ways to play instruments.

Play one instrument in different ways during piece, such as shaking or beating a tambourine.

Learn to handle records and operate old phonograph until this can be done carefully enough to operate good machine.

G. Dances

I. INTERMEDIATE

Do very simple dances, including such motions as walking, bowing, clapping, and jumping. (Follow directions in music books.)

Do circle dances, originated and called by teacher, such as this one:

Holding hands, circle right eight steps; circle left eight steps; walk four steps to center, four steps back; circle right eight steps. Then repeat whole dance, but this time clap hands during middle part instead of walking to center. For the third verse, substitute spinning in place during the middle part.

II. ADVANCED

Do more difficult circle dances. (Follow directions in music books.)

Dancing with a partner, do simplified versions of dances, such as this one to the tune of "Buffalo Gal":

Boys walk around room, each selects and bows to a girl as song words suggest, dances with her, and then returns her to her seat.

Do simple square dances where dancers circle, swing, promenade in couples, and the boys, then girls, walk to center, circling or clapping.

Simplified Virginia Reel: Row of boys and row of girls approach each other at one time, bow, and move back on line together. An adult at the head of the line can make sure that everyone faces that direction and turns to the outside (boys to the left, girls to the right) before separating and marching single file to the foot of the line. Another adult can receive them there, see that they get their partners, and then direct them under the bridge.

H. Singing

I. BEGINNER

Sing the few repetitive words or phrases in very simple songs which are selected by the teacher. (Teacher selects songs appropriate for particular situations or occasions, such as a song about a birthday, the kind of weather on a certain day, a toy animal that someone brought to school.)

Sing "Old MacDonald" with a simplified chorus.

Sing "Bye-bye (or 'Good-bye') everybody, it's time to go," (simplified words for the song, "Going to School").

II. INTERMEDIATE

Learn a variety of simple songs.

Listen first, then try to match tone of teacher as she sings certain words or phrases in very simple songs, with repetitive tones.

III. ADVANCED

Try to sing simple, well-known adult songs and choruses of more difficult ones. Some examples are: "For He's a Jolly Good Fellow," "Down in the Valley," "Take Me Out to the Ball Game," "Sailing." (In the case of a more difficult song, if the tune is easy the teacher can substitute easier words for it.)

RELATED READING

Martin, Bertha W. *Teaching Extremely Retarded Children.* Kent, Ohio: Kent State University, 1955, pp. 15–62.

Murphy, Mary Martha. "Rhythmical Responses of Low Grade and Middle Grade Mental Defectives to Music Therapy," *Journal of Clinical Psychology,* XIII (October, 1957), 361–64.

Weigl, Vally. "Functional Music: A Therapeutic Tool in Working with the Mentally Retarded," *American Journal of Mental Deficiency,* LXIII (January, 1959), 672–78.

VII. Language

Trainable children should be assisted in developing the ability to communicate verbally. They need to make their wants known and be able to understand and answer other people's questions and requests. A trainable person can learn a great deal about his environment and the people whom he meets if he comprehends spoken language. Other people will be more understanding of him if he can convey his thoughts to them through speech, simple though it may be. Spoken language will make it possible for the retardate to adjust more adequately to his home and to his community.

GUIDING LANGUAGE DEVELOPMENT

When guiding the children's language development, several problems need to be considered. It is necessary to realize that these children can generally enlarge their vocabularies with words of concrete rather than of abstract meaning, and can usually learn only simple language structure.

Since the children differ in their interests and behavior, the language problems of individuals in the group have to be met in different ways. There will be individual variations in language ability, some of which are the result of differences in chronological age and intelligence. Language difficulties will vary in degree and in kind. Emotional problems contribute to the language disturbance of some of the children, and in others special factors such as aphasia or motor handicaps are the partial cause of language disability. In order to understand better the limitations and differences of the children, the teacher may need special professional assistance. When she suspects that a child has a language disability greater than his mental retardation might account for, she or her principal may be able to arrange with a speech clinic or speech teacher to have the child's difficulty studied.

Guiding the Development of Receptive Language

Before a hearing person can learn to understand language, he must be receptive to auditory stimulation and be able to discriminate one sound from another. He must learn to attend to human vocal sounds and to distinguish the sounds of one word from those of another. When he has learned to do these, he can then attach meanings to certain combinations of sounds and thus begin to understand language. Activities listed in this chapter will help direct the children's attention to noises and speech sounds. Since authorities on delayed speech emphasize the importance of the child's hearing many repetitions of the same speech sounds, it is advisable to use the same stories, songs and phonograph records over and over.

In order to help the children understand more words, the school activities should provide opportunities for associating language with experience—visual, auditory, tactile, kinaesthetic. Pictures, movies, and real objects can be presented so that the children see what is being talked about. The teacher's gestures and facial expressions also help to give meaning to what is said. The meaning of some words, such as "whistle" and "loud" are made more clear by the use of auditory aids. If a child is shouting, the teacher may say to him in loud tones, "That is too loud," and add in a quiet voice, "Talk softly." Touching objects makes some words easier for the children to understand. In woodshop, for instance, the children may feel a *rough* piece of wood and then sand it until it is *smooth* to the touch. Acting out words like "jump" or "throw" make it possible for the children to get the meaning kinaesthetically.

Verbal directions are valuable in helping the children increase their comprehension of spoken language. Directions should be given slowly in very simple language and then discussed. The children will realize that they have to listen carefully and understand what is said if the teacher refrains from using gestures to help them get the meaning. However, for some children pantomime and illustrations may need to be used. There could be several possible reasons for a child's failure to respond to a direction: the teacher may not have given him time enough to absorb what he has heard; he may not have been listening; he may not have understood some of the words; he may not have been able to combine the perceived words into a meaningful whole; he may not know how to carry out the direction even though he understands it; or he may not want to respond.

A good way to help a child attend to directions is to teach him to look at the face of the person speaking. At first the teacher may often need to remind him, "Watch me." Sometimes a restatement of the direction in different words makes it clear to the child. In the case of a child who does not feel like responding, a repetition of the direction in a lively or dramatic manner sometimes provides the necessary impetus for him to carry out the direction.

The children can be questioned to determine if they have understood a story or discussion. Questioning also gives an opportunity for review of the meaning of words, but should be geared to each child's ability to comprehend.

If a retardate knows the meaning of most of the words he hears, he can sometimes understand a new word from the context of the sentence. But if there are too many new words, the meaning of what he hears will be lost and he may become habitually inattentive to what people say. It is important for the teacher to know the children well, so that she will not make the mistake of using language too difficult for them to understand.

A trainable child needs systematic help in developing language concepts. If a teacher keeps in mind the concept she is trying to develop at any particular time, she can encourage the development of this concept during many activity periods each day. When most of the children seem ready to learn the concept "around," they can make cars on which the wheels go around;

they can roll inflated tubes while singing about how they go around, and demonstrate the motion with their arms. They can watch a top whirl around, and spin around themselves, afterwards drawing pictures of how they went around. They can make their feet go around as they pedal their bikes on the playground or pretend to pedal while sitting in their chairs in music class. They can make balls of clay, rolling them around and around. They can join hands and dance around in a circle. In such ways their concept of the meaning of "around" is strengthened and broadened.

Ways of illuminating the meaning of "jack-o'-lantern" might include: picking a pumpkin in the field, buying one at a store, carving it, singing about it, smelling it when the candle is lit, making one out of clay; listening to stories about pumpkins, doing form board puzzles made to represent jack-o'-lanterns, drawing them, painting pictures of them; planting pumpkin seeds and growing a pumpkin, eating pumpkin pie.

Guiding the Development of Expressive Language

Many trainables who understand language do not express themselves in words. Some of them have very little speech and others do not use the language ability they have. Often a child who is able to speak in sentences will say only one word instead of using more words to make a clear statement. The problem for the teacher is to provide an environment and experiences which will help the children gain additional satisfaction from expanded verbal expression.

Some of the inarticulate children need the opportunity simply to babble. When a child without speech makes a sound, the teacher can repeat it over and over. Doing so may stimulate the child to continue vocalizing, trying different sounds as he gains pleasure and attention from his attempts.

For the benefit of those who can talk a little, the teacher should try to make the classroom atmosphere conducive to speaking. Small groups make it easy to have more informality than would be possible in the average size class of a public school. The children will need to be reminded to talk one at a time during group conversation periods, but they need not raise their hands or wait for permission before speaking. Free talking can be encouraged during the time for looking at books, free play, lunch, and before school.

Care should be taken to make the children feel successful in their efforts to speak. The teacher can give the children simple, correct words and language patterns to imitate, but should not insist that the children talk. A child who has difficulty in communicating, such as a stutterer, should find his teacher a sympathetic listener with time to try to understand the whole story. Beginning attempts at speaking, no matter how poor, should be delightedly accepted by the teacher. Even the more articulate children are better off with as little criticism as possible, and their conversation need not be interrupted for speech correction. If a child becomes confused and unable to talk when he is asked a question, the teacher can direct attention toward some other person in order to cover the child's confusion. Some children may seldom be called upon to take part in a group conversation because they are disturbed when asked to speak and do not seem ready for such an experience.

Before a child will want to talk, he needs to establish a good relationship with the teacher and the other children. The teacher should proceed cautiously in eliciting verbal responses from newcomers who may not want to talk, until it is evident that these children have become adjusted and comfortable in their new situation. When they begin to relate well to the others in the group, they may become interested in what the others say to them and will respond.

A few of the children may have emotional problems which further hinder their speech development. The teacher should try to satisfy the emotional needs of such children as best she can by giving them sympathetic understanding and providing a permissive and pleasant atmosphere. Perhaps the most effective instrument in inducing speech is the school situation itself. An atmosphere of emotional well-being and opportunities for group play and participation in interesting activities are conducive to verbal expression. Often the children are most talkative when happily engrossed in group play. At other times, a sudden, strong feeling of pleasure or of annoyance may bring forth a vocal response. If the classroom atmosphere is free enough for a child to express both positive and negative feelings, verbalization may develop more readily.

One of the most important parts of the language development program is the daily discussion period. The children can sometimes be encouraged to talk about anything they wish. Trainables who are inclined to imitate should be called upon first so that they will not merely copy what others say. By asking questions about something she knows interests a child, the teacher may suggest responses to a child who can think of nothing to say. The teacher can repeat the remarks of each child to the group, showing that she attaches importance to his remarks and feels that the others too, will be interested. After they have attended the "meetings" for a long time, most of the children learn to distinguish between what is relevant to the discussion and what is not. They also learn to take turns in talking and to be quiet while another child is speaking.

The discussions should be centered around ideas close to the children's experience. A subject should be kept simple, and new words and concepts should be reviewed often so the children will remember them. The single words of the less articulate children can be elaborated into phrases or sentences by the more articulate, with assistance from the teacher. For instance, if a child says "Fish," he may be asked to say more about the fish. He might then say "Swim." The teacher or another child would put this into a simple sentence such as, "The fish swim," or "The fish swim in the water." Some of the discussions can be made into stories. As the children contribute to a story, the teacher writes down what they say, in their own words (except for flagrantly bad English or confused ideas). She can rearrange the remarks so that the story will be in logical order. These stories should be reread frequently in the ensuing discussion periods.

Many trainables articulate so poorly that they cannot be understood by anyone who does not know them well. As they become more interested in having the teachers and other children understand them, they may put forth more effort to speak clearly and be more willing to accept correction. Sometimes, when such a child cannot be understood, the teacher can point out to him that the others do not understand him. She can then make a suggestion, such as that he talk more slowly, keep his hands away from his mouth, or put his lips together when he says a certain word. A recording instrument may be effective in stimulating the children to articulate better. The children understand that they will hear themselves when the recording is played back, and they may respond unusually well to suggestions while making a recording.

Additional help may be obtained to assist the children with their individual speech problems. Sometimes a speech therapist, or, if he is unavailable, a student from the speech department of a university or a volunteer with speech training may be able to stimulate interest in speech by taking the children singly for short periods. The older children appreciate the opportunity to talk without interruption to someone who has time to listen, and the younger children with delayed speech may develop their vocabularies with help from a speech instructor who gives them individual attention. If such a specialist is not familiar with trainable children, she will need much guidance by the regular teacher. For example, the classroom teacher may need to emphasize that teaching her children words they need and cannot yet say will be of far greater value to them than correcting individual sounds. The teacher can give the speech instructor a list of words for each child, which he needs to learn to say well enough to communicate. Refining his language—"Hi!" to "Good morning," or "wanna" to "want to"—is not as important as teaching him to express himself well enough to be understood.

Even were they available, daily individual speech lessons in themselves would have little enduring effect on the trainable's speech. Throughout the day, the classroom teacher needs to supplement the individual speech work. During the daily program, reminders to say words correctly should be made quietly and pleasantly by the teacher. The reminders work well if repeated frequently, but drill of this kind should be confined to a very few words for each child and continued over a fairly long period of time. Words have to be repeated very slowly, over and over again. The children may learn to make some sounds by watching the teacher's mouth and tongue, or by listening to the sounds she makes. For example, a child may learn to pronounce the "th" in "Thursday" while he and the teacher look into a mirror. He may enjoy imitating the exaggerated position of the teacher's tongue between the teeth; others learn to make the "ch" sound by imitating a dramatic sneeze or a simulated train sound.

In working with trainables each child's speech needs to be considered as an individual problem, but in all cases it should be remembered that the factor of mental deficiency is primary. The difficulty of trainable children in learning symbols and abstractions, their poor auditory perception, their lack of interest in learning for the sake of learning, their inability to read—all make it necessary for a teacher to discard her usual speech correction techniques. It takes ingenuity to discover how these children learn speech and to devise ways to guide them in developing the speech they need and can acquire.

Since the purpose of speech work for the trainable is to help him communicate with others, memorizing for recitation provides little help. Learning words by singing songs is easier and more fun than memorizing poems or learning just words. Songs can be found that contain very common and simple words useful to the children in communicating their own thoughts.

Although a child's articulation and sentence structure might be poor, it is usually advisable for the teacher to stress vocabulary development rather than correct enunciation and grammar. A child must have words to answer questions, to ask for what he needs and wants, and to express his ideas and feelings to others. Perfect grammar, and even silence, may be socially desirable in some circles, but extensive use of understandable language, perfect or imperfect, is far more important for the happy adjustment of the trainable child.

Selecting Books and Pictures for Language Development: When choosing a book for any child, one usually considers the subject of the story, the text, and the illustrations. Since a teacher of trainables can seldom find well illustrated books written in language that is meaningful and of interest to them, she must interpret the pictures in each book as best she can, by including elements of the original text that she feels are of value or by making up a more appropriate story. In her selection of books, then, the text is relatively unimportant if the subject and pictures of the book meet certain standards. Some criteria for selecting books and pictures appropriate for trainable children are as follows:

The subject matter and representation should be as realistic as possible—not fanciful. They should contribute to the child's development by being emotionally satisfying (never frightening), by stimulating him to use language, by providing him with useful knowledge. Comics or stylized drawings are not desirable.

Good books for beginners have a short bit of text which presents one fact on a page that is illustrated by a clear, simple picture. The subjects are those which the child will easily understand—toys, food, family members. Intermediates will like books dealing with family activities and the simplest books available about school, animals, transportation, and community workers who come to school or home. For the Advanced boys and girls the subject matter may be a bit more complicated—community features (park, zoo), public employees, early teen-age activities, simple nature study.

Illustrations should usually be fairly large, and, unless they are photographs (some of which are excellent), colored in clear, rich hues. There should be only a few objects in one picture. The subjects should be simple, but as complete as possible (preferably not a dog with apparently only three legs). The background should be unobtrusive but contrasting.

A partial listing of books having these qualities may be found in Appendix G, pp. 265–67.

READING, UNDERSTANDING, AND RESPONDING TO PRINTED SIGNS

Within the reading area a generally accepted activity for the trainable is learning to recognize a few signs. Because of the importance of some sign words to the severely retarded, this activity may prove beneficial. However, without an understanding of phonics it can be difficult to recognize these sign words when seen in varied print and in combination with unknown words on commercial signs.

There are other problems for the trainable child in learning signs. A boy may know the sign cards: "MEN," "Men," "GENTLE-MEN," and "Gentlemen." He may recognize the signs one sees written like this: "gentlemen," "men." He may possibly know "gents," but he would certainly be confused by the signs: "His," "Hers"; "Guys," "Gals." The teacher will have to weigh the value of sign-learning against that of other school activities and plan what she will teach, depending upon the majority of the children's ability to learn and to use many of the skills that will be taught.

How can sign-recognition be taught? In presenting a new sign word to be learned, the teacher should explain and demonstrate the meaning of the word immediately, whether the child is able to pronounce the word clearly or not. If she introduces "EXIT," she can hold the sign up on the door, tell the children it means to go out, and then have the children do so. The "EXIT" sign should be put on the door from which the pupils actually leave the room. "DANGER" is more difficult to associate with meaning through acting out, but a sign can be placed near the school furnace room, and the class taken on trips there. They can also go on trips farther afield, until they discover something dangerous, whereupon the teacher will display the appropriate sign or a child will select it from several signs held by the teacher. Places for "Danger" signs might be a busy street crossing, a construction job, or an open manhole.

While the children sit together as a class they can learn to respond to printed cards by standing when they see a word applying to them, such as "girls," "boys," or their names.

Meaning should always be associated with the configuration of the words. A card holder can be used to display two words, such as "MEN" and "WOMEN." A boy can be given the sign "MEN," and be told what it says. Then he can match his card with the one already displayed, by placing it under "MEN," and then saying "Men," perhaps after the teacher if he does not remember it. A girl could then be helped to do the same with a duplicate card of "WOMEN." Another boy and girl could then have turns, but each time they will be reminded of the meaning of the word.

Learning to recognize one's name in print usually precedes the learning of signs, but the methods used can be similar. Sign words to be learned should be printed in simple black lettering on manila or white cardboard. Later on, the children should learn to recognize them in a variety of commercial printing as well.

Reading: How Much Beyond Sign Recognition?

Let us assume that an older pupil has learned the important sign words. He can recognize them in any print and can pick them out when he sees them in combination with unfamiliar words. He understands their meaning and does as the signs suggest. A new teacher of the trainable, with experience in teaching language skills to average children, may wonder if such a trainable boy or girl is not ready to learn to "read," as the term is usually understood.

When we speak of "reading" we are naturally talking about reading with comprehension. There is no value in a child's memorizing any reading matter, reciting it word for word correctly, if he has no idea of what he is reading about. Moreover, when we say "reading" we mean understanding whole sentences or paragraphs—not simply recognizing isolated words, such as in sign recognition.

There are instances where a trainable boy or girl has learned to read after an intensive program for a number of years. Usually it is an older child who has reached his optimum mental maturation. When a young trainable learns to read sentences and paragraphs with comprehension, there may be a question as to his really being on the trainable level; if he is functioning at a higher or educable level, he may well belong in a class with educable mentally handicapped children.

Comprehending the relationship of words as they appear in the complex structure of a sentence requires a higher degree of mental maturity than most trainable children attain. Even simple reading material for children includes prepositional phrases, adverbial phrases and, later, complex and compound sentences. In addition, the vocabulary in children's readers includes abstract words that are difficult for trainable pupils to understand. With confusion or total lack of understanding of the meaning of such words as "thought," "though," "through," or "who," "was," "way," and "while," how can a pupil learn to read meaningfully?

Most severely retarded children do not seem to understand the principles of phonics, or benefit from context clues, so they can read only material which has the words they have been taught to recognize. Since it is difficult to find even pre-primers which do not have unfamiliar words such as names, the severely retarded boy or girl may find practically all reading matter too difficult for him. Consequently he may derive little continuing pleasure from reading.

Since a trainable pupil has great difficulty with phonics, with words having abstract concepts and with words related in a sentence, he would not ordinarily achieve a third-grade reading level, even after years of effort in learning to read. Yet unless he could read on at least a third-grade level, he would not be able to understand newspapers, written directions, and other informational material. Learning to read will therefore contribute little toward meeting the social goal for the trainable: how to get along better with other people.

When Parents Want Their Children to be Taught to Read

A result of learning to read that might be considered of social value would be the gratification of parents or other relatives. If this is the primary reason for having the trainable struggle with reading, would it not be kinder and wiser to help the parents change their goals for the child, rather than to subject the child to many frustrating years of fruitless effort?

Once in a while there may be a trainable boy or girl who could learn to read on a first- or second-grade level if tutored individually, but it would be impractical and unfair for the teacher to devote the amount of time and individual attention necessary to teach such a pupil to read in a class situation.

Because there are unusual exceptions when an older pupil might benefit in social aspects and derive pleasure out of reading, the teacher should discuss the problem thoroughly with a parent who asks advice about reading tutoring for a trainable son or daughter. The teacher may be able to point out some areas of the problem which need consideration:

1. Is the boy or girl mentally mature enough to benefit from individual instruction? Usually, if beneficial at all, the instruction should be when the pupil has reached his optimal mental growth.

2. Is the child emotionally ready to concentrate on this type of instruction without the tutor's having to apply undue pressure? If a pupil is pressed into reading prematurely, when he has no interest in it and it is too difficult for him, he may develop emotional problems which will prevent his functioning adequately or happily in other situations as well.

3. Is there a tutor available who would be competent to teach the trainable child to read meaningfully? Since the pupil will probably be a teen-ager, the tutor will want to make up reading material rather than rely on childish-looking pre-primers. There are many such problems that would challenge the imagination and initiative of such a tutor.

4. Are there other phases of the pupil's development which need greater emphasis than they have been given? The teacher may be aware of areas in which the pupil should be making more progress than he is, and to which the attention of the parent has not been strongly enough directed, such as, perhaps, one of the following: self-care, socialization, emotional development, knowledge of one's environment, oral language and other forms of self-expression. A teacher then will wisely leave the decision of individual reading instruction with the parent and continue with her own plans of training all members of her class in the many skills that they will be able to learn and will need to use.

LANGUAGE ACTIVITIES

Auditory perception is basic for language development. See list of Auditory Perception Activities, pp. 147–49, for activities used to develop awareness of auditory stimuli.

A. Following Directions

I. BEGINNER

When name is spoken, respond to teacher's simple directions, such as: "Come here."

II. INTERMEDIATE

Respond to direction given group, such as: "Everybody sit down."
Do errands when given verbal directions.
Put things where told to.
Play games that require complying with requests, such as:
Store: "Give me two cans of peas, please."
Restaurant: "May I please have some ice cream?"
Doll House: "Have the mother put the baby in the bathtub."

III. ADVANCED

Same as for Intermediate, but directions more complex, such as:
"Ask the secretary for ten paper clips."
Play game: "Put your arms behind you———. Now touch the floor."

B. Identification of Objects or of Pictures in Answer to Questions

Questions can be answered by pointing unless speech has already developed, in which case verbal answers are preferable.

I. BEGINNER

Point to object or picture of object that teacher names.
Point to thing or person in response to these questions:
Where is——— (name of child in the class)?

Where is the piano (or other object)?
Show me the————.

II. INTERMEDIATE

Point to object or person in response to questions emphasizing
the understanding of certain words:
Verb:
Find the boy *running.*
What *is flying?* Point to it.
Find the one who *is crying.*
Verb and object:
Who *threw the ball?*
Who is *feeding the fish?*
Adjective:
Where is the *big (little)* boy?
Where is the *red* flower?
Adverb:
Which boy is going *up* the stairs?
Preposition:
Who is going *in* the house?
What is *on* the table?
Who is walking *with* the teacher?

III. ADVANCED

More complicated sentences:
Find the one who got her dress dirty.
Who asked his mother for cookies?
What lives in the little house behind the big house?

C. Pre-Speech Activities

I. BEGINNER

Understand and use gestures, such as pointing and waving
"Good-bye."
Make wants known with vocal sounds, such as whining or questioning tones.
Imitate noises demonstrated by teacher, such as laughing, animal sounds, and noises of things (airplane, fire engine, clock,
auto's horn, train).

Look at self in mirror, making faces.

Look in mirror together with teacher, making faces, opening and closing mouth, pursing lips, smiling, showing teeth in imitation of teacher, thus making mouth, lips, and teeth in the various positions for speech.

Make various sounds through cardboard tube.

Make sounds when looking in mirror, noting appearance of mouth.

Blow out candles; blow feathers.

Make a sound spontaneously and, when teacher imitates it, repeat sound, thus playing little speech game with teacher.

Imitate teacher in repetitive words of song.

II. INTERMEDIATE

Blow out several candles with one breath; blow soap bubbles; blow ping pong ball across table.

Suck through straw.

Call children's names or other words through cardboard tube.

Imitate teacher's lips, teeth and tongue positions for various speech sounds (not as constant drill, but to become conscious of importance of watching faces when listening to speech, and becoming more aware of how to imitate speech).

D. Language in Connection with Music Activities

See also the list of Music Activities, pp. 97, 101, 105.

I. BEGINNER

Walk when own name is sung.
Point to body parts when they are named in song.
Do actions named in songs.
Point to objects as they are named in songs.

II. INTERMEDIATE

Indicate body parts, clothing, objects, and furniture when these are named in record or song, and join in singing the words.

Among several pictures displayed, point to the one described in song being sung.

Name objects (in picture) mentioned in a song the class sings or hears on the phonograph.

Act out and sing some words of singing games.

Act out the part of a character in a song.

III. ADVANCED

Same as for Intermediate, but the phonograph records, games, and songs will involve more complex ideas, longer descriptions.

Sing most of the words of a song while doing accompanying actions.

E. "Show and Tell"

I. BEGINNER

Watch and listen to teacher as she demonstrates objects and sings or talks about them (e.g., a jack-in-the-box).

II. INTERMEDIATE

Show things made in the classroom or brought from home, naming and answering questions about them.

III. ADVANCED

Show and describe or tell story about things brought from home or made in school.

Take turn being teacher, calling on pupils to "Show and tell."

F. Interpretation of Pictures

I. BEGINNER

Imitate teacher as she pronounces name of object in picture. (A mounted picture from the file is sometimes more effective than a picture in a book, since it can be handled more easily and there are no distracting, flopping pages and no second picture showing on opposite page. Mounted pictures are often larger than book pictures and, if filed by subject, can be located easily. First pictures used should be of only one object.)

Name objects in picture when teacher shows picture.

II. INTERMEDIATE

Answer questions about pictures, requiring the use of various parts of speech. (Question will be phrased so that answer need be only one word, or a short phrase.)

Noun: Is this a picture of a boy or a girl? (The answer to be elicited for question worded thus would usually be the first, rather than the last named.)

Yes or no: Is it a boy? (This question form is not to be used with very suggestible children, since they may always say "Yes," and, if the question demands a "No," they are encouraged in wrong answers. If the teacher asks questions requiring an affirmative answer, she will not know if the children really know the answer, since they invariably answer "Yes.")

While sitting at table with classmates, show and tell neighbors about pictures in a book.

In darkened room, when facial expressions of teacher cannot be seen, respond to teacher's questions about still pictures projected on screen (preferably opaque projector).

III. ADVANCED

Answer questions requiring longer replies such as:
What is each person doing?
Why is the boy crying?
What are they having for their picnic?

Describe a situation portrayed in a picture.

Tell story in sequence from series of pictures in book.

During Lotto game (see description p. 126), call cards, making a riddle of the picture instead of naming the picture. ("It sweeps the floor." "It is red and it tastes good.")

Bring pictures from newspapers and magazines and tell about them.

Interpret movie of familiar children and school activities.

Discuss pictures displayed with opaque projector.

Tell about simple movie, puppet show, or other visual entertainment being shown in school.

G. Responding to Stories or Songs without Pictures

I. BEGINNER

Listen to rhythmic words sung or said over and over. Imitate
these.
Listen to teacher describing child's activities in a few sentences.

II. INTERMEDIATE

Answer questions about songs played on phonograph.
Listen to a short story, answering questions teacher asks after
every few sentences. (After the teacher has told the story, she
may show pictures or real objects to help children answer
questions. For example, two pictures may be displayed, and
the child selects the picture which describes the story just told.)
Complete familiar story after teacher has told all but the end.
Answer riddles about familiar things or people: "He goes to
work every day. He wears trousers. He comes home at night
and kisses his children. He is the biggest in the family. Who
is he?"
Listen to teacher tell about a personal experience. Then tell
about own personal experience.

III. ADVANCED

Listen to short story and answer questions about it.
After hearing a story, tell as much of it as is remembered.
After hearing same story many times, retell it, looking at pic-
tures if necessary.
Tell about something that occurred in own experience, or some-
thing that is expected to happen.
Guess riddles; ask some.

H. Discussion

I. INTERMEDIATE

Answer questions about school and home happenings.
Answer questions about activities that will be occurring.

II. ADVANCED

Report and describe (with help from teacher's questions) individual school jobs or craft projects.
Plan and later report about parties, work, group projects.
Discuss standards of behavior (safety, hygiene, manners).
Discuss meaning of signs, symbols, numbers, coins, calendar.

I. Telephoning

I. BEGINNER

Watch teacher use toy telephone. Pretend to telephone.
Say "Hello" and "Bye" associated with picking up and hanging up receiver.

II. INTERMEDIATE

Answer teacher's "calls."
Talk to other child on toy telephone, stimulated to do so by teacher if necessary.

III. ADVANCED

Initiate and carry on telephone conversation in accepted manner. (Borrow from telephone company real set of telephones, which has dial tone, busy signal, etc.)
Make a planned telephone call to own name and discuss it with class afterwards.

J. Dramatic Play

See pp. 87–88 for description of dramatic play activities.
Include play involving much verbalization, such as ordering in a store or restaurant or introducing guests.

K. Tape Recording

I. INTERMEDIATE

Answer teacher's questions and then listen to play-back immediately and identify own voice.
Sing a familiar song alone.

After the class makes recordings, identify each child's voice. Improve speech after hearing own voice played back.

II. ADVANCED

Repeat words after teacher. Then listen to recording of teacher's and own words to see if they sound the same.

After having certain words or conversation recorded, listen and note, with teacher's help, a few of the unclear words, practicing them with teacher. Note poor volume or rate of talking. Then repeat several times the words or sentences previously used, each time listening to see if speech sounds are better.

Act as the leader for the group, selecting students to speak, or asking them questions. Leader may announce pupils by name so that later, when listening, the class can identify each speaker quickly.

L. Language Games

I. INTERMEDIATE

Picture Dominoes (commercially available): While playing, name picture or pictures that can be played at one or the other end of the line of dominoes already played. When placing domino, child names picture he is matching. (For a further suggestion on adapting Dominoes for Intermediates, see "Color Dominoes," p. 140.)

Lotto: The value of this game is that it teaches vocabulary and gives practice in combining several words into a sentence. The child who has a picture may say, "Please may I have the ————; I want the————," or repeat the name of the picture. Instead of the teacher calling the cards, or holding them up for display, she can give a small pile of them to a child who can act as caller. As the children take turns being caller, the teacher will sometimes have to name the cards first so that the words will be pronounced correctly.

Lotto can also be used to play "restaurant" or "store": Two large lotto cards are used as menus. The waitress (child) asks each child in turn, "What do you want?" The children use speech to indicate their selections—the words depending upon individual language ability.

Bingo: Both caller and player should name the number or say the word. (For a further suggestion on adapting Bingo for Intermediates, see "Color Bingo," p. 139.)

II. ADVANCED

Dominoes: Play in same way as Picture Dominoes, but use regular dominoes with dots. Name the number of dots at each end of row, and use other expressions such as "I pass;" "I have to draw one."

Steps to Toyland: Name objects on cards that are drawn from toy chest.

Explain any game such as a singing game, outdoor game, or table game to other children who are visiting or to new children.

M. Activities Involving Auditory Memory for Language

I. BEGINNER

Learn own first name, and those of classmates.

II. INTERMEDIATE

Learn full name of self and those of classmates. Be able to answer the question, "What is your last name?"
Learn own address and telephone number.
Learn name of school.
Learn names of school staff members.

III. ADVANCED

Tell name of city or town in which school and home are located.
Give address of school.
Remember names of visitors introduced in class.
Give mother's and father's first names.
Deliver verbal messages verbatim.
Tell words of songs verbatim.

RELATED READING

Beasley, Jane. *Slow to Talk*. New York: Bureau of Publications, Teachers College, Columbia University, 1956.

Chamberlain, Naomi H., Olivia Juliette Hooker, and Winifred Hull Wagner. *A Speech Readiness Guide for Parents of Severely Retarded Children*. Rochester: Olnay Books, 1956.

Karlson, Isaac W., and Millicent Strazzula. "Speech and Language Problems of Mentally Deficient Children," *The Journal of Speech and Hearing Disorders,* XVII (September, 1952), 286–94.

Schneider, Bernard, and Jerome Vallon. "The Results of a Speech Therapy Program for Mentally Retarded Children," in Chalmers L. Stacey and Manfred F. DeMartino (editors), *Counseling and Psychotherapy with the Mentally Retarded*. Glencoe, Illinois: The Free Press and the Falcon's Wing Press, 1957, pp. 312–20.

Van Riper, C. *Teaching Your Child to Talk*. New York: Harper and Brothers, 1950.

Figure 1. Wagons encourage group play for Beginners

Figure 2. Equipment for beginning physical activity

Figure 3. Beginners
need reassurance when
attempting to climb

Figure 4. Water play in
a social situation

Figure 5. Beginners learn to wash and dry hands thoroughly

Figure 6. A cooperative work activity (Advanced)

Figure 7. Color concepts are reinforced by a group game

Figure 8. Intermediates play a game to learn size discrimination

Figure 9. Developing number concepts by playing store

Figure 10. Stimulating verbal expression with a telephone

Figure 11. Intermediates practice lacing and bow-tying

Figure 12. Buttoning is an interesting task when performed on a manikin

Figure 13. Beginner and Intermediate levels of self-expression →

Figure 14. A variety of craft activities →

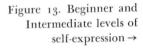

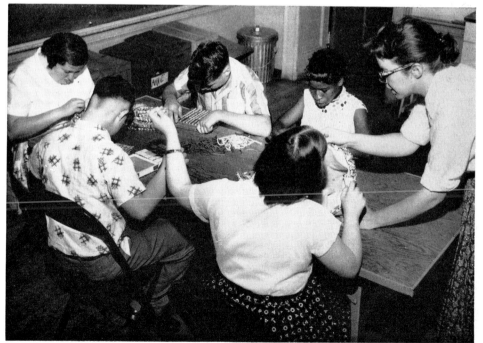

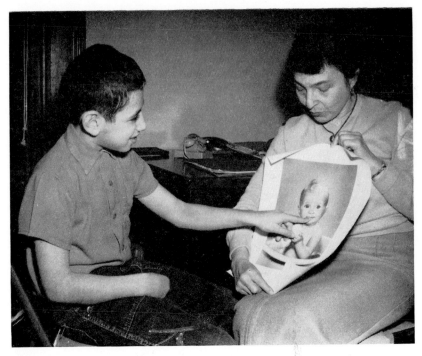

Figure 15. A new baby in the home provides motivation for beginning speech

Figure 16. Visual perception can be learned with a variety of materials

VIII. Understanding of the Environment

Perception is the process through which we come to understand the significance of the sensory stimuli with which we come in contact. After sensing something, the next step is perceiving it. Let us say, for example, that the sensory stimulus is an auditory one—an ear-piercing wail. It is essential, not only that we hear it, but also that we perceive it to be, in this case, a siren. We can have this perception of a siren if we have had previous meaningful experiences with the same or similar sounds.

After perceiving comes concept formation. When we perceive the sound as a siren, we can conceive of what this siren sound means. As a result of sensation, perception, and thought, it is possible for us to react appropriately to the original auditory stimulus.

WHY PERCEPTUAL TRAINING FOR THE TRAINABLE?

In severely retarded children—even those with normal sensory equipment—clear perception may not always follow sensation. The children may need perceptual training to become more aware of sensory stimuli and to develop adequate concepts. And concept formation is important for every child's adjustment in the world.

A trainable child needs help in developing an adequate concept of self. He needs to acquire a clear body image of himself. He can do so by integrating many sensory perceptions into a meaningful whole. He can see himself in the mirror, hear himself talking or making sounds, touch different parts of his own body, feel his own postural changes. Throughout the school day, the teacher can help the child by providing him with many rich sensory experiences which will help him perceive himself in relation to his environment. As he perceives his own body image, he can gain a better concept of himself.

In school the child can also be helped to develop a better perception of space. He needs to know not only who he is but where he is. In *Psychopathology and Education of the Brain-Injured Child*, p. 75, Alfred Strauss describes how the perception of space develops:

It is probable that the first attempts to structure space are closely related to manipulation of concrete objects. . . . This tactual manipulation is essential to the development of concepts of spatial relationships. The development of the space world proceeds out and from the body, those areas open to manipulation and handling being structured first.

The school should provide sensory training of all kinds to assist the child in his perception of space. The child cannot only play and work with educational toys, such as blocks and balls, but can also learn about space through moving about in active games and on equipment, or in exploring the school environment and taking trips into the community.

In addition to perception of space, it is important for the child to gain some perception of time. Time perception may be stimulated through the rhythm and other music activities listed in this book.

Perceptions of body image, space, and time—these are particularly necessary for a child to develop in order to feel secure wherever he may be. A child who is confused about himself and disoriented in time and space is usually an anxious, unhappy child. As he comes to understand himself better in relation to his environment, he will gain self-confidence and be able to function more adequately.

Increased perceptual skills result in his doing and making things more quickly and accurately. As a child becomes more aware of form, he improves in such skills as buttoning his clothes, lacing leather objects or setting the table. As he develops better visual-motor skill, he will don his coat or descend the stairs more easily. As his auditory perception improves, he can understand and respond better to directions given him.

The more perceptual skills he can develop and use in acquainting himself with his physical world, the more readily he can understand it. The more interest and knowledge he has about his surroundings, the better prepared he is for living. He will be able to respond to situations such as those involving danger. Most important of all, he can get along better with others because of his heightened appreciation of what they say and do.

GUIDING PERCEPTUAL DEVELOPMENT

Here are a few principles which the teacher may find of value in guiding the perceptual development of the trainable.

1. The severely retarded child seems to give particular attention to moving things. He can therefore be motivated to improve his perception through toys that he can see moving—tops, balloons, balls, pull toys. However, movement in toys can also distract a child from working with them and from gaining perceptual awareness of their various qualities. For example, a child may be given a wagon for the purpose of matching its colored pegs in the correspondingly colored holes. The child, however, may simply roll the wagon back and forth, or make it roll off the table. Even if it is put on the floor and he does not deliberately move it, the motion as he tries to place the pegs will make it difficult for him to manipulate them and will distract him from focusing his attention on the pegs and holes. Many educational toys are improved for use with the trainable by removing their wheels.

2. The child often learns better if he has a concrete activity upon which to focus his attention. Rather than simply showing a child two blocks and identifying one as "big" and one as "little," it is better to let the child handle the blocks. Then he should have a chance to do something with them which will reinforce his perception of the difference between big and little.

He could stack all the big blocks in one pile, and the little blocks in another pile. Such concrete activities focus the child's attention and emphasize the sensory training he is receiving.

Another result of integrating activity with perceptual training is that usually a number of senses, rather than one, will be involved in the learning experience. Instead of the child's simply learning to recognize "big" visually by looking at a big beach ball, he will also learn "big" kinaesthetically by putting his arms around it. His perception of "big" will be reinforced and expanded. Before a concept can be well developed, the child needs to acquire a perception of it in its many aspects.

3. A child will probably learn colors before learning abstract forms. Sorting and matching colors precedes sorting and matching of abstract forms. The child will usually learn his ball is blue before he learns that it is round. After the perception of color is well developed, colors can be used as cues to help in visual perception of other qualities. If a child needs help in observing corners as he cuts out a square picture, the teacher can reinforce the outline of each corner with a red crayon. When teaching consecutive progression in counting objects, such as beads on a counting frame, or tiny candies, it is better to have each of the objects a different color. This will keep the child's attention focused on his work and help him to keep his place, remembering which one he just counted and knowing where to move to the next one. Coloring the rims of holes for lacing, or for hammering nails in a row, serves the same purpose as in the counting of objects.

Trainable children often respond to color more readily than they do to abstract form. But there are times when a child may more accurately perform a task involving abstract form than a similar task involving color. For example, he may put various shaped blocks into their corresponding holes in a form board, and place a blue peg into a yellow hole on a color board. He is accurate in the case of the form board because there is only one space into which each form can fit, and therefore the child can perceive and correct his own mistakes. There is no such guide for correction of errors in the color pegboard. Many children respond better to form than to color when the form, instead of being abstract (a circle), is especially familiar, concrete, and meaningful (a spoon). The child may be able to sort knives from spoons before he learns blue from yellow. In this case, he may be sorting according to the concept—use—rather than to the percept—form. It is difficult to be sure unless the child talks, or responds to spoken language.

4. It is important to present one characteristic of an object at a time. In teaching a child a certain shape, it will confuse him if he is exposed to a variety of other characteristics at the same time. If he is learning to distinguish two particular shapes, such as a cube from a sphere, the color of the objects used should be de-emphasized by having them all the same color—preferably unpainted. If balls and cubical boxes are being used, they should be the same texture and approximate size. Beads of two shapes may be used in the same way. Then there would be similarity, not only in texture and size, but also in function. The child can sort these objects according to their shape and will not be confused by other differences. It is only the Advanced boy or girl who will be able to select all the round beads from a box of round and cubical beads of assorted sizes and colors.

When first helping a child to understand the idea of sorting, it is helpful to find some things which he already recognizes as different—it may be spoons and knives. Starting with spoons and knives familiar to him, he can learn first to sort them by shape. When he understands this process, plastic spoons of one color and knives of another can be substituted for the usual tableware. The teacher is thus introducing another characteristic—color. After sorting blue spoons from yellow knives, the child may be ready to sort blue blocks from yellow blocks (only the color being different in this case). He now understands sorting by color rather than shape—that is, by a new characteristic. In this way he comes to understand the sorting process.

In giving the child perceptual training, the teacher will wisely plan what she wishes to teach and then how this specific training is to be given. If she wishes the children to learn "loud" from "soft," she can beat a drum first loudly, then softly. If, instead, she uses a second instrument—a triangle—to make the soft sound, the children may not perceive what she expected them to—differences in volume. Rather, they may notice the difference between the pitch or the quality of tone, or they may respond primarily to the visual stimuli, distinguishing the red and white drum from the shiny metal triangle. If the teacher then says "soft," pointing to the triangle, a child may think of "soft" as a tinkling sound or a shiny piece of metal.

5. The child can be helped to learn one distinct color (or size or shape) by contrasting it with another color (or size or shape). If the color blue is to be taught, show not only blue, but yellow and blue at the same time, or one immediately after the other. If only a blue object is always shown, blue may become associated with the shape, size, or use of the object, rather than with the color. The child may think he plays with "blues," rather than blocks. Also, the child, if shown only the blue object and asked what color it is each time it is shown, may get in the habit of always responding "blue" and then, if another color is eventually shown him, will continue to say "blue."

6. The child perceives and responds to different qualities long before he can attach names to them. If a child is able to sort or match all the colors, he is not color-blind just because he calls the red ones "green." He is probably having difficulty in gaining the correct auditory perception of the two somewhat similar sounding words, or cannot remember which combination of sounds to associate with which color.

This principle applies to the perception of other qualities as well as color perception. A child can usually match abstract shapes and even alternate beads of two different shapes on a string before he can tell the names of the shapes.

An intermediate step between simple sorting or matching, and the naming of qualities is that of attaching the correct meaning to the name when it is spoken. A child will probably be able to follow the direction: "Point to the yellow one," before he can answer the question, "What color is this?" Or he will be able to walk fast when told to, before he can say that he is walking "fast." It is advisable for the teacher to be fully aware of these three steps in perceptual response: sorting and matching, recognition of the word denoting a quality, and identification of the quality by its name. If a teacher proceeds slowly and patiently, the average trainable child will master each of the steps in time.

7. It takes a long time for the severely retarded to perceive his environment in the way most adults do. Some of the retarded may always have very different percepts from the average person. A teacher who reminds herself that the child may not perceive things as she does will be able to give him better training than a teacher unaware of the child's imperfect perception. She will realize that to the child a flat picture of a ball may not be the same object to him as the three-dimensional, round thing he can feel and bounce. She will understand that a profile of a man can give the erroneous impression that this fellow has only one eye. (Puzzles and pictures need to be selected with great care. For further suggestions about kinds of pictures, see pp. 113–14.)

The teacher will understand that when the child puts a puzzle together, he may leave it upside down or sidewise. How can he know that on a horizontal surface the part of the picture nearest him is called the "bottom"? He may wonder why others say that the picture puzzle of a girl he has put together is "standing on her head," simply because, rather than her feet, her head is near the table's edge closest to him. One way of teaching him the concept is to have him lie down, while the teacher draws around him on cardboard. After cutting out his silhouette, she will have him stand it up, matching it with his image in the mirror. He can lay it down on his shadow, with its feet near his feet, and the head away from him. Later, a smaller figure can be made of him and placed on the table, with the feet nearest him.

It may be a long time before a child will know that when there are two cars in a picture and one looks half the size of the other, the cars are supposed to be equal in size but different in their distance from the observer. It may be hard for him to understand that an airplane makes a great big noise if he has only heard airplanes at a great distance.

The teacher will not expect him to recognize the pale blue of the sky, the midnight blue of a wool skirt, and the shades of blues of a printed fabric as all being blue. As in all her teaching, she will try to simplify his early perceptual experiences, introducing him to the rich, standard primary colors first.

8. Some trainable children will respond to tiny details rather than to the whole constellation. Children may fool you into supposing their perceptual ability is astounding when they identify accurately many makes of cars as they whiz by. They are probably responding to some little detail rather than the whole shape and various characteristics of the car. Although in the case of cars, such a child may identify accurately, he may become very much confused if he tries to distinguish two people from each other by details such as a barrette on one and earrings on another. He would be much better off if he could grasp an image of the whole person, seeing at a glance the relation of the parts to the whole.

A teacher should not be surprised to find one child frequently staring at a fancy pattern in the grille of a hot air register, and another who wants to keep playing with light switches. Strauss (*Psychopathology and Education of the Brain-Injured Child*, p. 25), reported on the exaggerated reaction to details of certain children. A child may be more interested in shiny door knobs than in the colorful toys so carefully selected for him. A thoughtful teacher will eliminate as many of these distractions as she can from the classroom, thereby helping some children to concentrate better on what is important for them to learn.

9. Some children confuse the background with the foreground. When they look at a silhouette of a circle on a large, bright square background, they may see a square shape with a hole in the middle of it, rather than a circle. In perceiving sound, a trainable may respond to that of muffled hammering in the basement, instead of the phonograph in the room where he is sitting. Often the child is confused by his attention switching from background to figure and then to background again. A child descending steps may feel very insecure by not perceiving where the edge of the stair step is in relation to the tread below.

Awkwardness and slowness on the stairs may result from this rather than from lack of physical coordination.

For such children, the figure can be emphasized by having it a bright color while the background should be subdued in color and have no pattern or design. It is wise to mount pictures on a neutral gray background. If a teacher wishes to use color to attract a child's attention to the configuration of his name, she may want to print his name with a bright-colored crayon or pencil on a subdued background, rather than printing it in black on a bright-colored card. Because he may associate his name with this color it is best not to have him see his name in this one color of printing for too long.

A clear-cut boundary between figure and ground can be achieved by reinforcing the outline of a form with a black crayon. This is helpful to the child when cutting out pictures, coloring inside a form, or sawing a figure out of wood. The boundary will also be emphasized if the figure and background contrast widely in hue and intensity of color.

Because many trainable children have difficulties in perception, it is very important to see that they are given the best experiences and materials possible. In mounting pictures, making patterns for craft work or printing signs, the teacher and her helpers should do careful, exact work. A hurriedly drawn, wobbly crayon outline, thick in some places and scarcely visible in others, will be of no value to a child in cutting out his picture.

Because abstract thinking develops along with intellectual maturity, trainable children will have special difficulty in the formation of number concepts. Our purpose is to teach the retarded child the number tools he needs to know and can, without undue time or emotional strain, acquire well enough to handle effectively in certain concrete situations.

Many trainable children can learn to use numbers where auditory and visual recognition and memory are the primary requirements, such as in memorizing and dialing his telephone number. They need not understand the mathematical principles behind the facts they learn. For example, finding the house number "243" is a valuable skill, but the trainable may not need to know that "2" stands for "200." On the other hand, any number of facts he learns should have some meaning, so that he can use them. Saying numbers to 100 may be within his ability, but there is little value in his learning to count in this fashion any farther than he is able to for finding out how many objects he has or taking a certain number of objects. He needs much practice in counting concrete objects in real life situations.

Although some of the older trainable children may have little conception of the value of time or money, they may show interest in certain aspects of these subjects and may learn to recognize and count coins and recognize time on the clock face. Such skills will probably be useful to a retardate and might make him more useful to others.

In teaching these, it is important to provide drill, associating it with the specific situations in which the skill will be used in daily living. Learning about quantity, money, and time can be fun for even very slow children if the teacher plans meaningful activities which use the specific skill to be acquired.

Included in the list of activities are examples directed primarily at increasing sensory-perceptual skills and certain kinds of concept formation. All through the school day perceptions and concepts can be developed. As the teacher guides the children in these activities, she will watch for opportunities to stimulate perceptual awareness and broaden the children's concepts.

ACTIVITIES CONTRIBUTING TO THE UNDERSTANDING OF THE ENVIRONMENT *

A. Size, Form, and Color

I. BEGINNER

Handle and look at materials, both indoors and out, which are presented or demonstrated to aid in the development of sensory awareness and discrimination of size, form, or color.

* See "Selected Educational Materials," pp. 255–58, for details about toys and games mentioned in this section.

Play with blocks, beads, balls, dolls, which differ in size, form, or color.

Make imprints of feet and hands in sand box and in clay. Replace hands and feet in imprints.

Engage in simple sorting activities, using objects which may be sorted according to use.

Engage in simple matching activities. For forms and sizes use homemade form boards. For colors, use large peg board. Match box covers that correspond in form, size, color.

II. INTERMEDIATE

Play with toys of different sizes and colors, such as wooden screws, inset barrels, dolls fitting different-sized furniture and clothes, construction toys like "Blockcraft," put-together toys like "Take Apart Train," and "Color Cone" (see p. 256).

Color Cone: Sort three different sizes and five or six forms or colors on "Color Cone" sticks, but play in a group game. Players each have perpendicular stick with one ring on it. Caller reaches into paper bag, pulls out a ring, looks at it below table so others cannot see and says, "Who has the middle-sized ring?" He gives it to player who answers correctly. That player slips ring on his stick with other middle-sized ring. Only three different sizes should be used. The child getting his stick filled first says "Bingo," or else game continues until bag is empty. Players can count their rings and see who has the most, or see whose stick has rings going up the highest. Same game can be played calling different colors or forms. A box can be used for each player instead of a ring stick. Different shaped beads can be used to call forms rather than using rings.

Color Bingo Game: Each child is given one large card divided into six squares of different colors. Caller has pack of small color cards, their colors corresponding to colors on large cards. The name of a small color card is called. First child who points to this color on his card and names it correctly gets the little card. With this he covers up the correspondingly colored square on his large card by turning the little card over. He can then see the squares needing to be covered. Winner is player who first fills his card. Of course, the game can be played until all the cards are filled, if children are too concerned about not filling their cards.

To lessen competition, the players who can recognize many colors quickly should have cards containing squares which should be of the more difficult colors, like purple and brown, and not the primary colors on the easy cards. A player who recognizes only two colors by name should have squares on his card of only those two colors. This gives the less advanced child a chance to obtain cards even though he cannot respond as quickly as other players.

The few children who can name most of the colors can take turns being caller. A less advanced player who cannot recognize colors when hearing their names will need to have the small card color shown to him before he can match it to the colored square on his large card.

When necessary, the teacher may arrange cards before the game begins so that there will be one for each child without too long a wait for him. She can also see that the cards at the bottom of the pack will not be those needed by a child who cannot yet tolerate being last in a game.

Children who cannot wait their turns can have cards with nine rather than six squares. They will then be kept busy answering and placing cards more frequently.

Color Dominoes: Wooden or thick cardboard blocks can be made 1″ x 2″, or larger for a class of children with less physical coordination. Half of each domino can be painted one color and the other end another color. A black line can be painted down the middle to reinforce the boundary of the two colors. The number of different colors depends on the general class level of color recognition. Along with the colors known, there should be a color that most of the children are starting to learn. Children who can match and recognize all the colors may still not be able to name them all.

From a pile of domino blocks turned upside down on the table, each child takes turns counting out five dominoes and standing them up in a curved row before him. When game is first taught, three blocks will be enough and can be laid face up on the table. The child who finds he has a "double" (both ends of the block with the same color) places it in the center of the table. The children all name the color, and the player to the starter's left places a block, matching the end of his block with the correspondingly colored block already in the center of the table. If the child has no domino with an end that matches the "double" in the center, he draws from an extra pile of blocks, the "lumber yard," to get another block. If after drawing he cannot match, he "passes," and the third child has a turn. Dominoes are added in a row to those already played. Before each play, the class should name the colors at each end of the row, the teacher or a child pointing out the ends to be played on. The child who first plays all his dominoes is the winner. The other children give him the dominoes they have left and the class counts them.

Form Dominoes: This game is played in the same way as Color Dominoes. In making a Form Domino Game for four beginning players, use four abstract shapes (see word list p. 142), making two each of every combination of the forms including "doubles." Blanks, which can be called "nothing" may be added after a while. The forms should all be painted one bright color, using a light gray or buff for background. Geometric figures can be ordered from educational supply companies and glued to blocks, after which blocks can be shellacked.

Parquetry Blocks: Match colored blocks of various shapes to cards portraying same shapes and colors. (The blocks with suggested designs are a commercial product, but teacher can make simple cards with only one or a few block shapes on them at first. The shapes can be black silhouettes, so the child will need to think only about the form; or they can be colored, in which case the child has to think of both form and shape.)

Peg Board Designs: Finish pattern of pegs started by teacher, such as a straight line, a border, or a square with all corners placed by teacher. Or copy pattern of pegs that teacher has made in peg board, making it on second peg board: Make vertical line, horizontal line, cross.

Colored Hat Parade: Select colored hat that teacher names, or name color of hat teacher offers, and put it on. When all children have hats, march. Paper lollipops, balloons, or flags can be used in same way.

Draw a line to complete a figure only partially drawn by teacher (square, circle, rectangle, oval). Gradually a larger amount can be left to be completed, so that closer attention will have to be paid to what the form should be.

Be able to understand and use the following words meaningfully:

Form	*Size*	*Color*
boy, girl	big, little	yellow
box, ball	tall, short	blue
round (like ball)	long, short	red
circle, square	fat, thin	orange
cross	large, small	green
stick		purple
egg		
heart		
triangle		
names of commonest body parts		
names of clothing worn		
names of familiar toys		
names of familiar furniture		
names of school materials		
names of school equipment		

III. ADVANCED

Play games such as the following:

Color Dominoes: Use seven dominoes for each player. Use colors listed on p. 143.

Form Dominoes: Use forms listed on p. 143, as well as simpler forms.

Regular Dominoes: Play with standard dominoes with dot patterns.

Parchesi or other games that use dice.

Go Fish: Good for matching and naming colors, forms, number figures and sign words. Homemade decks can be used, as well as regular playing cards. This game requires coordination sufficient for holding cards firmly while picking one card out. Only a few cards should be dealt to beginning groups of players. The object of the game is to make pairs with two matching cards. When a player gets a pair, he places it near him face down on the table. Players take turns, each one asking the next for a card to match one he holds. If player he asks has it, he gives it to the questioner who makes a pair, and the next person gets a turn. If player he asks does not have it, the questioner draws a card from the center pile. The player getting rid of all his cards first wins. If the players all seem to need more cards because no one can play, all can draw from the center pile simultaneously. To make a harder game, the cards can portray both different colors and different forms.

What's New: One player or the teacher asks the question: "What is new in the school room?" or "Can you see which boy or girl is wearing something new?" and other players try to find the answer.

Name color of various articles of clothing worn, and point out which of them match in color and in design.

String beads of various sizes, form, and color. Copy pattern of beads on a string, or a colored drawing of them; or make up own pattern and repeat it until string of beads is complete. Also string beads according to pattern described by teacher verbally or planned on own initiative and verbalized: "Red ball, blue square," etc.

Trace or copy and then cut out geometric forms, and also abstract shapes symbolic of holidays.

Use and understand the meaning of these words:

Size	*Color*	*Form*
thick, thin	brown	half circle
middle-sized	black	rectangle
larger, smaller	white	diamond
longer, shorter	gray	oval
taller, shorter	tan	club
tallest, shortest	pink	spade
longest, shortest	violet	walk in a circle
biggest, littlest	dark, light	straight, crooked
largest, smallest	darker, lighter	

B. Pictures

I. BEGINNER

Before being introduced to pictures:

Match three-dimensional imitation portrayal of live things with their live objects (a toy dog with a real dog, a girl doll with a girl classmate) first using things of life-like size, form, and texture where possible, such as a big, fuzzy, stuffed dog, or a life-like manikin of a child.

Match miniatures of familiar objects with real things: doll furniture with real furniture, toy telephone with real telephone, doll dishes with real dishes, tiny dolls with people.

Select large photograph of self from among those of others.

Match photographs of classmates with each child by pointing to child, or giving him his picture.

Match photograph of object with real object.

Match pictures of objects with the actual object. At first use forms which are almost two-dimensional in real appearance: clock face, fork, broom, wheel, penny, window, door, leaf.

Match colored picture of three-dimensional objects that are symmetrical or the same shape all the way around, with the real objects: grapefruit, apple, candle, bottle, bowling pin, pencil, ball, stick, paint brush.

Assemble very simple picture-form inset puzzles. Puzzles should be cut so that each piece represents a whole object.

II. INTERMEDIATE

Draw around own or other children's hands, feet, and whole bodies.

Color own silhouette's hair, eyes, clothes, after looking at self in mirror: recognize own silhouette among other silhouettes of children in group.

Find self in group photographs.

Match black-and-white pictures of objects with real objects, or name pictures, thus showing recognition of them.

Assemble more difficult picture-form inset puzzles, in which pieces represent recognizable parts of objects or people.

Assemble all parts of a face or figure puzzle which is cut straight
across or vertically.

These puzzles can be made from photographs in news magazines. All parts of a face should show. In the puzzles depicting
complete figures, both hands and both feet should be in evidence. Pictures can be sturdily glued onto cardboard with rubber cement. Sometimes a duplicate picture which has not been
cut helps a child to see what he is to do. Easiest puzzles can have
just two pieces, the picture having been cut once horizontally.
If the child is learning where the mouth should go in relation
to the eyes, the mouth should be cut off separately, rather than
having the cut made through the nose, which would give the
child a matching cue.

Assemble manikin from photograph of child cut out and
mounted on cardboard, and then cut into body parts. Assemble
two of these manikins of different sizes, from mixed pile of
parts.

Sort pictures into two categories, such as boys' clothes and girls'
clothes.

A good set can be made by using lady's hosiery box. In each
cover a picture of a boy or girl can be pasted. Clothes for a boy
and girl can be mounted on cardboard and cut out. Then they
can be stored in the box, until the child opens it, removes all the
pieces, and sorts them by placing the appropriate ones in each
box cover.

These Belong Together: Play similarly to Bingo or Lotto.
Game consists of 3″ x 5″ cards in pairs. A pair consists of two
objects that belong together: dust pan and broom, paper and
pencil, ball and bat, cup and saucer, dog and dog house. Players
are dealt three to five cards laid out in a vertical row. Caller has
one of every pair and asks, "Who needs a———?" or "Who has
something that goes with a———?"

Make scrapbooks of favorite pictures. Then talk about them.

Look at picture books and talk about them.

Look at very simple movies, film strips, opaque projector showings.

Movies, unless very simple and about the class, offer much less than a "still" which can be exposed until picture has been thoroughly discussed. Whatever the film, the teacher will wisely view it ahead of time to be certain its pictures are meaningful to her class. A large opaque projector can show pictures in magazines or books, but the projector fan may be distracting to discussions because of its noise. These technical visual aids are fun for the children because they are different from the usual class activities. At much less expense, however, a good teacher can show pictures to a small group very effectively by holding them up in her own two hands.

III. ADVANCED

Assemble difficult straight-cut and also inset puzzles.

Assemble simple jig saw puzzles.

Play card games that have pictures—Old Maid, sectional animal cards.

Sort pictures into categories according to different principles.

Look at movies, film strips, pictures on opaque projector screen, and picture books, interpreting what is shown.

Arrange three to nine pictures in a series to tell a story.

C. Space

I. INTERMEDIATE

Hunt for child or object that is hidden.

Hunt for many hidden objects, such as peanuts or eggs.

Play games in which one child acts out teacher's directions (or directions given on phonograph or tape recorder) which involve these concepts relating to space:

up, down	high, low
in, out	top, bottom
inside, outside	front, back
on, off	

II. ADVANCED

Play hiding games in which participators must give hints or

respond to hints as to location of objects, using words listed below after next activity.

In school jobs, projects, ball play, exercises, etc., follow directions, unaccompanied by gestures, involving these words relating to space:

under, over	forward, back
higher, lower	behind, in front of
left, right	beginning, end
above, beneath	next
below	too close
near, far	

D. Noises and Sounds

I. BEGINNER

Play in large barrel or paper carton, responding to teacher's or other children's knocking and calling.

Play with all kinds of noise-makers: whistle, bell, rattle, drum.

Listen to teacher whistling, playing drum, playing piano. With encouragement, be aware of, keep attention focused upon, and investigate other noises.

In using materials (toy hammer, clay being pounded), notice noise they make.

Listen to simple tunes and rhythms of a few records and songs, repeated often.

Imitate sounds heard on phonograph records.

II. INTERMEDIATE

Listen to a sound, with or without seeing person making the sound, and identify it or find where it comes from.

Make things sound loud, then soft.

Listen, blindfolded, to someone making noise with some object and then, after recognizing sound, make the same noise in the same way.

After hearing a noise, select picture of the thing or animal that makes the noise.

Listen to thing or animal that makes a noise, and make the appropriate noise.

Look at picture of thing or animal that makes a noise, and make the appropriate noise.

After being blindfolded, find a classmate who is walking with bells tied on him. (If the child chaser cannot catch the child wearing the bells, the teacher may tie a sash loosely around the latter's ankles to slow him down.)

Identify tunes on piano by naming, acting out, or pointing to appropriate picture among several displayed.

Play on toy piano, xylophone.

Play games involving sounds:

Who Called You: One child, blindfolded, guesses who called his name.

Puppy and Bone: One child quietly tries to sneak up and snatch "bone" from "dog" (child who sits with back to others, and with hands over eyes). As soon as "dog" hears someone creeping up, he gives chase.

Recognize the sounds below, and understand and use meaningfully simple words associated with:

Sounds that are loud or soft.

Sounds of rattle, whistle, bell, horn, telephone bell, drum, piano, cymbals, phonograph, fire gong, church bell.

Sounds associated with running, walking, stamping, clapping, crying, hammering, keys rattling, clock ticking.

Sounds made by bird, cat, dog, cow, horse, pig, duck (real ones and standard vocal imitations).

Sounds made by car, fire engine.

III. ADVANCED

Select something and make a noise with it while others guess what it is (e.g., rustle of dead leaves).

Name rhythm instruments by their sound, without seeing or feeling them.

Play "Make a Noise."

Make a Noise: One player is "It" and is blindfolded. Others join hands and circle silently on tiptoe around him. "It" says, "Stop!" and points his finger at someone, telling him to "Make a noise like a———" (naming an animal or something else which makes a distinctive noise). After the player he pointed to has made the appropriate noise, "It" must guess whose voice it was. If he guesses correctly, the player whom he indicated is "It." If he cannot guess, he is told, but must be "It" again while the game is played over again.

Distinguish between and identify:

Sounds included in Intermediate list.

Sounds made by moving fast, slow.

Sounds of clappers, doorbell, triangle, tambourine, xylophone, school bell, sand blocks.

Sounds associated with paper crackling, paper tearing, money jingling, leaves rustling, rain falling, metal banging, glass tinkling, a paper bag popping, someone blowing into bottles, tapping on window, sneezing, whistling, whispering, scratching, pounding.

Sounds made by bear, lion, airplane, chicken, sheep, goat, frog.

Listen to instruments played by visiting performers. Choose favorite tunes to be played or sung. Identify familiar tunes.

Try picking out very simple tunes on toy piano or xylophone.

Attend children's orchestral concert after teacher has prepared class by showing instruments.

E. Learning Through Other Senses

I. BEGINNER

Touch: Play with a variety of materials—cloth, paper, cellophane, plastic, glass (mirror), rubber, flowers, leaves, dolls (hard and soft ones), sand, grass.

Muscle Sense: Play seesaw holding teacher's or partner's hands, rocking and pushing and pulling; be twirled, be spun in a barrel, jump into teacher's arms, roll over and over; hang from horizontal bar or jungle gym; play with balloons and heavy balls.

II. INTERMEDIATE

Become aware of sensory impressions and discriminate between
them when the teacher presents objects in the school environment relating to the words in the following lists:

Touch and Temperature

hot, cold	brush	bottle
wet, dry	ball	fork
sticky	book	knife
paper	block	spoon
hair	box	pan
glue	sandpaper	

Smell / Taste

Smell	Taste	
perfume	salt	sugar
coffee	lettuce	water
cocoa	onion	milk
juice	green pepper	juices
good smells	lemon	cocoa
bad smells	carrot	soup

Play games such as the following:

What Do You Taste? (blindfolded)

Is It Hot or Cold? (while sampling foods and drinks, feeling
things)

What Do You Smell? (different foods which have each been
placed in bottles made opaque with one color paint or paper
covering). Answer, "Do you like it?"

What Do You Feel? (Select object hidden under cloth, or feel
in bag without looking.)

Find One Like This: Smell, feel, or taste object held by teacher,
and identify it on page of pictured assorted objects.

Find the Thing: Feel in bag, without looking, for object named
by teacher.

Select (using one or two senses only) objects with the same
quality—round, sweet, damp, or sticky.

III. ADVANCED

Recognize the following qualities and objects, by use of the sense under which they are listed. Understand and use these words:

Touch	
rough, smooth	articles of clothing
warm, cool	fur
damp	leather, skin
hard, soft	rubber, plastic, oilcloth
sharp	metal, wood

Taste	Muscle Sense	Smell
sweet, sour, bitter	heavy, light	sweet
salt, pepper		burnt, smoke
coffee, tea, soups		liquids
foods prepared at		fruits, vegetables
school		flowers

Play games: Same as for Intermediate, but respond to verbal directions and teacher's use of names of sensory qualities listed. Use these names when answering teacher's questions.

Make scrapbooks, putting pictures of things that have one common quality on one page, and those that have another common quality on another page.

F. Number Activities

I. INTERMEDIATE

Count slowly, along with teacher, the number of children, juice cups, and crackers.

Count different colored beads on abacus, starting with beads on left side and moving them across to the right side one at a time while saying number. When first learning to count, there will be only two beads on the wire. A third bead will be inserted on the wire by the teacher when the counting to two has been mastered. Later, a fourth bead will be added.

Count one, two, or three objects as game.

Count one, two, or three when opportunity arises. For example,

count hands when washing, or shoes when putting them on.
When cutting a pumpkin or doing a jack-o'-lantern form
board, count its eyes, nose, ears. When eating lunch, count
number of sandwiches, apples, and cookies that lunch-mates
brought. After counting, answer question, "How many?"
and realize what this means.

Count and take the number of goodies told to (one, two or
three jelly beans, raisins, peanuts, animal crackers), stopping
when that number has been taken, so that chance for a second
turn later will be forthcoming.

Count blocks and pennies by moving each one from left to
right when counting it.

Count things in simple pictures, answering question, "How
many?"

Count more than three objects or pictures of objects, always
synchronizing pointing with saying number and always answering question, "How many?"

Answer question: "How many eyes have you?" without counting.

Sort tally cards (i.e., put cards picturing one vertical line in one
pile, cards picturing two tallies in another pile and cards with
three tallies in a third pile).

Match and sort cards with dominoes, dots, or tallies.

Walk in a single line and in a double line; walk two by two.

II. ADVANCED

Count number of one kind of object in schoolroom: windows,
tables, lights.

Count while placing spools on pegs that are arranged in straight
row and set in pegboard.

Put twelve hard-boiled or clay eggs in carton; learn *dozen*.

Put number of beads teacher suggests on a string and stop when
number suggested have been strung.

Count and eat jelly beans, peanuts, or raisins given out a few at
a time.

Match tally cards with number of similar objects or pictured
objects in a group.

Place in large match box the number of blocks to correspond with number of tallies drawn on card pasted on outside of box.

Count own fingers; count those of another pupil.

Make continuous bead pattern as teacher suggests: two big, three little, etc.

Make loop loom potholder, putting certain number of loops of one color, as directed.

Without counting, tell how many fingers on each hand, how many legs a bird or chicken has, how many legs different animals have, how many boys are present in the class, if no more than four.

Point to and name first, second, third, and last objects in a row or line (such as a row of pupils).

Match tally cards with number figures; match dominoes with number figures.

Place correct number of beads in box to correspond with number figures.

Dial telephone numbers.

Put calendar numbers in sequence; read calendar numbers.

Play Dominoes.

During bowling game, count pins knocked down. Keep score for each team, using tallies. Count tallies at end of game to determine winning team.

Play Parchesi, counting dots on dice and counting steps when moving pieces or "men."

Count number of players on teams in relay races; keep score of races won.

Count number of cards when dealing in card game.

Use counting in doing jobs: stack cups in piles of three; stuff three papers in envelope; put pages in number sequence; count three cups or cans of liquid in cooking.

G. Quantity

Learn meaning of the following words when counting and in concrete situations throughout the school program:

Intermediate	*Advanced*	
empty, full	enough	more
boxful	all, some, none	whole, half, quarter
cupful	much, little	pair
everybody, nobody	somebody	dozen
	many, few	cup, pint, quart

H. Coins and Money

I. INTERMEDIATE

Play store using a few pennies.

Sort and match small coins.

Buy balloon, stamp, candy, gum, cookie at real store.

II. ADVANCED

Play store. Read and respond to price tags made by teacher.

From two different coins, then three, select coin teacher names.

From a group of coins, pick out each and name it.

Select coin from a group when asked which one is one cent, five cents, or ten cents.

Tell how much each coin is worth.

Pay storekeeper (real or impersonated by classmate) a penny for one-cent purchase, a nickel for five-cent purchase, and a dime for ten-cent purchase.

Select from pictures or real store items, things that can be bought for a nickel, penny, dime.

Select correct amount for bus money; count it.

Select correct amount of money for other small purchases like movies or food or stamps.

Count nickel and pennies.

Count dime and nickels.

Count by nickels to 25, adding on pennies after that.

Count by dimes to 50, adding on pennies.

From a variety of small change, select correct amount for specified small purchases.

Learn quarter, dollar, and half-dollar.

Give storekeeper big enough coin or bill to cover cost of purchase to five dollars.

I. Time

I. INTERMEDIATE

Answer questions such as "What do you do before lunch (or after lunch)?"

Distinguish night from day in pictures and in relating personal happenings.

Associate morning and afternoon with meals and school activities.

Tell in sequence of time what pupils do at school, using "then," "next."

Tell own activities in sequence of time, from morning to night.

Put three or four pictures of a story in correct time sequence.

Through discussion associated with action and with school activities, learn concepts involving these words:

early, late	wait	fast, slow
now, later	first, last	hurry (used only in emergencies)

II. ADVANCED

Use meaningfully such terms as: "last night," "tonight," "tomorrow night," "this morning," "yesterday morning."

Name the days of the week in sequence as teacher or pupil points to abbreviation of each day; name the day of the week corresponding to the words "yesterday," "today," and "tomorrow," associating each with events of personal significance and school happenings.

Through discussion, gain concepts of "on time," "beginning," and "end."

Read names of the days of the week on the calendar.

Learn that there are seven days in a week.

Realize that there are several weeks in a month.

Point to the number on the calendar corresponding to "today," "yesterday," "tomorrow," and find date on calendar for a holiday or birthday.

Make monthly calendar with teacher's help, and regularly mark off the day that has just passed.

Give present date—day, month, year.

Give date of birth, and tell age. Tell who is oldest: mother, child, grandmother.

Name present season and a few outstanding weather characteristics or activities for this season.

Telling Time:

Distinguish hands of clock by pointing and naming short and long hands.

Say the number of the hour as teacher moves short hand on cardboard clock.

Place clock numbers in correct sequence in clock puzzle (see Appendix E, p. 257 for commercial clock puzzles).

On own small cardboard clock, move short hand and say number of each hour, looking at teacher's clock hands as pattern, when necessary. Point to clock hand that tells the names of the numerals on the clock.

Tell time as teacher moves hands from 12 o'clock to one o'clock, etc. (A real clock whose hands can move around together is good to use for showing the way the clock moves from hour to hour. If teacher simply moves the short hand on a cardboard clock, children may get the impression that long hand does not move.)

Tell time by hours in sequence while moving short hand around the clock.

Tell time as teacher moves hands to indicate hours, not in sequence.

After noticing that the school clock is on the hour, announce time to class.

Tell which is longer, an hour or a day.

Match on own clock the long hand of teacher's clock as it goes from "o'clock" to "half past"; match both hands of own clock with those of teacher's clock as she indicates hours and half-hours in sequence.

Follow same procedure in learning "quarter past" and "quarter after."

Tell time that school begins and check to see if all pupils are on time.

Associate verbally or with pictures certain activities with the time they begin and end.

Notify the class when period ends by checking real clock with adjustable cardboard clock.

Watch clock to announce when it indicates a particular time for a special activity.

Play Clock Bingo: Play as regular Bingo, each player's large card having nine clock faces indicating times that he is just learning. The cards could be numbered inconspicuously, and after player learns one card he could be given another which is more advanced.

When the concepts of "o'clock," "half past," and "quarter after" are well understood and have been used easily and correctly over a period of time, learn the position of the hand for "quarter before."

Match teacher's short clock hand with own clock's short hand, noting it is in a position *before* the number of the hour, when the time is "quarter before——— (some hour)." Then proceed in learning "quarter before" and later, "quarter of" as in learning other clock positions.

When long hand does not point exactly to a familiar clock time, learn to recognize and tell the time to the nearest quarter hour or 5 minutes saying, "It is about———" (first, *after* the hour, and only much later, *before* the hour).

RELATED READING

Engle, T. L., and Iona C. Hamlett. "Comparison of Mental Defectives and Normal Children in Ability to Handle Clock and Calendar Situations," *American Journal of Mental Deficiency*, LVIII (April, 1954), 655–58.

Epps, Helen O., Gertrude B. McCammon, and Queen D. Simmons. *Teaching Devices for Children with Impaired Learning: A Study of the Brain-Injured Child.* Columbus, Ohio: Columbus State School, 1958.

Halpin, Virginia. "The Performance of Mentally Retarded Children on the Weigl-Goldstein-Scheerer Color Form Sorting Test," *American Journal of Mental Deficiency*, LXII (March, 1958), 916–19.

Hauessermann, Else. *Developmental Potential of Preschool Children: An Evaluation of Intellectual, Sensory, and Emotional Functioning*. London: Grune and Stratton, 1958.

House, Betty J., and David Zeaman, "A Comparison of Discrimination Learning in Normal and Mentally Defective Children," *Child Development*, XXIX (1958), 411–16.

House, Betty J., David Zeaman, Robert Orlando, and William Fischer. *Learning and Transfer in Mental Defectives*. Storrs, Connecticut: The University of Connecticut Department of Psychology, 1957.

Hunt, Betty, and Ruth M. Patterson. "Performance of Brain-Injured and Familial Mentally Deficient Children on Visual and Auditory Sequences," *American Journal of Mental Deficiency*, LXIII (July, 1958), 72–80.

Riess, Anita. *Number Readiness in Research*. Chicago: Scott, Foresman and Company, 1947.

Schucman, Helen. "A Method for Measuring Educability in Severely Mentally Retarded Children: A Preliminary Study," *Training Bulletin*, LIV (November, 1957), 52–54.

Stevenson, Harold W., and Edward F. Zigler, "Discrimination, Learning, and Rigidity in Normal and Feebleminded Individuals," *Journal of Personality*, XXV (1957), 699–711.

Strauss, Alfred A., and Laura E. Lehtinen. *Psychopathology and Education of the Brain-Injured Child*. I: *Fundamentals and Treatment*. New York: Grune and Stratton (1951) 18–74, and 127–44.

Strauss, Alfred, and Newell G. Kephart. *Psychopathology and Education of the Brain-Injured Child*. Vol. II: *Progress in Theory and Clinic*. New York: Grune and Stratton, 1955.

IX. Crafts

Craft activities can serve a number of significant functions for the trainable. Besides aiding in the development of the small muscles, they teach him skills which may be useful in the future: the making of certain objects and the operation of simple tools. A craft may also have a social value, since a child may work on it with his classmates, or give the product to another person. Another craft may have value in making him happier when alone, because it occupies his leisure time meaningfully. Satisfactions from achievement may be rare in the life of a trainable child. It is important for his emotional well-being that he have the tangible evidence of the useful things he makes to prove to himself his value and ability to succeed.

Since the trainable should be taught thoroughly and since his time for learning in school is limited, his craft activities ought to be carefully chosen. Only those which seem especially appropriate for such a child are listed in this book. Major criteria for selecting them are given here, in order of importance:

1. The craft should be useful. Although the coordination of a retarded worker is seldom fine enough for him to compete in speed and quality with average craftsmen, he can make, or help others make, acceptable gifts for family and friends: a dish towel, a greeting card, a rhythm instrument for a child.

2. The craft should be simple enough to be learned with detailed instruction and practice. (Sometimes this can be determined only after a trial period. Even though a retardate may be unable to learn it at a certain age, he may be able to after further maturation.)

If a presentable gift is to be made, the teacher should select a project requiring very simple workmanship, so that the child can carry it out satisfactorily without the teacher's guiding his every move or actually doing most of the work herself.

3. The craft should be one that can be done outside of school. For example, ceramics would be impractical for the inexpert, as it requires an expensive kiln, or money to pay for firing. Loop-loom pot holders require only a small, inexpensive frame and cloth loops. The desire among a person's acquaintances for imperfect ceramic pieces would certainly be limited. The need for pot holders might be small but somewhat continuous, for they do wear out. The retarded could make these in their own homes.

4. A simple craft should at least be a step toward learning a more useful craft. Certain ones that might appear to have little value in and of themselves may lead to useful work. For example, sewing cards, while not of use themselves, are steps toward learning to baste. Paper work involving folding can lead to preparing materials for mailing, which a retarded worker may do as a volunteer or in a sheltered workshop. A teacher may realize that a certain pupil with a severe hand tremor may never be able to get beyond sewing cards to the next step of basting. In this case the teacher may well ask herself, "Should this boy continue lacing sewing cards, or is there some useful task that he could and should be learning?" Perhaps he could do a fine job of sanding furniture or waxing floors.

5. The craft should be of interest to the child. Making holiday greeting cards, decorations, or presents for the family will motivate the child to work as fast and well as he can. This may lead to an increase in attention span, in general manipulative ability, in perception, or in special skills like folding.

6. Craft activities should be challenging. After a child has learned to string big beads easily or cut paper into strips, he should not continue this indefinitely, but be constantly encouraged to try something a little more difficult or something original, which challenges him intellectually as well as manually. A child whose skill improves slowly, because of physical handicaps,

needs various materials which will make use of his intellectual capacities. (If he makes an original design with pegs, rather than simply inserting them, he is still getting the manual practice, but is gaining much more than that.)

7. Activities should help in the development of muscle skills. A retardate's usefulness will depend considerably on his ability to use his small as well as his large muscles.

8. Given a choice of activities, select the one which involves as many concomitant learnings as possible. For example, putting pegs in a board or stringing beads can become meaningful activities for improving perceptual and number skills, while increased attention is being developed at the same time; the child can be learning to count the number of beads of a certain color as he strings them to match a bead pattern.

A thoughtful teacher, in looking over the list of craft activities that follows, will keep the problems and goals of each child in mind, so she will teach him only those crafts of true value to him. Rather than teaching the child crafts that have few concomitant learnings and that he can seldom use, time would better be spent perfecting his domestic skills, such as wiping off tables or washing windows.

The projects in the list are simple enough so that the child can carry out many of the steps himself. The teacher, however, will need to prepare materials and assist the pupil at certain points. To distinguish between the directions for the child and those for the teacher, the steps of a project where the teacher will have to help out are usually given in parentheses or are suggested by use of the passive tense.

CRAFT ACTIVITIES

A. Sewing

Sewing is included in the program for trainable boys and girls because, as they gain proficiency in such skills as basting or hemming, they can be useful to themselves and to other people. Utilizing their sewing to keep themselves well groomed makes the retarded less dependent upon others and increases their sense of worth. While sewing, children become familiar with a variety of materials and small tools. Through sewing and weaving activities they learn to work in an organized way. The concrete evidence of their progress makes such activities especially effective learning tools for retarded children.

In order to learn the skills that are usually referred to as "sewing," the youngster may first need simpler activities. One preliminary step to sewing is bead-stringing. Even simple bead-stringing may be too difficult at first. Since steps preceding bead-stringing sometimes need to be introduced, a few of these are given below as the first steps in bead-stringing.

1. Bead-Stringing

I. BEGINNER

Put rings on sticks.

Insert pegs in peg board.

Insert Tinkertoy sticks into holes in round Tinkertoys.

String big, flat, large-holed beads by using short lace with long tip. The ease with which beads can be laced depends upon appropriateness of materials and tools:

Lace: short and sturdy with large knot at one end and a long, stiff unbroken tip 1″ to 2″ long at the other end.

Beads: thin and with large enough holes so each bead can be held with one hand while other hand grasps tip of the lace as it comes through; beads large enough to be held firmly, without being covered up by hand; beads shaped so that they do not roll easily and excite or frustrate the child.

String assorted large beads with lace having 2″ tip.

String button molds by using lace having ¾″ tip. (Button molds are obtainable from educational supply houses.)

Make spiral bracelet: With spring wire, string smaller beads. (End of wire should be bent at one end before beads are strung and at other end when stringing is finished.)

Make decoration: String assorted beads on a pipe cleaner. Bend over end, so decoration can be hung.

II. INTERMEDIATE

String beads ½″ long, with lace having ¾″ tip.
String button molds using lace having ½″ tip.
Make articles such as:

Shoe-Button Bracelet: String colored shoe buttons using elastic thread. Tie the elastic.

Decoration: Take 1″ strips of colored construction paper. Cut across each on heavy lines, marked by teacher at 1″ intervals, and make 1″ squares. Or cut pieces without lines if this can be done successfully. Punch hole near center of each square. Alternately string paper squares and macaroni on pipe cleaners.

Clay Bracelet or Necklace: Roll small balls or make other shapes out of self-hardening clay and poke holes through with long nail, ⅛″ thick. Paint, shellac, and string.

III. ADVANCED

Long Necklace: With needles, string cranberries or paper straws, cut into 1″ sections, alternating with paper triangles. Make triangles by cutting diagonally across a paper strip on lines drawn by teacher.

Sunburst Table Mat: To make a mat, it is necessary to have 30 wooden slats (popsickle sticks, obtainable from an icecream company), 30 ball beads at least ⅜″ in diameter and 24 inches of elastic cord for stringing (obtainable from a craft supply house). With pencil, mark sticks and drill holes using a standard hand drill. Follow directions included with materials from craft supply house in stringing beads and slats together to make circular mat. When finished, shellac.

2. Overcast Lacing

I. INTERMEDIATE

For learning lacing, use a piece of cardboard approximately 3″ x 6″, white on only one side. Cardboard has 8 holes punched in it about ½″ apart. (The teacher has colored the cardboard around the rim of each hole a different rainbow color or brown or black, but the upper surface and underside of the cardboard around the hole are of the same color.) For lacing, use round shoelace with tip at least ¾″ long, or string whose end has been dipped in shellac, or nail polish. Other end of string of lace must have a knot in it.

Holding card almost vertically, start at lower right-hand corner. With left hand hold cardboard firmly; with right hand put tip in from under side and then up through hole, pulling it through with same (right) hand. Each time, while holding card, tip it over a little, so it is almost on edge, to see where to insert lace. Pull the slack of the lace tightly after each stitch, leaving new hole where tip is to go, clear of lacing so stitches won't get crossed. Examine work after each stitch, to see if any holes have been skipped or stitches crossed.

If left-handed, start at lower left corner and work with just the opposite orientation.

More Advanced Steps: Use cardboard in which holes have been punched all the way around by the teacher. Make holes that are smaller and spaced closer together. The cardboard can be the same color and texture on both sides, which will be more difficult when determining where lace should be inserted. The rim of the holes need not be colored. Lace two thicknesses of cardboard that have been clipped or glued together to hold them in place. Use a flat instead of a round shoelace, and hold the tip without letting go or turning it in fingers, to prevent twisting of the lace. When lacing with a leather or plastic lace, glue the end of the lace in place with rubber cement, and lace over it. When the project is all laced, lace over through the last hole once again and then poke the end back through the last few stitches.

If child becomes confused when lacing two pieces of leather together, place a bit of sticky tape on the side into which the tip is always to be inserted.

Make a big object, involving much lacing, in order to gain practice and to learn how to work independently.

Wall Container for Pot Holder: Place half of one paper plate on top of another paper plate, so that inside surfaces face each other and holes at their edges correspond (holes punched ⅜″

from edge, ½″ apart). Lace plates together, decorate, and shellac.

Cardboard Coaster or Place Mat: Trace and cut from a pattern a small cardboard circle or larger rectangle. Mark through pattern that indicates where lacing holes are to be. Poke holes into cardboard with awl or large-hole paper punch. Paint and shellac lightly, not filling up the holes. Lace with plastic lace.

Felt Bookmark: Draw around pattern (a 1″ wide strip pointed at one end) and cut out. Over-cast edge with yarn by inserting either a blunt needle in punched holes, or sharp needle where dots are marked.

Oilcloth TV Cushion: Clip together wrong sides of two large squares of oilcloth. Punch holes and lace 3 sides. Stuff plumply with long strips of newspaper. Lace fourth side.

Lace cork coasters, hot dish mats, purses, wallets, oilcloth book covers.

II. ADVANCED

Leather Projects: Always put cardboard (such as index card) under leather where punch is to cut hole in order to preserve smooth surface of metal on punch. When leather project is double thickness, glue pieces together with rubber cement to hold them in place, before punching. When lacing, if hole is too small, use nut pick or knitting needles to enlarge it. If snaps for purses or napkin rings are preferred instead of snap and strap or button and loop, a craft shop or the teacher (if she has tools) can put them on. Advanced lacers can decorate their projects with a cross-stitch instead of plain overcasting: after overcasting the edge, lace around at reverse angles the second time. (Teacher can buy ready-cut pieces of leather in project kits at craft shops and make additional patterns from these to cut projects from leather scraps obtained free from local concerns, such as upholsterers.)

Wallet, Book Cover, Purse, Comb Case, Eyeglass Case, Napkin Rings: Trace shape around cardboard pattern and cut out with scissors (or teacher cut with knife). Mark lacing holes through pattern and punch with leather punch. (If leather is thick, teacher will have to do this.)

Felt Projects: Make projects similar to leather, using overcast stitch with needle and yarn. Make fastening for purse with button and loop.

3. Running-Stitch

I. INTERMEDIATE

Sewing-Card Place Mat: Using lace or yarn with tip, sew with running stitch through holes punched ½″ apart and 1″ from edge of large round card. Next, run stitches around edge of a smaller card, in which holes are placed closer together and nearer the edge. If it is confusing to know where needle is to be inserted, teacher can mark a line from hole to hole where thread should go, on each side of card. Later, sew around square cards without guide marks.

II. ADVANCED

Greeting Card: Thread large, blunt needle with heavy thread. Tie knot by making a loop at one end, putting other end through thread several times. Or make regular sewing knot in this fashion: wind thread around index finger twice; twist thread off finger with moistened thumb and index finger of other hand or thumb of same hand, and pull thread down into a knot. Sew through holes which have been pin-pricked in card to make a simple, clear shape (ball, star, heart or other standard symbol in one piece—not a subjective portrayal of people, trees, or houses with perspective). When sewing is finished, there should be a clear outline of stitches showing the entire design. Run stitches around design a second time, bringing needle up where it originally went down to make a solid line. When sewing is finished the form inside thread outline can be crayon-colored. Yarn of different colors could be used when sewing, but is so hard to insert thread into needle that teacher rather than children get practice in threading needle.

Muslin Place Mat: Unravel edges (beginning at outside), making fringe. Decorate with running stitch sewn with yarn, along a guide line drawn ½″ from fringe. Or, instead of fringing, turn down each edge ½″ and crease, following a guide line if necessary. Then sew edge down with yarn running stitch, following guide lines or dots if needed.

Head Scarf: Fringe or turn down each edge as for place mat above, and sew with running stitch.

Yarn-Covered Hot-Dish Mat: Sew through holes across cardboard rectangle and back again until cardboard is covered with yarn.

Oilcloth Apron: Draw around pattern on oilcloth and cut out. Decorate edge with running stitch. Tack on ribbons for sash, sewing back and forth across ends of ribbon.

Felt Pot-Holder: Cut out and stitch several thicknesses of felt of appropriate size and shape.

Felt Purse: Draw and cut around pattern placed on felt. Sew sides with running stitch using strong thread. Sew on loop made of narrow ribbon doubled and knotted. Sew on button to be used with loop.

Cloth Shoe-Bag: Draw around cardboard pattern placed on cotton cloth remnant; cut out, and sew around all but top edge, with right sides of material clipped together. Turn down top edge 1″ and iron, pin, or clip it down. Sew it down strongly with running stitch ¼″ in from rough edge. Insert draw string in top and turn right side out. Make bag for each shoe, or a larger one for a pair of sneakers.

Scrapbook: Fold in half several sheets of paper of same size that have been clipped together with edges even. Open up; sew along middle fold once and back again, poking needle up in same holes it was poked down, to secure pages.

Towel (Basted): Cut or tear toweling material to size wanted and turn up edge, creasing well. Pin, baste with black thread, and after turning up a second time, baste with red in preparation for hemming.

4. Hemming

I. ADVANCED

Towel: Fold back hem onto right side of towel that has been basted twice. Crease and hold down with pins or paper clips. Then overcast top edges. When finished, unfold, showing completed hem. Rip out basting. Carpenter aprons, aprons, place mats, head scarfs, doll bedding, sheets, and pillow cases can be hemmed in this way.

5. Sewing on Buttons

I. ADVANCED

Button Card: Sew cardboard buttons on cardboard in which corresponding thread holes have been made.

Button Picture Card: Sew buttons of various sizes and colors onto pictures on thin cardboard. Original designs can be made by arranging large, colorful buttons on large card. Draw around them and sew them on places designated.

Sew buttons on clothes. Sew big buttons on smock, apron, pajamas, big doll clothes.
Sew small buttons on blouse, shirt.
Sew large buttons on jacket, coat.

6. Weaving

I. INTERMEDIATE

Mat for Flower Pot: Use cardboard loom 7″ x 7″, on top and bottom edge of which notches have been cut an inch apart. (Teacher ties heavy string around card at first notch, located ½″ from side edge of loom, and then carries it from notch to opposite notch then behind nearest point and from next notch to opposite notch, etc. She may take two crayons and color all the warp strings alternately to make it easier for child to tell which string to go under to weave each row.) With safety pin attached as shuttle to one piece of heavy yarn, weave under every alternate string. It seems easier to concentrate on going *under* the string of one color, rather than also thinking of going *over*.

(Teacher will need to tie end of woof through beginning warp string, which is tied around first point at edge of cardboard loom. At end of weaving, woof will have to be tied again in similar fashion. During the weaving, a new piece of yarn, as long as child can handle, may be tied to the end of the woof when it has been almost used up. Tuck in the knot. A paper clip may be needed at corner where string is attached, to keep it from slipping off. Also, a small paper clip attached to string nearest each edge of cardboard holds string tighter so that weaving will not draw it in toward the center.)

After weaving one row across loom, learn to turn around and return under the alternate strings by first stopping at end of row and showing teacher which string was last one that yarn went under. Pointing to it, tell what color it is. Then tell what color the yarn will go under the next time across, and point to the string of that color that is "closest," or to the "next string, close to the one where the yarn just came out." Even if the words are not understood, the method of finding where to start the next row can be established after it has been used under supervision a number of times.

II. ADVANCED

Loop-Loom Pot Holder: Use a homemade loom with ¾" nails having small, smooth heads, or a bought metal loom for making loop-loom potholders. (Looms' points should be smooth and could be bent outward a little by the teacher to keep loops from slipping off. For those first learning, it is best not to have more than 19 nails or points to each side and preferably 15. Loom should measure 7" from nail on one side across to opposite nail on other side. Nails should be about ⅜" apart. Loops for this type of weaving are available in various stores and craft shops. The color should be fast.)

Select 19 loops of one color, 10 of another color, and 10 of a third (preferably ones the pupil can name). Be sure each is long enough by stretching it from nail on one side of loom directly across to nail on opposite side. If this cannot be done easily, discard it. Save the 19 loops for the woof. String loom, alternating the other two colors.

To weave, insert loop of third color (woof) on first nail on right side of frame and weave to left, using bobby pin or large safety pin as shuttle. (Teacher questions child each time as to what color he is going to go *under*.) At end of row, pull loop over nail and remove bobby pin. If loom slips about on table too much, put rubber mat under it or clamp it to table.

Point to nail just used and find nail next to it. Over this nail put a new loop. Weave with new loop, being reminded by teacher to go under *other* color this time, and naming it each time before going under it. Continue weaving using loops all the same color.

If there is difficulty in keeping warp loops from falling off nails (either during weaving process or during crocheting to remove pot holder from loom), stretch rubber bands over nails from one nail to another along sides of loom; however, rubber bands on sides where loops are being added or removed will have to be moved each time new loop is put on or removed from nail. If elastic is to be tight enough, a very short rubber band will be needed when only a few loops are on the nails.

To remove pot holders from loom, use crochet stitch. First take stick or pencil and push rows of weaving down, to give more room for removing loops from nails at top of frame. Start with side that has alternate colored loops, beginning with first loop at top right. Take first loop off nail and follow teacher's directions: "Make the loop big. Take off the next loop, pinch it, and hold the old loop open. Put this new loop (third) in the old," etc. (Since loops next to side of frame will not alternate in color, but will all be one color, there is no use in noting the loops' colors for cues as to which loop goes inside which.)

When the last loop is removed from its nail, insert previous loop in it and then insert other loop (or last) into that loop to secure the weaving. However, if there is difficulty in remembering which loop should be inserted in which, make potholders using only two colors instead of three for loops, and alternate these two colors with the woof as well as the warp. Then when crocheting, alternate colors when inserting one loop in the next.

Bath Mat: After making 35 pot holders, overcast them together with needle and thread, so that there are five rows of squares with seven squares to a row.

Hand Bag: Using six loop pot holders, place them in three rows of two each. With overcast stitch, sew together in that arrangement. Fold bottom rows up to top of middle row, and overcast sides together. Top row is flap that folds over rest of purse. Pull one loop that is in middle of top row's edge, so it is larger and can be used to fasten purse. Sew button at middle of bottom of purse. If desired, make lining for purse.

Yarn Place Mat: Weave with yarn on very simple loom larger than size of place mat wanted. (Such a loom can be bought at craft shops or other stores, and additional ones could be handmade by copying it. Loom is strung with thread.)

Rag Rug: On large, handmade frame stretch string back and forth around nails for warp. Sew, end to end, rags cut or torn into narrow strips, all of one width. Wind into balls for easier handling while weaving rug.

7. Braiding

I. ADVANCED

Colored Sash for Costume: Tie together at one end three different colored starched sashes about ¾" wide and 2½' long. Hook the knotted end over a knob on a chair or door, or on a vertical nail at about waist height. Sit where sashes can be laid flat across a table, separated from each other. Pick up the two outside sashes. Place one over the middle sash and push it between the two sashes. Spread it out and pick up the free sash now on the outside. Place other outside sash over middle sash. Then push it between the two sashes. Always keep sashes separated. When finished, knot it.

Jump Rope or Rope for Sled: Braid together three long, thin ropes dyed different colors.

Lanyard for Whistle: Braid leather or plastic lacing together, inserting whistle when half of lanyard is laced.

8. Machine Sewing

I. ADVANCED

Some older pupils will be able to run a sewing machine, especially an electric one where pedal manipulation is easy.

A few boys and girls may learn to thread machine. Practice sewing first on rags. Learn to tie ends of thread.

Hemming Dish Towel: Turn edge up once and baste; then stitch hem on machine, tying thread ends. Remove basting stitches with pin. Turn up a second time and stitch again, after basting.

Hemming Sheet: Turn edge up and baste; turn hem a second time and baste again. Sew on machine.

Doll Quilt: Cut 2″ to 4″ patches, all the same size, from cloth scraps or samples of material. If necessary, baste two patches together wrong sides out, along one edge. Sew same edge on machine. Baste a third patch onto the second, and stitch. Continue until long strip of the length desired is made. Make similar strips of patches same length, in same way. Finally, sew long strips together to make large rectangle. Make duplicate of this rectangle. Sew both together on wrong side along with same size flannel cloth (for padding). Leave fourth side open to be overcast when quilt has been turned right side out.

Bean Bag: Clip together right sides of two 4″ squares of strong material. Baste. Sew around all but top edge after regulating machine for short stitches. If necessary, have supervision for turning corners. Tie ends. Turn right side out. Fill partially with dried beans. Baste fourth side and stitch on machine, or overcast with small stitches placed close together.

B. Paper Work

Working with paper not only is fun but also develops skills such as cutting, stapling, and punching holes. Paper helps a child learn to work carefully because it is fragile and easily torn or mussed. Many paper activities give training in visual perception (e.g., folding, cutting on a line, pasting in corners). Through making designs the child becomes more aware of form and balance.

Paper work is a desirable craft because it is usually accepted in the home as a leisure-time activity, since materials are inexpensive and neither a large working space nor much assistance is required.

1. Crayoning

I. BEGINNER

Gift-wrapping Paper: Cover a small sheet of wrapping paper with crayon marks as desired (probably scribbles at this stage).

Greeting Card: Color solidly inside gray 5″ x 7″ cardboard stencil, held by small paper clips or staples to paper of same size placed underneath stencil. (Patterns used should each have one solid, simple shape, outlined in black, that can be easily perceived and understood. Design should not be broken up into parts but be one complete object when child has finished it. Subject should be a standard symbol or simple object portrayed easily and clearly in silhouette form as, for instance, a plain heart shape for valentine. It should not be an artist's drawing using perspective, shading, etc. nor a complex outline, with many small parts jutting out.) When stenciling is finished, teacher removes pattern from paper and writes greeting or words child says, his name and name of person to whom it is to be given.

Stenciled Decoration: Use same type of design and stenciling as for greeting card, with colors that stand out, such as yellow construction paper, and red crayon, or red paper and white chalk. Run pipe cleaner or shoe lace through hole punched near top for hanging decoration on wall or other place.

Paper Bag Hat: Color paper bag, after teacher has trimmed it to fit a child's head.

II. INTERMEDIATE

Cleaner's Garment-Bag Costume: Cut holes for head and arms. Crayon borders of arms, neck, or hem, and decorate "dress."

Greeting Card: Without stencil, color inside black outline of simple form, made originally if possible.

Place Mat: Color border of paper of appropriate size and shape, inside line drawn by teacher, or follow edge of paper, using side of crayon.

III. ADVANCED

Colored Coaster: Crayon white cardboard disk completely with waxy crayon, on both sides. Place the disk between a folded piece of newsprint and press with warm iron, giving coloring a soft, smooth appearance.

Party Crown: Cut 2″ strip and draw linear design on it with crayon as desired. Design may be simply sticks of one color, with another color stick placed between these, or with circle between. Staple ends of decorated strip together for crown.

Decorated Napkin: Crayon simple design in corner of folded napkin, or crayon linear border about an inch from napkin's edge.

Decorated Paper Plate or Circular Place Mat: Make linear design along edge and original design in center. Shellac.

Wastebasket: With help, cut a piece of heavy brown paper large enough to cover the sides of a large can such as a potato chip can. Make repeated linear designs along 1½″ rows on paper with bright crayons. Wrap the paper around can and glue with rubber cement. Shellac.

2. Cutting and Folding

I. BEGINNER

Practice opening and shutting small, blunt scissors repeatedly, keeping fingers in finger grips with teacher's help. (If scissors are too tight, teacher can loosen center screw one turn. Scissors can be sharpened by cutting through sandpaper a few times.) Make cuts on piece of 3″ x 2″ stiff construction paper or heavy wrapping paper while teacher holds paper. Say "Open, cut" with teacher while proceeding. Later on, hold paper with teacher's help and, still later, experiment alone with scissors and paper. Cut and then tear off little snips of paper.

Picture of Fall Leaves: After playing outdoors in leaves, cut little snips from variously colored small pieces of construction paper. Drop pieces on sheet of light blue paper on which paste has been spread over an irregular area to resemble leaf pile. Press them down. When dry, shake off loose "leaves." (Before "leaves" are dropped on paper, a real twig may be stuck on with tape to represent a tree.)

Paper Pieces for Stringing: Cut across 1″ wide strip, making square or rectangular pieces. For stringing see p. 162.

Greeting Card: Fold sheet of construction paper in half, by bringing bottom corners up to top corners. (Teacher may have to mark top corners at first to emphasize where bottom corners are to be placed, and draw lines on both sides of paper to show where fold is to be made.) Crease by pressing hard with thumb several times. Open paper and cut on fold. Fold one piece in half for booklet card. Paste sticker or draw picture on front with crayon. Fringe edges by making small cuts close together along the edges of card. (Teacher can draw light border line to indicate where cut of the scissors should stop. Inside the card teacher can write greeting that child dictates.)

II. INTERMEDIATE

Wallpaper Place Mats: Draw around cardboard pattern of large circle, clipped to reverse side of wallpaper. (Teacher centers pattern to correspond with design of wallpaper.) Cut out circle on line.

Orange, Pumpkin, Apple, Grapefruit Cut-Outs: Cut out circular shape drawn on paper of appropriate color. Cut piece from strip of green paper for pumpkin stem, or from brown paper for apple stem, and paste on.

Picture to be Mounted or Placed in Scrapbook: Select square or rectangular picture from a group partially cut out by teacher, and finish cutting out. The usual magazine pictures are not stiff enough. Greeting cards, backs of magazines, and some advertising circulars are more easily cut. Pictures should be small for beginners, with outline emphasized with crayon, and with wide margin of paper on side or sides to be cut. In cutting out picture, teacher will leave only one side of rectangular or square picture or two parallel sides for beginner to cut, but later will leave three or four sides involving cutting around corners.

Valentine: Cut several narrow rectangular pieces from 1″ wide strips of white or vari-colored papers. Paste at random onto red paper heart 4″ or 5″ wide, made by teacher.

Ladder, Fence, Railroad Track: Cut across a 2″ wide strip along lines 1″ apart. (Lines have been drawn by teacher with different colored crayons to focus child's attention on lines during cutting.) Placing these "rungs" parallel, hammer onto beaver board or paste across two long paper strips cut and mounted on cardboard in parallel arrangement. Make picket fence or railroad track in similar way. Use for play with small dolls and trains.

Train: Make "blocks" by cutting on lines 3″ apart across a paper strip 2″ wide, and connect them with sticky tape, to represent train. Move them along track.

Candle: Cut a ¾″ x 3″ strip of paper for candle and a 1″ x 3″ strip in contrasting color for base. For flame, cut diagonally across a ¾″ wide red or yellow strip.

Paper Chains for Decoration: Following lines, cut strips ¾″ or 1″ wide, the length of a 7″ square of construction paper. Make link by bending strip into a circle and pasting one end about ¼″ over the other end. Press together tightly. Put paste on end of a second strip, insert it through first link, and paste ends together to form second link. Repeat until chain is length desired. (Thinner paper strips are more readily bent into chain links, and narrower ones are prettier, but both require more cutting skill. Shorter strips are harder to hold when pasting.)

Stamps and Tickets: Cut rectangles on lines drawn horizontally and vertically according to size of object desired. Later, use as stamps or, with paper punch, as train tickets and bus transfers.

Jack-o'-Lantern Picture: After talking about and looking at real jack-o'-lanterns and making them of clay, cut large orange circle for pumpkin. Green strip for stem and yellow or black pieces for features can be cut and pasted on pumpkin.

III. ADVANCED

Small Napkins for Juice-Time: Fold large opened paper napkin into quarters. Cut along the folded edges so that four little napkins result. If desired, napkins can be folded in half again to form rectangles or triangles.

Paper Strips for Bottom of Pet's Cage: Fold newspaper page in half, bottom to top. Holding horizontally, with fold toward body and with fingers on fold, cut from fold up across paper, making strips about ¾″ wide.

Snowflake: With class, watch and imitate teacher as she folds a sheet of typing or mimeograph paper first in half, then in quarters and if possible, in eights. Cut out notches and odd shapes along edges, leaving parts of each edge uncut. Unfold and staple or paste onto colored paper for party place mat, or attach "snowflake" made on quarter of above size to a red booklet for lacy valentine.

Collage: Cut out shapes such as vari-colored triangles, spirals and thin strips (to be pleated). Paste or staple to large paper, fastening only one end of spiral or of pleated strip. Hang on wall. (This can be a group project.)

Money for Play Store: On gray and brown construction paper or light-weight cardboard trace around pennies, nickels, etc. and cut out.

Object Game: Without pattern (if possible) cut familiar object into standard geometric shape (e.g., an orange, tomato, wheel, or ball in the form of a circle; a block in the form of a square; a book in the form of a rectangle). Draw simple detail on it and color appropriately. Ask class to guess what it is.

Lantern for Decoration: Fold construction or lighter weight paper in half. Draw line the width of ruler in from unfolded (top) edge, and another line the same distance in from each side edge. Cut on parallel lines drawn ½" apart, running from fold (at bottom) to line drawn across top edge. Throughout cutting, be sure to stop at top line. When all slits are cut, open paper and make cylindrical shape by bringing the side edges together. Staple or paste, and attach paper strip as handle.

Icicles: Cut two ¾" wide strips, the full length of onion skin typing paper. Keeping strips flat on table, paste one end of one strip over one end of the other, at right angles. Then fold strip pasted underneath over top strip, again keeping it at right angles to other strip. Continue folding strips one over the other until their entire lengths have been folded together. Paste top ends together. Then staple loop of string on end of strips for hanging. For festoon effect, all pupils' icicles can be pasted or stapled together and draped.

Star Decoration: Trace and cut out two stars from construction paper. Make a cut from edge to middle of each star. Holding one perpendicularly to other, slip its slot into slot of other star.

3. Pasting

I. BEGINNER

Colored Shapes on Contrasting Background: Using paper colored on one side only, cut paper any shape large enough to be grasped (2″ or 3″). Put paste on uncolored (i.e., "wrong") side. When pasting, work directly on washable table rather than on newspaper, to which materials may stick. Insert paste brush into a small amount of smooth, wet, slightly fluid paste placed in jar lid or paint pan. (Paste will usually not be eaten if alum is mixed with it.) Apply paste to reverse side of colored shape. Wipe paste off fingers with wet paper towel kept close at hand. Place shape on piece of construction paper of another color and press down hard. Wash paste off table.

Later, try pasting onto one piece of paper, two shapes, then three, then four, learning to place them apart from, instead of on top of, each other.

II. INTERMEDIATE

Greeting Card: Put paste all over back of small picture cut from stiff paper, such as old greeting card, and mount picture on half or quarter sheet of construction paper placed with edge parallel to edge of table and worker's body. Paper can be folded first into booklet form and picture placed on cover, if desired.

Picture for Classroom Decoration: Locate and mark each corner on back of a favorite picture and apply paste on marks. After wiping fingers, place mounting paper straight on table. Point to where picture will go and then paste it on.

Scrapbook: Have name written on cover of scrapbook. Select and cut out several pictures from stiff paper. Arrange them on first right-hand page. Turn first picture over, apply paste and mount. As reminder of which side is for paste, mark that side with kindergarten pencil. Let page dry before turning page or closing book. Placing pictures on only one side of sheet will avoid their getting torn by sticking together. (Teacher writes down whatever the child says about the picture, for use in speech work.)

III. ADVANCED

Thanksgiving Border: After studying fruits and vegetables by examining, feeling, and talking about them, cut out some of simple shape from paper of appropriate colors. Arrange along strips of paper and paste. Connect strips at ends, in straight line, with transparent tape, paste or staples. Attach as border with sticky tape to wall or to doors and window frames.

Flower Border: Study a simple flower's three main parts— head, stem, and leaves—and look at individual flowers and a row of tulips. Then take pleated cup cake papers, or paper cup from fancy cookie box, for flower head. Put paste on one end of green paper strip cut for stem. Paste bottom of cup to it. Cut pointed strips for leaves and paste onto stem. These can all be pasted in desired arrangement on a wide strip of construction paper. For grass, add short, thin green strips, or cut a fringe on a long green piece of paper to fit across front of picture.

Spring Greeting Card: Cut out eggs of various colors either free hand or by following an outline. Paste in basket drawn free hand from simple one on display.

Valentine Card: Cut sheet of red construction paper in half. Take one half and fold in half to make booklet. Punch holes with paper punch around edge of a quarter sheet of white typing paper. Paste onto red paper booklet. Decorate with a little gummed heart seal; or fold small piece of thin red paper in quarters and cut as desired along open edge. Open, and paste it in center of white piece of paper.

4. Other Paper Work

I. INTERMEDIATE

Gift-Wrapping Paper: Wet a piece of wrapping or finger-paint paper and apply finger paint in dots, streaks, or daubs to form rough design. Or cover paper completely with paint. Do not apply too thickly, since it may crack off when paper is folded.

Wastebasket: Find out color of parent's bedroom or study and paint 9″ ice cream carton. Shellac. Wrap as a present for parent, using large paper bag which can be decorated and tied at top with bow after inserting wastebasket.

Paper Bag Puppet: Place small paper bag on table, with opening at bottom edge. Draw face on top third of bag and have teacher cut a hole in middle third for each "sleeve" (where thumb and little finger are to be inserted). Place rubber band around bag to represent neck. Bag may be crayoned to look like clothing.

Basket for May Flowers or for Colored Eggs: Cut strip of construction paper as wide as a cottage cheese container and long enough to wrap around it. Decorate this strip with crayons or paint. Wrap strip around container. Remove container and staple the overlapping ends of strip which teacher holds together. Replace strip on container. Cut strip 2″ wide for handle, which teacher can staple to sides of basket. After filling with eggs or flowers, carry for safety in small plastic bag gathered and tied at top. (Handle can also be made by punching two holes 1½″ apart, on each side of basket, thus making four holes. Attach two pipe cleaners, crossed in center, by inserting ends of each through holes diagonally opposite. Bend ends and twist tightly.)

Party Hat: Fold a 21″ square of wrapping paper into four parts making smaller square. Take top flap at open-edged corner and fold it diagonally to opposite corner. Paste it down. Take three remaining corner flaps and fold them under, tucking them into closed corner, thus making triangle. Crease; decorate.

II. ADVANCED

Design a pattern for decorating a teapot stand: Fold a 3″ square of typing paper into four parts, making smaller square. Fold again, diagonally, forming triangle with all open edges together. Holding open edges together, cut along them. Open paper to see design. Make several, selecting preferred one to use as pattern. Fasten this one with transparent tape to object to be decorated, and trace onto object (see "Woodworking, p. 184).

Design a stencil for decorating a teapot stand: Cut piece of typing paper 4″ square. Fold it into quarters. On each of the two folds cut out two vari-shaped pieces. Open paper. After making several such stencils, fasten the one desired to the object being decorated and trace.

Stick-printed Gift Papers: For printing stick select cork or piece of raw potato. (Corn plasters affixed to end of a block 2″ x 1″ x 1″ make pleasing designs.) For varied design, cut shape in top of cork or potato. Use regular ink stamp pads with various colored inks, or use mixture of thick tempera and liquid starch, placed in saucer containing thin cloth. Stamp onto wrapping paper, making pretty gift paper or covering for wastebaskets or gift boxes.

Card-board Box City: After visiting and studying the city neighborhood, collect various sized boxes (pill boxes for chimneys and mail boxes; shoe boxes and milk cartons for apartments; cracker boxes for train box cars, etc.). Paint with tempera. (Waxed cartons will have to be thoroughly scraped after washing in hot water, before painting, or colored paper can be wrapped around them to cover them.) Stick overlapping edges together with paste or transparent tape. Paint outline of windows, doors, and bricks, or cut paper or sticky tape to represent them and affix to "buildings." Attach pleated paper strips for steps in similar way. For vehicles' wheels, poke holes in boxes, insert Tinkertoy stick for axles, and attach Tinkertoy wheels. Traffic lights, telephone poles, and lamp posts can be made with Tinkertoys and construction paper or colored sticky tape. Paper can be cut to represent streets and sidewalks.

C. Woodworking

Since carpentry requires measuring and judgment, one might question woodshop activities for the trainable. However, even when not economically useful, there are a number of good reasons why, with careful preparation and enough supervision, woodworking should be included in the program. Boys and girls feel it is a grown-up activity and are usually enthusiastic about it. They enjoy making something big that is tangible evidence of achievement, and they need activities like pounding and sawing which are acceptable outlets for energy and aggressive feelings.

Because of the positive attitude toward woodworking, it can be a strong motivating factor in learning good safety habits and careful workmanship as well as in acquiring skill with both small and large muscles. The pupil gains new experience—that of working in a new medium, three-dimensional like clay, but not soft and pliable. He learns the names of woodworking tools, where they must be kept and how to handle them safely—which should be of help to people at home or wherever he may be.

In woodshop, the boy or girl learns how to meet failure—an experience he might not be able to face in other situations if not prepared for it. Wanting so much to make or do something in woodshop and enjoying the activity, he learns to begin over and try again when necessary.

As with most activities that are new, there should be opportunities for the boys and girls to experiment, under close supervision and in a safe situation. A child will enjoy learning to wield a hammer by pounding pegs into holes and then driving nails wherever he wishes into blocks of wood, long before he attempts to make something. He will learn to saw by merely sawing pieces off a board before he is ready to saw on a line to make something. A box of soft wood scraps will give him an opportunity to gain skill and be taught certain techniques necessary for his own safety and that of others. He can simply hammer and saw, or try nailing different sized pieces together. It is enough that the beginner gains a knowledge of the safety rules involved and the manipulative skill necessary for even the simplest construction, without his feeling that he must make something.

1. Hammering

I. BEGINNER

Bingo Bed or Pounding Bench: With wooden hammer drive protruding pegs into bench. Turn bench over and hammer pegs through again. (When a peg becomes too loose, tooth picks may be inserted between the peg and its hole.)

II. INTERMEDIATE

Driving nails partially sunk in block of wood: From tools laid out on shelf, select regular lightweight hammer with large head. Find own place at work bench, where there is a block of soft pine, basswood, or whitewood, labeled with own name. Drive into this large, thick wood block some big-headed 1¼″ nails that have been partially hammered in. Keep eyes on work. When finished, carry hammer carefully back to shelf.

Free hammering: Select scraps of soft wood and experiment by hammering into them short roofing nails.

Hammering nails into holes in wood block: Put a strong 1¼″ nail into the first of a number of holes, drilled ¼″ deep and painted different colors, in a long wood block. Press nail in until it stands erect. Hammer it in all the way. Hammer down a second nail, placed in next hole. If nail starts to bend, ask teacher immediately for help.

Starting nails and driving them into wood block: First place a few nails on bench where they can be easily picked up, but not knocked off. Start nail at first dot in a row of colored dots made, if possible, across grain of wood to prevent splitting. Hold nail with one hand and gently tap with hammer. As skill develops, straighten nails when they first start to bend.

Making crude telephone pole or airplane: After teacher has demonstrated purpose of nailing, select from scrap lumber two pieces that seem suitable. Nail together as desired, perhaps in T-shape as airplane or telephone pole. Experiment with various sizes of wood and lengths of nails to find those most suitable. After a period of experimentation, learn to check nails and wood for appropriateness of size to be used together, and plan where nails will be inserted to be most effective, before starting to hammer.

Playing with hammer-nail set: Into beaver board hammer vari-colored and vari-shaped wood pieces (accompanying commercial sets), each of which has hole in center. (Nails of these sets are very short, and hammer has very small head.) Remove nails with claw of hammer.

Making toy car: From scrap wood select piece for body of car.

Choose four old toy wheels, or button molds or beads that will fit as wheels. Select four nails that are long enough, and nail wheels to wood.

III. ADVANCED

Hammering design on teapot stand: Trace a border or other design onto a sanded square of wood 1″ thick. On the traced line, drive short nail a little way into wood. Take it out and, moving it about ¼″ along line, repeat pounding the nail in. Continue to move nail up and remove it until design is outlined in nail marks. Hold hammer near end of handle to be effective when hammering. Remove nail each time by turning hammer so it stands on its head with its claw end pointed away from worker. Pull hammer handle down toward worker, turning claw upward, while top of hammer head acts as a brace against the wood. When finished tapping out design, shellac wood.

2. Sanding

I. INTERMEDIATE

Sanding large blocks for floor play: Take coarse sandpaper which teacher has wrapped around a small block of wood and fastened with a thumb tack. Then take a large wood block, preferably rough so that the effect of sanding it will be apparent. Sand with the grain of the wood. While sanding, feel wood to determine when it is smooth, rather than asking teacher. Shellac or paint one or two sides when they are smooth. This is a restful change and is also an incentive to further sanding. While block is drying, another block can be sanded.

Sanding corners of furniture: Smooth corners of chairs, stools or tables with sandpaper block where they have become rough. Shellac.

3. Sawing

I. INTERMEDIATE

Practicing sawing with coping saw: Use coping saw with round blades for safety. These blades saw in any direction no matter which way saw is turned and do not break as easily as the usual coping saw blade. With teacher's help put narrow strip of wood in a vise, or clamp it to bench or table. If table is high, hold saw vertically, with handle pointing toward floor. If bench is low, hold saw as one would a crosscut saw, sawing more horizontally, with handle tilted upward.

Making fence posts: Put into vise, or clamp to work bench a strip of wood 12″ x 1″ x 1″. Saw on line teacher has made across middle of strip. (Wood where line is should be close to vise.) Use short saw strokes to start the cut, then longer ones. When finished, take wood from vise and insert similar or longer pieces, marked every eight inches by teacher. Saw on lines to make small fence posts for a new grass area. Hammer sticks a little way into ground about 14″ apart. Tie string from post to post. Tie cloth strips on string to keep birds away from grass seed.

As more skill is gained, saw longer and thicker fence posts and make points at lower ends by sawing diagonally.

II. ADVANCED

Practicing sawing with crosscut saw: Get 20″ crosscut saw from shelf where tools are placed. Holding saw down at side, walk with it slowly to low work bench. Lay it down without touching saw teeth with hands. With teacher's help fasten a piece of wood in vise, or clamp it to bench. Stand with own body slightly sidewise, forearms in direct line with saw. Face wood so as to look straight down groove in which to saw. (Groove is made by teacher.) Saw slowly and easily, not forcing saw. Go very gently near the end, so that wood will not split off. In sawing, keep free hand away from saw and wood.

Later on, try to start sawing without help of teacher. First draw guide line for sawing across wood by using try square. Use short strokes until groove is made.

After sawing, put saw carefully away. With brush sweep off bench. Sweep up dust on floor with broom and dust pan.

Saw off board for a shelf: Draw straight line with try square on a 1″-thick plank that will measure about 10′ x 12″. Lay plank flat on work bench, holding it there with C-clamps, rather than putting it in vise on its end, since it might wobble and split while being sawed in that position. If sawing can be done skillfully by now, try pushing down on the stroke for more effective sawing. Make long strokes. Go gently when board is almost sawed; end piece, since it will be long in this case, can be held, carefully, without danger of sawing hand.

4. Using Screw and Drill

I. INTERMEDIATE

Wooden Nuts and Bolts: Unscrew and screw large colored wooden nuts and bolts of different sizes (sold in toy stores).

Playskool Truck: Take apart and reassemble, with help, a Playskool or other toy, using wooden screw driver and wrench that come with truck.

II. ADVANCED

Drilling holes: Mark place that hole should be made in yard stick, cutting board, or clay board so that it can be hung up. Use small augur, twisting it and pressing down as it is held vertically.

Inserting small screw in woodwork (for hanging yard stick, mirror, etc.): With gimlet or bradawl make tiny hole in spot where screw is to be inserted. Set screw in hole and twist it in with screw driver held constantly at right angles to wood surface where screw is to go.

Making peg board: Mark, through cardboard stencil pattern, the location of each hole to be drilled in a square piece of wood. Drill holes with hand drill or brace having suitable-sized bit selected by teacher to fit large pegs she has on hand, or to fit doweling from which large pegs can be sawed. (Drill bit should be thick and sturdy for beginning drilling.) Care must be taken to remember which way to make the drill turn, or it will come apart and then require teacher's time. Also, watch progress of drill to make sure it does not go through board into work bench. Drill must be held vertically. As soon as drill breaks through wood, remove drill carefully, turn wood over, and drill a little into hole from the other side to prevent splitting. Sand and shellac peg board.

5. Painting

I. INTERMEDIATE

Painting a flat, sanded surface (stool, bench, block) with primer coat: (Before this is started these preparations should first be made by teacher: paint checked, and any skin on paint removed; paint stirred if it has settled, and thinned with turpentine if necessary; brush checked as to its condition and size for task at hand; plan of painting object decided upon—inside before outside, bottom and under parts before top, inconspicuous parts first.)

Spread newspapers over floor and over low bench where work is to be done. Put on smock with long sleeves, backwards. Tie back long hair or braids—or wear bandana.

Stir paint gently with stick and then watch teacher pour paint from big can into shallow tin or cup big enough for brush to enter easily. Brush should be immersed only about halfway. Press excess paint from brush against side of can each time after dipping it in paint. Paint part indicated by teacher, probably not in conventional way, but finding and covering most spots needing paint. Apply paint very thinly.

When finished, look over surface for spots not covered, and paint them. Then wipe brush back and forth on newspaper to remove most of paint. Put brush in water with a bit of turpentine or paint solvent if more painting of same color is to be done next day. (Have teacher suspend brush in narrow can between two sticks held together with rubber bands.) If brush is not to be used next day, wipe with cloth. Rinse in used turpentine and wipe again on paper and cloth. (Teacher subsequently finishes cleaning it with clean turpentine and then washes it with cleansing or scouring powder and warm water, rinsing thoroughly.) Throw used papers into trash can. Wipe hands with cloth with a little turpentine on it. Keep hands and turpentine away from eyes. Wash hands with soap and warm water.

(Teacher adds a little turpentine or linseed oil to paint in can, to cover surface of paint and prevent thick scum from forming on its surface. She then closes can by pounding lid down tightly.)

Painting object with rubber-base paint: Using this kind of paint facilitates cleaning up, since water and household cleanser remove it. Leave brushes immersed in water after use, until cleaned.

Cigarette Case: Paint a can, such as a Band-aid can, of approximate cigarette-package size.

Clothes Sprinkling Can: Paint large liquid detergent can. Have holes drilled in top, with electric drill.

II. ADVANCED

Painting second coats on flat surface of plain furniture: After sanding, paint block, picnic bench, table top, or stool systematically, with up-and-down strokes, working from left to right, with grain of wood. Hold brush properly, re-dipping as needed, so that job can be done more evenly and quickly. Watch for spots missed and cover them, but try to cover surface the first time. Also, try to avoid drips from edge of painted surface by using proper amount of paint. Watch for drips and remove with brush with little paint on it.

Shellacking large blocks and benches: Have teacher thin shellac sufficiently (reading directions on can—usually three parts alcohol or solvent). Apply as paint was applied, working along quickly, since it dries fast. When finished, wash the brush out well with water and household cleanser, and use cleanser to remove shellac from hands, rinsing hands well afterwards. (Avoid using shellac on damp days because it does not dry well.)

Vase: Paint glass jar with tempera, and then shellac.

Crayon Finish: Crayon small blocks of wood, instead of painting them. Then wipe with cloth dipped in turpentine. Polish with flannel cloth.

6. Projects Combining Woodworking Skills

I. INTERMEDIATE

Outdoor Sign Post: Saw off a suitable length of wide board ¾″ thick for the sign part, and a stick 3″ wide and 1″ thick for the post. Paint sign all over. (Teacher draws on letters afterwards.) Trace the point for the end of post that is to be inserted in ground by placing cardboard pattern made by teacher on the stick, or have teacher draw diagonals, making point. Saw on diagonal lines with coping saw. Place post on sign, turned face down, in middle. (A pattern the size of the sign board, creased in the middle, can show where middle of sign board is.) If it is difficult to keep in place, have teacher clamp it to table. Mark where nails should go, and pound in four 1½″ or 1⅝″ nails. These will be long enough to hold wood together, but will poke through to other side. If longer nails or thinner wood have to be used, it might be better to start the nails from the front side of sign, putting post under sign. Drive all four nails 1½″ apart, turning sign board over and watching to see when they protrude a little through the underside of the wood. Then set the post and complete the nailing.

Sign can be screwed together instead of nailing. Mark and drill holes through sign. Then place post under sign and mark through holes in sign. Drill holes in post a little way. Then insert screws slightly longer than length of holes, and screw them in all the way.

Hanging Sign: Saw a flat board of appropriate size. Sand, paint, have words painted on. With string, experiment to see where holes should be made for hanging sign. Mark location of holes, then drill. Insert string. Cut and tie it.

Memo Pad: Saw piece of soft wood to a size appropriate for scratch pad and tiny calendar to be arranged attractively. Sand and paint board. Put pencil in vise and saw in two. Sharpen the half that has eraser on one end. Attach scratch pad to board by putting wide, short rubber band under board and over cardboard piece that comes attached to bottom of scratch pad. Insert pencil under rubber band, at side of pad. Place tiny calendar at bottom of board, centering it below pad.

Jingle Stick: Soak two soft-drink bottle caps in hot water. Saw from a long piece of soft wood, 1¾″ x ¾″ a stick 8″ long. Sand and paint it. Take bottle tops from water, wipe dry, and dig out the cork inside with a tiny screw driver. Place tops on large, heavy, hard board, and pound them flat with hammer. After being given a screw about ⅝″ long for securing the tops on the stick, select a nail that is of the same or slightly greater thickness than the screw. Pound the nail through the center of each bottle top to make a hole in each. Insert screw through bottle tops, and show to teacher, who will see that they are loose near the screw head so they will ring when shaken. If not, make bigger holes in bottle tops.

Mark and drill a hole ¾″ from one end of stick and midway across width. Make hole smaller in diameter than screw, and no more than ¼″ deep. Insert screw with both bottle caps on it into hole in stick. With small screw driver tighten screw until only ¼″ remains above wood. Lick gummed label with one's name printed on it and stick it to handle of jingle stick. Shellac the stick and the label, but not caps.

INTERMEDIATE OR ADVANCED—depending upon complexity of design

Flag: Saw a post 2″ x ¾″ x 20″ (or half as long, if desired). Sand it well. Cut finger-paint paper or heavy wrapping paper. With paints or crayons, make flag design as desired. To make American flag (for younger child), paint blue field and, when it is dry, put a few dots on it with white paint or chalk. Make some red stripes with finger paint. An Advanced pupil can study and discuss American flag and assemble ready-made puzzle of the flag's parts before making one. Paint blue field, letting it dry. Stick on gummed stars, or make correct number of dots to represent stars, first with chalk and then with white paint. (Count while making them.) Make seven red stripes with finger paint. The finger's width of about half an inch will make just enough stripes. Or paint with ½″ brush.

Place paper banner at top of stick. Plan where nails should be placed and mark. Use 1″ large-headed, plaster-board nails. First nail one in top corner, then in bottom corner. Then place along edge as needed.

Sand-Blocks: With crosscut saw, or coping saw, cut block about 5″ x 2¼″ x 2″ (or smaller, if too difficult to cut). Sand the block. Cut piece of new, coarse sandpaper after tracing size from pattern, 3″ x 7″. Place and then tack sandpaper up on the sides of the two ends of block. Use tacks that can be held when hammering heads, rather than the shorter thumbtacks.

For handle, nail a bead to top, or cut a block 2¾″ x ⅝″, sand it, and glue it to top of larger block.

Make another just like the first wood block. Shellac or paint the top and sides of both. Then they are ready for use in the rhythm band.

Train: Use coping saw or crosscut saw to make thick wood blocks of train car proportions. Sand and paint. Make windows by painting, or sticking on sticky tape or adhesive tape squares. Drill tiny hole in front and back of each car, so that cup hooks can be inserted and cars thus joined. Add wheels if desired (see p. 184 for details about adding wheels). Make larger block for engine, with big wheels. If it is to be a steam engine, nail on spool for smokestack, and saw smaller block for tender. Sand all cars and shellac or paint all but bottom of each.

Airplane: Become acquainted with appearance of airplanes and different parts by looking at them, talking and hearing stories about them, playing with toy models, and seeing pictures of them. If Intermediate, almost any two-piece combination will be satisfactory. If Advanced, learn names of parts—wheels, tail, wings, body, propeller—and select different pieces of wood that seem appropriate for parts of airplane. For some children, making an airplane out of a Bolt-it set may help to give idea of proportion. Understanding the purpose of the wings and the body may help in the selection of appropriately shaped pieces of wood. If the right sizes are not available, saw them to size desired.

Propeller can be traced and sawed with coping saw. Drill hole in center. Nail wings and body together as described under "Sign Post," p. 188. Sand and paint. Make windows with tape or by painting. Other parts, if desired, can be added: wheels (button molds, jar lids, wheels from other toys), tail, propeller (inserting nail through hole and nailing to body).

Bread Board or Cutting Board: This is better if made of hard wood, but then it is difficult to saw. (It may be cut elsewhere and then simply sanded in school.) If soft wood is used, saw it with crosscut saw to size desired. After sanding thoroughly, drill hole at top for hanging in kitchen.

II. ADVANCED

Boat: Thumbtack cardboard pattern made by teacher onto piece of whitewood or white pine 1″ x 4″ x 9″ to 15″ long.

Draw around pattern and remove it. With coping saw cut out boat. Sand it smooth. Drill two holes the size of some doweling that is on hand. Watch and imitate the teacher do the following to make two sails: cut a piece of typing paper in half lengthwise and, with try square, draw a line 1″ or 2″ across end. Cut off and discard this piece. Cut diagonally across the piece remaining. Cut two small slots through which doweling for mast can be inserted when paper is unfolded. Saw masts to a length of 6″ and sand their ends. Hoist sails on mast and insert masts in two holes made in boat. Shellac whole boat. If string for pulling is desired, bore hole and add screw eye, or staple string to bow of boat.

A block of wood can be nailed on for a cabin if a fancier boat is wanted. For other kinds of boats, use a different pattern. Use thick doweling for smoke stacks. Pound nails all around edge of boat and tie and weave string around them for railing.

Book End: Saw a block 2″ x 3½″ and another piece 4½″ x 5½″ x ½″. Sand pieces. Put thick piece on its 4½″ x 3½″ side. Match thin piece to it, so thin piece stands vertically against side of thick piece, and ½″-long edges correspond. Mark where nails should go. Nail first at corners, then along edge. To do so, tip block over so that nails can be hammered vertically into thin piece first. Glue felt or rubber to base to prevent slippage.

Another way to prevent slippage is to make a book end with thin wooden piece used as the base to fit under books. Use thick block measuring 4½″ x 4½″ x 2″ and, after nailing thin board 4½″ x 5½″ x ¼″ to it, use thin board as base. Cover nails by gluing felt to bottom of book ends.

Key Board: Saw piece of wood to size desired (8″ x 8″ or 6″ x

8″). Mark wood by using cardboard stencil made by teacher, making dots 2″ apart, starting 1″ from each of the side edges and 2″ from the top and bottom of the wood. Sand and shellac. Drill tiny holes at each dot, or screw cup hooks directly into wood without drilling. Drill large holes in top corners for inserting screw that will fasten key board to wall.

Cardboard Wastebasket: Cut top and bottom off two heavy cardboard boxes measuring at least 8½″ x 11″. On each piece draw around teacher's pattern for wastebasket's sides 8½″ x 11¼″ x 7½″. Put dots along side of wastebasket, by marking through stencil. Dots can be 1″ to 1½″ apart. Paint and shellac wastebasket's sides. Punch holes with leather punch. Lace sides together with overcast lacing or shoelace stitch using coarse twine or plastic lacing. Saw wooden square to fit exactly inside wastebasket sides (teacher measuring). Shellac wood square on both sides. Place inside the cardboard sides and tack in place with studs.

Toy Animal: Trace around simple cardboard pattern of duck, pig, or other animal, taped onto scrap of basswood or white pine ½″ or 1″ thick. Remove pattern and, using round-bladed saw, cut along traced line. Do not push saw hard. To saw protrusion such as a tail, start at tip and saw toward the wider part.

To make stand for animals, saw piece about 2½″ wide and 1″ thick, and longer than animal. Saw two pieces of same length and thickness as first piece, but narrower enough to leave a place for animal to stand between them. Nail these to wider piece, leaving groove between just wide enough for animal to stand in.

Stippled Aluminum Teapot Stand or Tile: Glue aluminum foil around 6″ wood square. Trace outline of a design, and then make dots evenly spaced along line. Lightly tap small nail through foil on each dot marked.

Shelf: Several pupils can work on this project. Saw shelf board to desired length. Sand and shellac or paint. Arrange angle irons where they should be placed. (Teacher checks with person who can determine where joists in wall are for attaching a shelf securely.) Mark through angle irons' holes in order to know where screws are to go through angle irons into board and wall. Lay board on low bench. Drill fairly shallow holes in board and wall, screw angle iron to board, and then screw shelf to wall.

Coat Rack (group project): Plan how many coat hooks are needed, and arrange on strip of wood as far apart as teacher suggests. (Two coat hooks may be advisable for some children who have many winter wraps. There should be plenty of space between each child's hooks.) Mark off wood and saw it to length desired. Sand and shellac or paint. After making dots where screws are to hold hooks (teacher holding hooks in place) drill holes partway for screws. Also drill holes in rack where directed, for the screws that will hold rack to wall (after it has been determined where wall joists are, to support rack). Drill shallow holes in wall corresponding to holes in rack. Lay board on low bench to screw hooks into board. Screw rack to wall with large screws. (Teacher can nail frames for name cards to rack at sides of hooks. Frames make it easily possible to change name cards.)

D. Other Craft Projects

I. BEGINNER

Hand Plaque: Make large ball of self-hardening clay and flatten it out by patting. Press hand into clay to form impression. Withdraw carefully. When plaque is dry, paint it white and present it as a gift to parents.

Candle Holder: Insert short candle into middle of 2″ ball of self-hardening clay. Remove candle and paint clay when dry.

Oatmeal Box Drum: Take off top cover. Paint box with tempera, except top and bottom. Thread string through hole punched by teacher in bottom of drum near edge, and through hole in corresponding spot in loose top cover. (Teacher ties string, leaving it long enough to go over child's head and allow "drum" to hang at waist height.) Paste top cover onto box and shellac entire drum.

Rattle: Gather small stones, pebbles, or gravel, or use small shells or beans. Put them in small cardboard box that can be easily held by a child for shaking. Glue top on. Paint with tempera, or crayon. (Baking powder cans are durable, but hard for young child to paint. A large toothpaste-tube box would be good size to handle.)

Cotton Snow for Decorating a Tree: Make small balls from large wad of cotton and place on twigs or evergreen tree.

Tin Foil Decoration: Take tinfoil or thin aluminum foil that teacher has cut into various shapes, 4″ to 6″ in length. Crumple, roll, tear or fold to form decorative pieces. (Teacher staples loop of string on each for hanging.) Foil that is colored on one side may be obtainable and is quite effective.

Pipe Cleaner Decorations: Twist and curl colored pipe cleaners together, or make chains of them.

II. INTERMEDIATE

Clay Paper Weight: Flatten ball of self-hardening clay and decorate by pressing with end of pencil or stick, making original design. When dry, paint and shellac.

Clothespin Planter: Place clothespins on edge of shallow can, such as a tuna fish can, and paint both pins and can. Insert flowerpot in which geranium slip or flower seed has been planted.

Jewel Box: Paint and shellac cigar box. Line with aluminum foil. Glue colored bead or painted spool to lid near front edge, to serve as knob for opening box.

Marshmallow Man: Use one marshmallow for body. To make each leg, join two marshmallows together with toothpicks and attach to body with more toothpicks. Add marshmallow head, and marshmallows for arms. Insert cloves for features and buttons.

Tiny marshmallows can be used with large marshmallows to make man of better proportion.

Marshmallow Santa: In similar way make Santa, using apple for body and adding one marshmallow each for head, cap and each arm and leg. Attach with toothpicks.

Vase: Cover a glass with aluminum or tin foil that has been crinkled.

Fancy Eggs: Decorate hard-boiled eggs (dyed or plain) by using blunt, colored pencil or "painting crayon" dipped in pan containing about ¼″ water. If egg is placed in egg carton or egg cup, the top half can be painted without touching it. When dry, it can be turned over and the bottom half painted.

Pipe Cleaner Candy Canes: Twist a red and white pipe cleaner together, bending them into a crook at the top. Hang as decoration.

Clay Pencil Holder: Shape clay as desired, but at least 1½″ thick. Make holes in it with round pencil, deep enough to hold pencils upright.

III. ADVANCED

Sewing Kit: Paint and decorate a cigar box. Make pin cushion, felt needle book and felt or leather scissors case. Place thread, thimble, and other equipment for sewing in box. Sewing tray can be made of a rectangular piece of self-hardening clay in which center is hollowed out for pin container, and pegs are placed into clay around edge to hold spools of thread.

Clay Bowl: Make round clay base by flattening a ball of clay. Roll "snakes" or "ropes" about ½″ in diameter, and wind them around the base and then around on top of each other, gradually building up the sides of the vase in this fashion. When one rope is used up, attach new rope to old by pinching ends of each a little and overlapping them. Smooth joinings and sides of vase by dipping fingers in slip (water and clay mixed in a little pan) and applying gently to bumpy spots on vase.

Locker Box: Paint and shellac large beer carton that has folding covers. Use as container for personal belongings. Attach label with own name on it.

RELATED READING

Dewing, Dorothy. "Use of Occupational Therapy in the Socialization of Severely Retarded Children," in Chalmers L. Stacey and Manfred F. DeMartino (editors), *Counseling and Psychotherapy with the Mentally Retarded.* Glencoe, Illinois: The Free Press and the Falcon's Wing Press, 1957, pp. 366–72.

Taylor, Jeanne. *Child's Book of Carpentry.* Philadelphia: Chelton Co., 1948.

x. Work

Society wants individuals to be productive, and for this reason alone, it would be to the advantage of the trainable child to learn to work. As a retardate grows older he may find it necessary or advisable to perform certain tasks and it is helpful if he has had work experiences in school. Then, if he has to, or wants to, work later on in life, he will know how to do some tasks, and will not be frustrated by not being able to do them satisfactorily when no one is available to teach him how and supervise him closely.

Participating in school jobs will teach the trainable specific work methods, skills, and good habits and attitudes toward work. These include ability to follow directions, ability to work alone, responsibility for contributing to group undertakings and habits of promptness, carefulness and neatness.

The severely retarded can be appreciated if he has learned how to perform even little jobs. Whether he remains at home, lives with relatives or foster parents, works in someone else's home or in a sheltered workshop, or eventually comes to reside in a private or public institution, he will be accepted far better if he is willing and able to work well. If he can be recognized as a person who can accept responsibility, small though it may be, he will make more friends among both peers and supervisors and will be given not only more work but also special privileges and more freedom.

In planning the kind of work activities to introduce in the school program one must first consider what the child can learn well and will have an opportunity to do in the future. The child must have an opportunity to practice and review at home what he learns in school; it is hoped that through conferences with the parents the teacher can find out which tasks the child can and will be permitted to do at home. The more the parents and school cooperate, the more prepared the child will be for the future.

For his own and other's protection, certain limitations of the retarded should be kept in mind when selecting work for them, and when planning with the parents for the kind of training they need. For example, a trainable boy may gain the manual skill to handle a dangerous machine, but would lack the ability to react quickly in case of emergency. Although an older girl may have a way with children and learn to care for their physical needs, she should not be left in charge of them, because of her lack of judgment.

Since we do not know what work will be expected of a trainable adult in his future household, sheltered workshop, or institution 10 or 20 years from now, emphasis should be placed on developing work habits and providing experiences that might be of value in any given work situation. For instance, it is advisable for school tasks to provide opportunities for cooperating with other people in addition to some in which the retarded boy or girl must work alone.

In order that a severely retarded adult may adjust well in a work situation wherever he may be, there is an area in which it is more important for him to develop than that of learning specific work skills and attitudes: it is his personality that will make him acceptable or barely tolerated in his place of work, for his skill in any line of work usually can be only minimal. If the school program provides activities which bring him to as high a level of personality development as possible, he may become a pleasant, interesting person whom others will like, and he will be able to make a better adjustment to any life situation.

WORK ACTIVITIES

A. Care of Interior of a Building

I. BEGINNER

Pick up toys.
Pick up scraps and put in waste basket.
Wash off tables.
Move and put away chairs.
Use tools and materials as they are meant to be used, so they do not become broken or soiled and do not damage furniture or building.

II. INTERMEDIATE

Stack books and put materials away.
Wash paint brushes and pans.
Wipe up floor when something is spilled.
Wash off chairs, shelves, and lockers (rinsing sponges after use).
Water plants. Break off dead leaves.
Sweep large trash. (Teacher can help hold broom until the sweeping motion is established.) When learning to sweep, if floor is patterned or so mottled that crumbs and dirt cannot be seen, scatter tiny scraps of bright paper (crumpled, not flat) all over the floor. As all scraps are swept up, crumbs will be swept up too.

III. ADVANCED

Put books, furniture, materials neatly and quietly away.
Wash tables, stack furniture, sweep floor after lunch.
Use broom, dust mop, push broom, vacuum cleaner, carpet sweeper, dust pan, dust cloth, sponge efficiently.
Collect all trash from building and place for city disposal.
Make beds, mitering corners.
Do complete and orderly process of regular household cleaning, including furniture, blinds, windows, floor, woodwork, rugs. Prepare cleaning solution and materials that will be needed.

Clean up afterwards, taking care of water and cloths, return-
ing each piece of furniture to its place.

Clean walls.

Mop floors, using wringer.

Polish furniture, floors.

B. Yard Care

I. BEGINNER

Pick up stones and sticks, and put in small wagon or wheelbarrow.

Put play equipment away.

II. INTERMEDIATE

Use play equipment carefully.

Notify teacher when equipment breaks.

Put equipment away neatly.

Sweep trash or rake leaves into pile; put into box and carry
box to trash can by using wheelbarrow.

Rake leaves into big pile and jump in them (motivation for
raking).

Shovel snow (not necessarily in systematic fashion).

Pick up trash papers, using stick and bag as an incentive. (The
bag, which may be made by older pupils, should be of heavy
canvas or oilcloth which can be overcast along sides with
heavy thread. A long, double piece of material is attached as
a shoulder strap. Strap can be shortened by knotting when
worn by a small youngster. A wire is put through the hem at
the top of the bag so that the opening can be found easily
by the child. The opening should be worn toward the front.
For picking up papers, a small-headed nail can be hammered
into the end of a smooth stick, 1″ thick and less than a yard
long. The nail should stick out of the wood about 1–1½″.
The head is filed into a blunt point.)

III. ADVANCED

Use special judgment in handling small or fragile equipment
so it will not be broken.

Notice and report equipment that is breaking.

Dig up garden spot or place for grass seed. Rake dirt, plant seeds, pull weeds with supervision.

Water lawn, taking care of hose.

Rake lawn, pick up stones, mow lawn, clip grass.

Use these garden tools carefully: lawnmower, rake, shovel, grass clippers, broom, spade.

Sweep walks systematically and dispose of dirt. Start sweeping where there is plenty of dirt, and not much wind to make things difficult. Keeping the body in a natural position, sweep straight along one edge and then the other of a walk which serves as a guide, pushing all the dirt along at each stroke of the broom. Finally sweep down the middle of the walk. When more proficient, or when the walk is fairly narrow, start at one side of the walk and sweep across to other side, pushing dirt into grass with every stroke. To dispose of a lot of dirt or trash, work with another pupil, taking turns— one holding a little shovel to collect dirt that other pupil sweeps into it. Carry shovel to trash can or dump contents in nearby carton. A third pupil might serve several working pairs by coming along with wheelbarrow containing a carton. Shovelers empty dirt into carton. Hauler empties contents of box into large trash can.

Shovel snow systematically.

Rake leaves or grass and remove efficiently: Start learning to rake systematically, standing in row with class and helping to rake strip of grass between street curb and sidewalk. In order to rake in straight line, use own basket placed as marker at edge of sidewalk. Rake, moving backward, toward basket. Removing basket of leaves in a wheelbarrow is often a strong incentive for working consistently.

C. Serving Food

I. BEGINNER

Pass plates of food consecutively to children around table, without touching food.

Sort silver into spoons, forks, knives; sort dishes.

II. INTERMEDIATE

Get out plates, cups, and napkins after washing hands.

Fold napkins.

Carry things to and from kitchen, using trays.

Pour from pitcher.

Pass cups containing beverage.

Place napkins, glasses or paper cups, and spoons where they
belong. When first learning to set table, stand directly in
front of place mat that has been set correctly on table. Put
napkin where teacher directs. Proceed around the table, each
time standing directly in front of place mat where napkin
is to be placed. Follow steps below in learning to set table.
(Learn only one step at a time.) Use cardboard forks, knives,
and spoons if metal ones are distractible because of jingle,
or are dangerous. When table-setting is well learned, set table
for tea party using colored plastic dishes, with each place-
setting of a different color. Take one piece to be placed at a
time, always in same sequence. Looking at a picture or dia-
gram each time before setting a place is helpful to some
children.

Learn to set correctly one kind of tableware before setting the
next piece: place mat, napkin, knife, glass or paper cup,
spoon, saucer, and cup. Set table daily for juice or lunch.
When learning the position of napkin and place mat, serve
cookies, apples, or cakes that can be eaten without flatware.
When learning to include a knife and glass in the place setting, serve fruit to be cut with a knife, or peanut butter to
be spread on crackers, and then serve something to drink
from the glass.

Placing the knife before adding the glass helps the learner see
where the glass is to be placed—above the knife. Understanding that the knife goes on the "other side" from the
napkin makes it unnecessary to learn the words "right" and
"left" at this point. A left-handed child may easily learn to
place the napkin on the side by the hand that naturally picks
up and is holding the napkin when placing it. A right-handed

child, if having difficulty learning where the napkins go, might be taught to place the knife or spoon first, since either of these goes on the side by the hand that naturally picks them up, as well as holds them when eating. Then this right-handed child could learn that the napkin goes on the "other side." For practice in setting the table with spoons, drinks in which sugar or marshmallows are to be added can be served.

III. ADVANCED

Learn to set complete table, one step at a time: Add fork, second spoon or soup spoon, butter plate and butter knife, salad fork and plate. Serve foods which require the tableware set out.

Count number of people to be served.

Arrange table mats and chairs for correct number of people.

Count correct number of things to go on trays or tables.

Open container and pour liquids into pitchers.

In waiting on people, serve to left side, remove from left, except cups and glasses (right).

Watch for necessary refill of cups.

Pour hot as well as cold liquids.

Clean up lunchroom after use, removing dishes by using trays. Wipe off place mats and tables thoroughly. Sweep floor efficiently.

D. Food Preparation and Cleanup

I. BEGINNER

Play with and be encouraged to examine food that can be handled, smelled, and tasted (fruits, canned cocoa, etc.). (See "Learning Through Other Senses," pp. 150–51.)

Sort foods (all apples together, etc.).

Watch while foods are cut and served.

II. INTERMEDIATE

Stack, wash, and wipe doll dishes in orderly process.

Polish silver.

Play grocery store, sorting and stacking groceries.

Boil eggs.

Cut apples, bananas, slices of canned pineapple into chunks.

Make jack-o'-lantern, cutting out features with help.

Cook from prepared mixes.

Make sandwiches.

Shop for food to be prepared at school, learning not to touch
items displayed.

III. ADVANCED

Help with marketing for groceries, learning to keep out of
other shopper's way and to guide shopping cart.

Prepare simple foods, following rules of safety and hygiene.

Scrape, stack, wash, rinse, and put away dishes, using systematic
and hygienic methods.

Clean up kitchen after dish washing: Clean sink, wipe off tables
and stove, sweep floor, etc.

Clean out refrigerator.

Practice a few prepared mixes often enough to learn recipe, so
can make at home.

Fry bacon, eggs; make toast.

Make beverages, soups (preparing vegetables), hot dogs, simple
salads.

Prepare box lunches and picnic lunches, hygienically and efficiently.

Know names and location of kitchen utensils. Use measuring
cup, can opener, egg beater, spatula, and knife efficiently.

E. Laundering

I. INTERMEDIATE

Wash doll clothes and hang up. Play at ironing them.

Wash sponges and rags used in cleaning.

Iron own craft products, ribbons and rags with warm iron.

Take care of bathing suit after water play.

II. ADVANCED

Take trips to laundries, cleaning establishments.

Do laundry by hand: Rinse, wring out, hang out, fold and put
away.

Launder own fine things, knowing relative temperature of water
for different materials.
Launder dish towels, pillow cases, curtains efficiently and safely,
using washing machine, wringer, clothesline, and drying rack.
Dampen and roll up laundry for ironing.
Iron flat things, shirts, shorts, simple sport blouses.

F. Washing Cars

I. INTERMEDIATE

Wash off children's vehicles with wet cloth. Wipe.

II. ADVANCED

Wash bicycles.
Take trips to car-washing establishments.
Do whole process of car-washing.

G. Office Tasks

I. INTERMEDIATE

Fold paper in making greeting cards.
Use large-hole paper punch and stapler in craft activities.
Sharpen pencils in pencil sharpener at eye level.

II. ADVANCED

Prepare materials for mailing:
    Collate sets of mimeographed pages.
    Check work by counting pages. (Use rubber caps on fingers.)
    Get edges of paper even, staple, or put between covers or in
        envelopes.
    Fold circulars and business letters.
    Insert in envelopes and seal.
    Affix postage stamps, using small sponge in water.
    Use addressograph, or affix typewritten gummed labels on
        mail.
    Use transparent tape for sealing.
    Bundle and tie up circulars for mailing.
    Wrap and tie packages, using square knot.
    Sort clips, tacks, etc.

Use paper cutter, paper punch, rubber stamp, stapler, transparent tape.

Take messages, run errands.

H. Skills Involved in Workshop Operations

Most of these skills are developed in other activities, such as crafts or perception activities, which have been described in previous sections of this book. When pupils need special workshop preparation, or the teacher wishes to find out how they respond to workshop conditions, assembly-line relay races can be played. These will develop more facility and speed and an appreciation of the need for efficiency. But better than relay races for developing workman-like attitudes is the performance of duties for a motivated purpose. Sometimes, rather than competing in teams, working in pairs achieves good results, since a pupil likes to feel he is helping someone, and working together provides immediate and tangible evidence of helping.

I. ADVANCED

Examine materials and sort them according to various specifications.

Assemble parts of object into whole.

Measure and cut.

Lace or string.

Pack according to a pattern.

Glue.

Polish and clean.

Sand.

Use tools.

Manipulate simple machines.

Run errands.

RELATED READING

Delp, Harold A. "Criteria for Vocational Training of the Mentally Retarded," *Training School Bulletin*, LIV (August, 1957), 14–20.

Fitzpatrick, F. K. "The Use of Rhythm in Training Severely Subnormal Patients," *American Journal of Mental Deficiency*, LXIII (May, 1959), 948–53.

Jacobs, Abraham, and Catherine Sherman. "Training Facilities for Severely Physically and Mentally Handicapped," *American Journal of Mental Deficiency*, LX (April, 1956), 721–28.

Jacobs, Abraham, and Joseph T. Weingold. *The Sheltered Workshop*. New York: Bureau of Publications, Teachers College, Columbia University, 1958.

Loos, F. M., and J. Tizard. "The Employment of Adult Imbeciles in a Hospital Workshop," *American Journal of Mental Deficiency*, LVI (January, 1955), 395–403.

Minnesota Department of Public Welfare. *Now They Are Grown.* Minnesota Department of Public Welfare, 1959, pp. 32–35, 57–59. (Reprinted by the National Association for Retarded Children, Inc., 386 Park Avenue South, New York.)

Walton, D., and T. L. Begg. "The Effects of Incentives on the Performance of Defective Imbeciles," *British Journal of Psychology*, XLIX (February, 1958), 49–55.

XI. Group Projects

In modern programs for average children, the class often works on a group project or unit of experience, through which each child gains skills and knowledge in a variety of subjects which are integrated and directed toward an over-all goal. A project on the grocery store, for example, may include some learning of arithmetic, spelling, language, reading, and social studies. Much of the art, dramatics, and woodshop activities may center around the grocery store project.

WHY GROUP PROJECTS?

Group projects are of value to the retarded child because they provide meaningful concrete experiences which lead to greater understanding of his environment. They also afford opportunities for each child to work at his own level and yet enjoy the socializing experience of contributing to the group effort.

Projects are important for a trainable class because they emphasize the carry-over of a learning experience from one situation to another. If the class is learning to care for turtles, for example, it is helpful to encourage the children to associate this experience with others. The class will talk about turtles in discussion period, hear stories, and see pictures about them at book-time. The turtles will attend music class, so the children can imitate and sing about them. The class may count their turtles and feed them worms. In a trip to the zoo, the class will visit the turtles and later will return to observe them not once but several times. In art period, a child may one day want and be able to make turtles from clay or draw them and even the worms for the turtles to eat. Another child may make a turtle out of tinkertoys. Thus the children improve in ability to express themselves, in their understanding of numbers, and in their general knowledge of their environment. Retarded children do not get bored by repetition of subject matter when it is introduced in so many different ways. They need repetition to learn.

DEVELOPING MEANINGFUL PROJECTS

Projects must be planned and carried out with consideration for the needs of the individuals in the class. Retarded children who are distractible, hyperactive, or insecure may be upset by projects which involve or require many materials, diversity of activity, and changes in schedule. For such children especially, project activities will need to be carefully structured.

In planning a project for a trainable class, it is not important for the teacher to tie all the learning activities for one day, week, or month into one topic or interest. Concentrating solely on one project over a period of time might not provide the necessary drill in certain skills and would limit the learning experiences of the children. The place assigned to a particular project should be balanced with other important school activities.

What criteria are important in selecting a project for a group of trainables? Here are questions the teacher might ask herself to help her in deciding:

1. Have the children shown any interest in activities which would be associated with this project?
2. Can many concrete, firsthand experiences be connected with this project?
3. Will the project give the class a good opportunity to gain worthwhile skills, knowledge, attitudes, and appreciations?
4. Would the project at present help to serve the needs of most members of the class?
5. Will it help to prepare the pupils for the future?

Let us say that a teacher heard some of the children mention plays they had seen on television in which there were cowboys. She may feel that a cowboy play would be a good project. She may answer "Yes" to the first question, although the children may not have too much interest in the activities themselves which would be connected with the project, and perhaps only some of the children would be interested. If she is clever, she may think of some skills, knowledge, and attitudes which she can develop through preparation of a cowboy play, such as sewing costumes, learning to gallop, and tying a rope. That would mean a possible "Yes" for question 3. But this project probably would not meet the other three criteria. It would be difficult to provide the children with many concrete firsthand experiences. Many of the activities in most play productions would be nearly meaningless to the children. It is difficult, when producing an entertainment for others, to have time for the needs of each child. Often the children will be waiting on the sidelines while one child receives individual help with a costume, with his lines, or with a stage routine. As for question 5, it has previously been suggested that class entertainments may do more harm than good in preparing the child for the future. Examples of more meaningful projects will occur to the teacher, and samples of other projects which could meet the criteria are described in this chapter.

Careful planning on the part of the teacher is very necessary for the success of a project. Below is a sample plan of a project for an Advanced group, which a teacher might have evolved:

Sandpaper Project

Skills to be learned: sanding, shellacking, counting money, folding and tearing sandpaper.
Knowledge and concepts: "rough," "smooth"; things cost money; equipment has to be taken care of or it gets in bad condition; different pupils have different abilities.
Attitudes and appreciations: care of furniture, consideration for people on streets and in stores, safety at street crossings, sense of accomplishment when results of sanding and shel-

lacking are seen, pride in keeping school in good condition. *Procedure:* Talk about splintered edges of the school stools. How did they get rough? They should have been treated more gently.

Feel stools. Which ones are rough? Which ones smooth? (Take turns, with eyes bandaged, feeling stools.)

Discuss why we don't like stools to be rough; what to do about rough ones.

Since we lack sandpaper, plan how to proceed.

Plan purchasing of sandpaper: which store, how much to buy, what kind?

Learn about different grades of sandpaper—three kinds shown by teacher.

Before going to store, decide the following:

Where do we go?

How do we get there? Can we walk? Which route do we take?

Who can be responsible leaders, stopping at corners, waiting when told to by teacher?

Who will ask storekeeper for sandpaper? Practice the appropriate words and sentences to be used. Decide who can say it clearly.

Who can carry the money and be responsible for it?

Who can pay the money? Who knows the coins? Take turns counting money to find out.

Who will accept the change?

Who receives the package and carries it home?

Who will lead coming back?

Behavior on trip: Walk with partner; move over when someone wants to pass; look ahead to see where one is going; don't touch things in the store.

When back at school, discuss what the class did, listing rules remembered, behavior that should be improved before next trip.

Open package; count sheets of sandpaper; sort into grades and discuss purpose for each kind.

Count out as much as class might need, and take rest to supply room.

Fold and tear sheets into quarters and thumbtack onto blocks of wood if easier and more effective that way.

Another day, start sanding stools. While sanding, keep feeling wood to see when it gets smooth, and then move to new spot, rather than always sanding in same place. Learn to judge smoothness, not asking for teacher's opinion constantly. Learn to keep at it until finished.

When sanding of a stool is finished, shellac it.

Carry-over: After all stools are sanded and shellacked, look over other furniture and equipment to see if anything else needs smoothing.

Talk about rough and smooth in connection with other materials.

Take other shopping trips for other purposes, reviewing standards of behavior ahead of time.

Watch for furniture needing repairs of any sort; be careful of equipment.

There are an infinite number of projects and ways to carry them out. Below are listed some of the activities which might be included in some projects, depending upon the level of the class, the school environment, facilities available, and the background of the children. The sample projects, sketched very briefly, should be considered merely suggestive. The teacher will want to plan projects appropriate to her class situation and will outline them in the way most helpful to her.

SAMPLE PROJECTS

A. The Home

I. BEGINNER

People in the family:
Recognize names of own family members when spoken.
Recognize photographs of own family members.
Say names of family members and identify.
Tell whether a family member is big or little.

When family member comes to school, inform teacher who
he is.

Point to mother, etc. in other children's family pictures.

Point to mother, father, etc. in book pictures.

Parts of a house:

Identify door, steps, floor from inside or outside school.

Identify doors, windows, upstairs in doll house.

Walk around block, finding these various parts on other
houses when teacher asks.

II. INTERMEDIATE

Functions of family members:

Play house, acting out functions of various family members.

Discuss pictures of family members working.

Talk about how children can help family members.

Do tasks at school that children can do at home.

Act out receiving friends, relatives, or workers coming to
home.

Rooms in a home and their uses:

Play with doll house, sorting furniture in various rooms.

Have dolls function in doll house as family members.

Make scrapbook of a home and its occupants.

Sort pictures of furniture according to the rooms in which
they belong.

Work to be done in the home:

Bring pictures of work done in a home and discuss pictures.

Make scrapbook of family jobs.

Learn about how a home runs and about safety in the home
by doing similar tasks at school and applying safety rules.

III. ADVANCED

Work to be done in the home:

Bring record to school of jobs done independently at home.

Visit in classmates' homes while they tell jobs they do there.

Learn how to do home tasks and to use tools and simple
machines by working at household and yard jobs at school.

B. The School

I. BEGINNER

Sing and play games in which the children and adults in the class are named.

Show recognition of classmates' photographs by matching with the children themselves.

II. INTERMEDIATE

Take trips about the school to meet staff members and to see other classes.

Find out about the rooms in which other people work and jobs they do about the school.

Practice safety on these trips.

Learn about school visitors and workers; act out how to greet them.

C. Holidays

I. BEGINNER

Participate in songs and games appropriate to holiday.

Talk about objects and colored decorations displayed for the occasion.

Participate in party to celebrate holiday.

II. INTERMEDIATE

Participate in activities suggested for Beginners.

Make decorations, greeting cards, or presents.

Participate in preparing for party.

Talk about party before and afterwards, telling what one does at parties and on special holidays.

III. ADVANCED

Associate holiday with calendar dates.

Find pictures and news about holiday.

Decorate the room.

Plan appropriate program to celebrate an approaching holiday.

D. Food

I. BEGINNER

Feel, smell, and eat various foods identified by teacher (see "Learning Through Other Senses," p. 150).

II. INTERMEDIATE

Talk about foods brought to classroom.
Play grocery store, bringing cans, cartons, and boxes from home.
Play at cooking, making foods from clay and painting them.
Play blindfold games to identify foods.
Talk about food eaten at lunch, juice-time, parties.
Prepare simple foods from box mixes.
Go to store with class to buy something to prepare at school, such as pudding.

III. ADVANCED

Discuss proper diets. Show pictures, make scrapbooks.
Prepare and sample foods that are healthful.
Visit farm, dairy, bottling factory.
Discuss proper methods of food preparation.
Prepare simple foods; plan and prepare food for party, picnics, box lunches or soup or dessert for lunch.
Bring note from home giving own diet for a day. Discuss with classmates.
Visit kitchens of cafeterias, restaurants; eat in such places.

E. Nature Projects

I. BEGINNER

Plants, weather: Have close contact with grass, leaves, flowers, birds, snow, rain, and wind. (This experience with nature can be expanded by the teacher's calling attention to natural objects and phenomena.) Take walks to look for objects of nature that class has been learning about. Gather leaves, flowers, grass. Listen to and join in with teacher when she sings songs about nature.

Animals: Observe, pet and hold an old, quiet dog, cat, or guinea pig. Feed it, watch it drink. Talk with teacher about its parts, and then find and touch them (ears, tail, etc.). Pretend to be the animal. Make noises like the animal.

II. INTERMEDIATE

Plants: Visit farm to see plants that farmer is growing. Pick from field or orchard the products of the farm. Bring these back to school, and prepare them for eating or use in other way (jack-o'-lanterns). Place sweet potato in jar containing water. Place onion bulb or carrot tops (with just a bit of the orange root part attached) in pebbles and water placed in bowl or saucer. Plant sunflower seeds or kernels of corn in paper cup, flower pot, or jar with owner's name affixed to it. Plant orange seeds, acorns, apple seeds and see if they will grow. Radish, parsley or grass seeds can be planted in cigar boxes or in ground outdoors where garden is staked out. Learn that sunshine and water are needed for plant growth. In the fall, collect nuts and leaves, sorting according to size, shape, or color. Wax leaves with paraffin or coat with shellac and then mount with transparent tape.

Pets: Help care for and play with schoolroom pets (turtles, fish, guinea pigs, frog, toad, snails, bird, worms). Visit pet store to buy pets or food for them. Visit museum, aquarium, or zoo to see pets similar to those at school. Talk about school pets, home pets. Bring a home pet to school for a visit. Take school pets home to care for in the summer. Look at picture books, search for and cut out pictures and listen to phonograph records about these animals. Sing about them and pretend to be the animals.

Weather: Talk about weather when first entering school. After whole class has assembled, participate in telling about the weather and indicating this on a very simple weather chart showing four kinds of weather. Listen to simple stories which refer to the weather. Discuss kind of wraps to wear on the day at hand when going out to play. Sing songs about the weather on this day. Paint and draw pictures of the weather.

III. ADVANCED

Plants: Study about, plan and then make a little garden at school, selecting and buying necessary tools and seeds. Visit other people's gardens or conservatories. Bring products of own garden at home to school. Cut out pictures of flowers and vegetables from seed catalogues and identify them, showing them to rest of class. Make a scrapbook with pictures of vegetables and flowers which have been sorted into meaningful categories.

F. Community Workers

I. INTERMEDIATE

Observe community workers who come to school: milkman, postman.

Walk with class around the neighborhood, observing work of community helpers that is meaningful to children: policeman on the corner, milkman in his wagon, postman going down the street, sanitation men.

Invite community worker to visit the class. Serve him juice and crackers, ask him questions, observe his uniform and what he carries.

Visit places associated with community helpers: firehouse, post office, and other places that are simple enough to be meaningful.

Talk about jobs of community helpers and the visits made to see them.

Pretend to be one of the workers. Play postman, delivering letters labeled with names of other children. Play barber or doctor with other children. Be a policeman directing traffic (vehicles propelled by other children).

Sing about different community workers.

II. ADVANCED

Participate in activities similar to those for the Intermediate, but study more types of workers in the situations where they work.

Make plans, then take trips to places such as the police station,

airport, gas station. Visit and shop, eat in restaurants, be
entertained (concerts) in public places, ride on public con-
veyances, use public washroom facilities.

After trips, discuss them, sing about them, draw or paint pictures.

Act out jobs of different workers: bus driver, dentist, restaurant
workers.

Discuss and act out ways citizens can cooperate with community
workers: obey laws, learn how to act in public places.

Plan and carry through work for neighbors or community:
polish silver for a community club dinner, clean up a public
yard, prepare circulars for mailing.

G. Parties

All school parties may not be projects, but many can be. Because parties appeal so strongly to children, good projects often
can be developed around party planning.

School parties give additional experiences for social growth
and provide new situations for practicing skills, developing attitudes and gaining knowledge in many areas.

The program for a party depends upon the kind of group—
the developmental level of most of the children, their cohesive-
ness, their individual excitability. With careful planning the
children can have a genuinely happy time without becoming
uncontrolled or overly excited.

The school party should not be considered an opportunity
for parents or outside charity groups to present the children
with food, entertainment and gifts, while the children sit pas-
sively, not being expected to contribute in any way. Rather, a
party should be an opportunity for the children to learn for
themselves how to participate with their peers in having a good
time. Ordinarily guests should not be present.

Most of the children will enjoy some anticipation of a party,
but excitable pupils cannot stand too much anticipation.
Through making preparations for such an important affair,
the group learns the need of working together to achieve a
common goal. Making decorations, buying or making refresh-

ments, and setting-up for the party are incentives to work more efficiently, with greater perseverance.

One key to a successful party is simplicity. Costumes should be comfortable. Decorations should not be too distracting or in the way. Refreshments should be such that they can be served and eaten with few catastrophes. The amount of food should be kept to a minimum, partly for reasons of health. Also, a child who must manipulate a straw in a coke bottle, crumbly cake iced with fluff, heaping ice cream topped with sticky sauce, and a crowded candy cup will naturally give himself over to the job of eating, rather than enjoying his friends at the table; and there will be no time left to play games afterwards.

There are values in having some parties to which the pupils invite guests, such as parents or a younger class. Each trainable boy and girl can then learn the fun of giving a good time, refreshments, or even gifts, rather than considering what he himself may be getting out of the party. When parents are invited, the pupil should be aware that he will not be entertaining them by showing off. He may perform dances or sing songs with the class to demonstrate some school activities, and to help the guests learn how to do these things themselves before they join in. At the party, parents can experience the values of participating with their children and other parents, and may learn how helpful their children can be as hosts when given this responsibility.

RELATED READING

Strickland, Ruth G. *How to Build a Unit of Work.* Bulletin No. 5. Washington, D.C.: Federal Security Agency, U.S. Office of Education, 1946.

University of Kansas School of Education. *Curriculum and Methods for the Trainable Retarded.* Lawrence, Kansas: School of Education, University Extension, June, 1958.

XII. School-Community Relationships

Just as the cooperation of the parents can facilitate school training and the realization of effective services for trainable children, so also community support of the program for severely retarded, whether conducted in an institution or in public or private schools, can be of great benefit. Only with community cooperation and through community agencies and organizations can many needed or desirable services be provided for these children. It is to the community that the school needs to turn for solutions to many problems: How can 'the mentally retarded be protected from unkind ridicule, suspicion, and even condemnation by people in the community? What can the older boys and girls do for recreation after school hours? What can be done for retarded youngsters in the summer vacation period? What can they do when they have outgrown their special school programs? The retarded need the community's support and understanding if they are to be reasonably happy citizens outside the protected environs of home and school. It has been established that a community can develop wholesome attitudes toward trainable children and extend valuable services to them. Whatever the school can do through community contacts to benefit its trainable children will also benefit all retarded children, for the public will become more aware of the problem as a whole.

It is important to realize that the reverse is also true. The needs of all children must be supported if the needs of the mentally retarded are to be served. For example, if the community has been helped to understand the general need for good educational and good mental health facilities for its children, it will be more receptive to the idea that retarded children have similar but also special needs which must be met. Likewise, if the community can be stimulated to the point of recognizing the importance of training the educable mentally retarded, it is more likely to become interested in supporting a program for the severely retarded—perhaps a school already in operation.

Stimulating community interest in the problems of the mentally retarded is the responsibility of local organizations for the mentally retarded, school boards, administrators, and P.T.A.'s already involved in programs for the retarded or fostering the development of such programs, as well as teachers and other professional staff members who are working directly with the retarded.

WHAT THE INDIVIDUAL TEACHER CAN DO

Too often an enthusiastic and capable teacher is so engrossed in the children in her class and in their program and problems that she may overlook the values which may be gained for them from her contacts in the community. Helping to foster good school-community relations may appear to the teacher to be a task she cannot possibly add to her major responsibility of training her class and having frequent contacts with the children's parents. Unless she is also the school director or one of very few persons working for trainable children in a particular area, the teacher's contributions, as far as time and energy go, will not be too taxing. Even a school director is generally able to encourage her school board or parents' group to assume a great deal of the responsibility for this function.

Regardless of the scope of the teacher's responsibility for the trainable's program, it is nevertheless important that she know the community's varied resources and that she is clear as to what authority she may approach when community aid for the retarded is to be sought. This does not imply that a teacher go directly to—let us say—the community welfare director for assistance. But she should be thoroughly informed before she presents her request for community assistance, whether it be to her principal, supervisor, parent group, school board, or directly to an agency or organization.

Where the trainable program is part of a larger program such as a public school system, or where the teacher is one of several in a large institution for the retarded with a hierarchy of staff officers, she can still do her share in stimulating community effort on behalf of the trainable. Perhaps she can make a contribution to the heightening of citizen interest in this area by serving on the public relations committee of her school P.T.A. or parents' group, or of the local association for the mentally retarded. She might work on a civic affairs or service committee of a local non-professional organization to which she belongs. Or she might be instrumental in setting up within the public school where her class is located a committee to consider the problems of the atypical child.

WHY THE COMMUNITY SHOULD HELP

As a society becomes enlightened, it demonstrates a growing concern for all its members. In our civilization it is expected that the community should assume the responsibility of offering each individual an opportunity to receive training and education which will help him develop to his maximum. Why, then, should the severely retarded be ruled out?

Well-adjusted, happy individuals are the kinds of citizens a democratic community needs. Before urbanization took place in this country, most trainable mental retardates were able to make an adjustment in rural situations where they were more readily accepted. Since urbanization has created problems for the retarded, the urban community should help to solve their problems.

A community, by studying the severely retarded and ways to aid them, gains insight and experience in how to help its average children. When methods for psychological testing of the retarded were developed by Binet, a great contribution was made to the understanding of the average child.

As severely retarded boys and girls, through training outside as well as within the home, become more responsible, more independent, and happier, their families become more harmonious units, and individual family members will be able to function better. Freed from complete responsibility and constant concern for a demanding, dependent, or unhappy retardate, a parent can direct some of his efforts to community affairs where he has his own special contribution to make.

What the Community Needs to Know

Besides acquiring an appreciation of why it should help in developing and supporting a sound program for severely retarded children, the community will have to understand, in broad terms, what these children need that the public can provide. Some of these needs parallel those which are accepted as necessary, or at least desirable, for all children: more and better schools, more and better teachers, more ancillary services (visiting teachers, school psychologists, family case workers, child guidance clinics, vocational guidance, and public health, welfare, and recreation services). In regard to retarded children specifically, the general public will have to have their very particular needs emphasized: specialized training for their teachers, the development of school training programs for the severely retarded as differentiated from the regular school education program, and the unique facilities and services which may not as yet be available in the community. In some cases, special legislation may be required to make training of the retarded become a public responsibility, to insure its financial support and to raise the level of standards for this training. Much more extensive research is needed into the causes and prevention of mental retardation, and, in many instances, especially in large metropolitan areas, such research can be promoted by an informed, active citizenry.

How the Community Can Be Informed: It is no easy task for

the school to communicate effectively with the groups and individuals in the community who are best able to interpret to
others. It will frequently take very skilled people to present to
the public clearly and forcefully what the general problem is,
what progress has been made, what the school and others are
doing about it at present, what the immediate needs are, and
what plans for the future entail.

In any planned public education program, great care must
be taken to give a correct interpretation of the trainable and
their needs. The children and the program for them should
be presented as they are, and the goals described to the public
should be the true goals. We are not propagandists; we are
educators. The community must know the truth if it is to help
retarded children.

To aid in the continuing responsibility of keeping the public
informed, there is included here a list of ways which may be
used effectively by the school staff and others closely connected
with the program:

A. The spoken word
    1. Informal conversations with people in staff members'
       own social or other groups—college alumni associations,
       church associations, fraternal organizations.
    2. Initiation of, or participation formally or informally in
       conferences, panel discussions, institutes, lecture meet-
       ings, discussion or study groups, which may be set up
       particularly around the subject of the school and mental
       retardation, or around some other area in which certain
       aspects of mental retardation are included.
    3. Initiation of and participation in radio programs.
B. The printed word
    1. Printed material that staff members write or arrange to
       have written:
       a. Newspapers: special feature articles, letters to the ed-
          itor, announcements of meetings and press releases on
          school activities.
       b. Magazine articles or books in the field.

      c. The school newsletter, describing school activities, philosophy of the school, parent activities.

      d. Handbook, brochure or other material about the school.

  2. Printed material that the school can lend or distribute:

      a. Professional publications in the field.

      b. Newsletters and newspapers of local, state, and national associations of parents of the mentally retarded.

      c. Authoritative material on mental retardation from responsible sources such as the federal government.

      d. Authoritative books which can constitute part of a school library, can be recommended for the public library, or can be displayed at various places, such as universities.

C. Visual material

  1. Movies on the school or on mental retardation, especially if a good discussion follows.

  2. Television programs in which the school staff participates, or programs for a national audience publicized locally.

  3. Slides accompanied by a good lecture.

  4. Observation of the school in action (primarily by students going into the field, or professional people who will probably understand and benefit most by this, especially if there is verbal interpretation by the staff afterwards).

  5. Photographs and descriptions of school activities in newspapers.

Kinds of Organizations Which Might Be of Service

Health and Social Welfare Agencies: Many excellent, well-established agencies and organizations in most sizable communities have the funds, facilities, and professional staff available to help, in specialized ways, a struggling program such as that involving the severely retarded. These public and semipublic organizations are an invaluable resource for assistance which certainly should not be overlooked by any school for the trainable. What are these groups with which the school should establish contact? The following list will give an idea of the great variety of possibilities which may be at hand.

1. Children's agencies, such as guidance clinics, for treatment of special problems or handicaps and behavior problems.

2. Diagnostic and treatment centers for the mentally retarded, such as mental retardation clinics connected with hospitals.

3. Family service agencies, such as Family Service Society, for helping families with their problems.

4. Health agencies, such as local hospitals, for emergency or other health and medical services, and American Red Cross for swimming instruction and possibly for transportation for the school children.

5. Group work and mass recreation agencies, such as Boy and Girl Scouts, camping, swimming, and neighborhood house activities, for recreation opportunities after school, retarded teen-ager socials, and facilities for carrying on summer programs for the children.

6. Associations for the handicapped, such as a state commission for the blind, Goodwill Industries, and the Cerebral Palsy Association, for special services for the multiple-handicapped, and for sheltered workshop opportunities.

7. Vocational rehabilitation programs, such as those that can be arranged by a state division of vocational rehabilitation, for vocational aptitude testing, vocational training, sheltered workshops, and placement.

8. Other governmental agencies, such as the departments of Public Welfare (for family problems, placement of a member in an institution, and financial assistance), Public Health (visiting nurses), Recreation (parks and playgrounds), Traffic Safety (helping at street crossings); the courts; and a department of Mental Hygiene. (In a few states there are local, tax supported mental health agencies which can help provide facilities for the mentally retarded.)

9. Interagency organizations, such as the Community Chest to assist with financing, and an agency which helps with social

planning (sometimes called a Community Planning Council or Council of Social Agencies) for helping the school gain information and advice about making referrals, working with other agencies on a problem, at the same time that they interpret the school and the problem of mental retardation to other agencies.

How Health and Social Agencies Can Help: As has been suggested, contacts with health and welfare agencies can give special help to the child or to his family, either while the child is attending school or after his schooling is ended. If a family agency or child guidance clinic refers a trainable youngster to a school or class and he is placed there, the agency can be encouraged to continue working with the child and the family rather than considering the case closed. Reports from the school to the agency and from the agency to the school can lead to increasing effectiveness in planning for the child and his family.

These agencies can be of help to the teacher by providing professional advice pertaining to areas such as the problems of the multiple-handicapped, pre-vocational training, school equipment and kinds of facilities that might best serve needs of particular children.

In addition to direct service, an agency can help the school by interpreting to families and to other agencies what the school goals and program are, so that they can use the school's services more effectively.

Other Organizations: Besides the professional service agencies in the community, there are other professional groups and many civic and religious organizations which welcome opportunities to assist valuable community enterprises such as a retarded children's program. But it is first necessary that they become aware of the program and its needs through the media already mentioned. Some idea of the many resources in this category can be obtained from the following list:

1. Organizations for the retarded which have very broad purposes (see pp. 15–16 for description of these).
2. Professional groups, such as the local chapter of the Council

for Exceptional Children, local branches of teachers' and principals' associations, and medical, dental, and psychological associations.

3. Schools, universities, and libraries, including P.T.A. groups, fraternities, study groups and bodies connected with services for the trainable—such as an institution's administrative body.

4. Educational, social, and service groups, such as the League of Women Voters, and special cultural groups.

5. Religious groups.

6. Business and fraternal organizations.

7. Industrial unions.

8. Community and civic associations.

9. Philanthropic foundations.

Individuals Who Can Be of Service

Professional Persons: The school may benefit greatly by using the volunteer professional services not only of groups but also of individuals. Volunteers should be selected with care if they are to prove of value to the school staff. Students being trained in professions closely related to the field of mental retardation, such as medicine and psychology, have seldom until recently been oriented to the severely mentally retarded in their course studies, or been given the opportunity to gain firsthand experience with the retarded. Consequently, professionals otherwise well trained are often limited in their knowledge and understanding of the problem of mental retardation. However, through community agencies, such as a city's community planning board, some professionals well qualified in their fields, with an interest and knowledge of—or desire to learn about—the problems which face a school for trainable children can be found and can be of invaluable assistance to a school both in the planning stages before classes for the retarded are established, as well as in the operation of the classes after they are in full swing.

There may be a recreation leader, craft teacher, psychologist, or speech specialist who could work effectively with one child or a group of children several days a week. Some students, especially graduate students, can be of service to the school at the same time that they are making a study in some area of special interest to them. Students just beginning their training may benefit from observation or participation, when it does not interfere with class activities. Even if not performing any direct service to the school, they may gain an orientation to the problems of mental retardation which may lead them into further study and possibly into preparing for a career related to the field of mental retardation. They will, at any rate, influence community awareness of this problem, simply through their informal contacts with people they know, after watching the school in operation and talking with the staff.

In addition to those professionals who may function directly in the school setting—and these may be few—some professionals may act in an advisory capacity, serving on a council with other professional people. This council could act as a fact-finding and deliberative body to consider problems brought to its attention by the school staff or parents' group and make reports which might serve as a basis in staff planning for the school.

Instead of establishing its own advisory council, a school may be able to gain assistance from one already functioning in connection with a parents' organization for the retarded. Many of the professional people best qualified to help a school for trainable children already may be members of such a council, and the school staff may be able to suggest to the council other people with experience and training who are also dedicated to the interests of the retarded. The personnel on an advisory council should represent a variety of professions covering many fields closely related to that of mental retardation—education, social work, psychology, psychiatry, nursery education, education of exceptional children, public health, pediatrics, neurology, etc.

Other individuals with a background of appropriate experience, who are willing to devote the time, may prove invaluable by serving on a parents' council or a school committee composed of lay people, parents, and professionals. The school committee may help review and determine policies and activities of the school which are being planned or are already in operation, and help solve school problems.

Since the amount of time a professional will be able to devote to the school may be very limited, it is important that he be used to the best advantage by having him contribute from his own field of competency. Those who are not able to give the time necessary for regular attendance at advisory council or school committee meetings may be willing to participate once in a while. Perhaps a group worker or psychologist may be called upon to lead a series of small, parent discussion groups. A neurologist may be invited to speak at the P.T.A. about— let us say—problems of the brain-injured child. A physiotherapist may willingly attend a school staff meeting to talk on problems of the physically handicapped.

Not only will the school gain from its contacts with professional volunteers, but the professionals also will gain a broader knowledge of the mentally handicapped. And their increased awareness will eventually be reflected in greater community understanding of the problem of mental retardation.

Individual Contacts Made by Teachers: In her day-to-day contacts, the teacher can probably make as many sympathetic friends for her special pupils as she can through some of the more formal channels, unless, of course, she has a natural talent for either public speaking or writing. There is a special significance and value to be obtained from these contacts. Some of the people she meets most frequently are those who come to the school or have dealings with the school: food handlers, maintenance men, bus and taxi drivers for the transportation of the children, shop owners and clerks in the school vicinity with which the school or its families do business, custodial employees in the school building, delivery men, the postman, and crossing guards at street intersections near the school. These people not only deal with the school personnel, but they will also see the children and in some cases have personal contacts with them.

All these people will welcome information about the children and the school program. As they come to accept the children and understand what is being done, they too can serve as interpreters to other citizens in the community.

Besides this circle of what might be called school business contacts, the teacher and other staff members will be constantly on the alert to interest other lay citizens in the program for retarded children. Among her own friends and acquaintances, a teacher may discover people with special understanding, abilities, and assets which would contribute to the welfare of the retarded. And there are those with outstanding influence in the community who would be valuable spokesmen for the retarded once they were acquainted with their needs.

It will not take long for a teacher of the retarded to find that the ordinary citizen is genuinely curious about severely retarded children. Once the subject has been raised, the teacher will often find herself bombarded with questions. This is her opportunity to see that those who are listening go away with a better understanding and growing sympathy for the group with which she is professionally involved. These will be the citizens who join in an organization or community effort on behalf of the retarded when a concerted program gets under way.

Volunteer Services by Non-Professionals: Education and interpretation are the main contributions that some organizations, as well as individuals, will make to the retarded children's program. When individuals learn about the problem, they will be more helpful to the retarded in the community, and will know where to refer those in need. As service clubs assume responsibility for volunteer work with the school, they become better informed about the problems of the mentally retarded and, with guidance from the school, can become helpful interpreters of the school program.

Civic groups of all kinds, as they study and interpret the program and the needs of the special school and of mentally retarded children in general, will help form public opinion. This may eventually lead to more adequate programs for these children through appropriate legislation, fund-raising, and additional professional services. It may also lead to better facilities, more training materials, and better staffing of a school or institution.

Many groups are interested in doing something specific for the school or the children, rather than simply studying the problem. Before civic groups can start actively serving the school, they need to be informed as to just how they can be of most help. Often these civic groups, through discussion with school staff members, can come to realize what is helpful and why, and what is really not useful to the school. It is certainly worth the staff time to go over plans with such groups, or at least refer them to someone who can direct their good intentions into useful channels. A teacher may find she has time to work effectively with only one or two groups and should not try to extend her activities too far. Her role is first that of teacher rather than supervisor of volunteer workers.

Here are some suggestions as to the kinds of non-professional services that volunteer groups or individuals can best perform for the school, other than assisting with the children:

1. Do office work, especially typing.
2. Drive the children on trips or accompany them on bus trips with the teacher. (Special insurance coverage may be necessary for car drivers.)
3. Entertain the children by playing musical instruments or giving school-approved puppet shows.
4. Take photographs of school activities.
5. Arrange details of trips, under the teacher's direction.
6. Paint and repair furniture and equipment.
7. Shop for materials and supplies at teacher's request. Pick up donated supplies.
8. Donate new materials and equipment after consultation with the school staff.
9. Prepare materials for children to finish (e.g., cutting out and punching holes in leather for the children to lace).
10. Donate or make clothes for dolls, for manikins, or for children to use for dress-up.
11. Make curtains.

12. Collect and mount pictures for the picture file.
13. Mend books and game boxes.
14. Make covers for phonograph records.
15. Print signs or job charts for children's use.
16. Make scrapbooks, puzzles and games, according to school specifications.
17. Raise money, if plans approved by school authorities.
18. Serve as members on committees of organizations interested in the school.
19. Serve as members on committees directly connected with the school, such as a school committee.

Training the Non-Professional Volunteer: In working with the school, service groups or individuals need guidance in how to be most helpful. The following are suggestions for teachers or other school staff who work with or instruct service groups before they start a project:

1. Explain that the group will help the school and the children best by working inconspicuously, away from the children.
2. Encourage groups to work elsewhere than on school premises when engaged in activities which may create noise and confusion, or require a clean-up job afterwards.
3. Give extremely explicit directions, writing them down if there is any question about details.
4. Instruct one responsible person who can direct the work of the others.
5. Emphasize the importance of confidentiality when typing records. (The school will leave out names when giving records to volunteers to be typed, but volunteers are reminded not to discuss the contents of reports with anyone. Parents should not do any work on school records.) The children should not be identified in material to be used outside the school. Photographs and other identifiable materials are not to be used without permission, and case histories cannot be used when enlisting club support for a particularly needy child.

6. Encourage the giving of money gifts, rather than presenting material gifts, so that the proper types of materials can be selected.

7. If a group is only interested in presenting gifts, discourage the giving of parties or candy.

8. Explain that the trainable child has more fun and learns more when not subjected to unusually exciting mass entertainment, such as being taken in a large group to the circus as guests of members of a service club.

9. Describe the benefits that the children derive by doing things for themselves such as giving their own parties.

10. Suggest that people who wish to give talks or solicit funds for the school discuss their ideas first with school authorities.

Some volunteers wish to work directly with the children. Since only certain people will have the kind of personalities that would be an asset in the schoolroom, it would be wise to have applicants for this type of work observe the children in class, have a personal interview with the teacher or supervisor, and fill out a special application blank, giving references, before being considered as a volunteer aide to the teacher. It is important to find out why the volunteer wishes to help; frequently a person is trying to fill his own emotional needs, some of which cannot be met in the school program. Volunteers who are able to work directly with the children will need special orientation and close supervision from the teacher in the classroom.

It has been the author's experience that once the school has given volunteers a thorough explanation as to the kinds of services they can contribute and the manner in which they can serve, their work has often been found so satisfying both to the school and to the volunteers that they return to help year after year.

The last chapter has digressed from the main theme of the book—the actual training of the trainable. And here the author wishes to restate her words of caution presented in the Introduction. It would be disastrous if a new teacher were to take this text and attempt to teach the children in her classroom each activity in the order listed.

The readers of this book are advised to experiment and to use their imaginations—not to follow the given suggestions too literally. The ideas for activities which have been described may supplement those that a teacher has used successfully in the past, discovered elsewhere, or created herself.

The thoughtful teacher may try a few activities selected from the text which she thinks might be appropriate for her class, repeat those proving valuable, and gradually introduce more of the activities as the children's needs indicate. If the teacher has tried many of the foregoing suggestions, she may have been disappointed to find that some did not work, or that they only worked when she used methods differing from those suggested. This will happen over and over again, and not only because children and teachers are not the same, but because the writer's twenty years' experience with trainable children is not nearly enough. As teachers discover new, more effective methods, it is important that they make their discoveries available to other teachers so that all of us can benefit.

The dearth of existing information regarding what and how the trainable child can learn most effectively becomes more and more apparent as we search for ways to improve our teaching. A great deal of experimentation and research needs to be done and probably will be done in the future. A wise teacher will test any new information against the background of her own experiences, and—most important of all—she will invariably supplement the knowledge she gains from research workers, teachers, and parents with her own creative ideas.

RELATED READING

Boggs, Elizabeth M. "Relations of Parent Groups and Professional Persons in Community Situations," *American Journal of Mental Deficiency*, XLVII (July, 1952), 109–15.

Ecob, Katherine G. *The Retarded Child in the Community.* New York: New York State Society for Mental Health, 1955.

National Association for Retarded Children, Inc. *We Speak for Them.* New York: National Association for Retarded Children, Inc., 386 Park Avenue South, New York.

Powers, Grover F. "Professional Education and Mental Retardation," *Pediatrics,* XX, No. 6 (December, 1957), 1088–94.

Rath, Alfred E. "Retarded Children's Educational Project," *Public Aid in Illinois,* March, 1951.

Tudyman, Al. "A Realistic Total Program for the Severely Mentally Retarded," *American Journal of Mental Deficiency,* LX (April, 1956), 574–82.

Weingold, Joseph T. "Parents' Groups and the Problem of Mental Retardation," *American Journal of Mental Deficiency,* XLVI (January, 1952), 1–8. (Reprint distributed by the Association for the Help of Retarded Children, Inc., 200 Fourth Avenue, New York.)

Appendix A

PERSONAL DATA FORM

Date _____

Name of child _____   _____
　　　　　　　　　Last　　　　　　　First

Birth date _____ Age _____ Sex _____ Ht. _____ Wt. _____

Name of father _____   _____
　　　　　　　　　Last　　　　　　　First

Address of father _____ Phone _____
　　　　　　　　　　Street　　　　　City

Father's business address_____ Phone _____
　　　　　　　　　　　　　　　City

Name of mother _____   _____   _____
　　　　　　　　　Last　　　　Maiden　　　First

Address of mother _____ Phone _____
　　　　　　　　　　Street　　　　　City

In emergency: Name _____ Phone _____

Siblings:

　Name _____ Age _____ Sex _____

　Name _____ Age _____ Sex _____

　Name _____ Age _____ Sex _____

　Name _____ Age _____ Sex _____

　Name _____ Age _____ Sex _____

Any others living in the home?

　Name _____
　　　　　　　　　　　Relation　　　　Age

　Name _____
　　　　　　　　　　　Relation　　　　Age

Has your child been diagnosed as mentally retarded? _____

By whom? _____ When? _____

Kind of specialist? _____

Address _____

Has your child been excluded from public school attendance? _____

Reason: _____

What clinics, hospitals, or specialists have seen the child?

   1. Agency or examiner _____
      Address _____ Date _____
      Kind of examination _____
      Diagnosis or report _____
      _____

   2. Agency or examiner _____
      Address _____ Date _____
      Kind of examination _____
      Diagnosis or report _____
      _____

   3. Agency or examiner _____
      Address _____ Date _____
      Kind of examination _____
      Diagnosis or report _____
      _____

   4. Agency or examiner _____
      Address _____ Date _____
      Kind of examination _____
      Diagnosis or report _____
_____

Is your child in school? ___ How long has he been attending? _____

Hours per day _____ Grade _____

Name of school _____

Comment on his adjustment in school _____
_____

Schools your child has attended:

1. School _____ Grade _____
   Length of stay _____ Reasons for withdrawal _____
_____
   How did the school help him? _____
_____

2. School _____ Grade _____
   Length of stay _____ Reasons for withdrawal _____
_____

How did the school help him? _____

_____

If your child has studied school subjects, are there any in which he
has had particular trouble? _____
In what other group programs has your child participated? Give
name and dates of attendance. _____

_____

Do you feel that he has benefited from them? _____
If so, how? _____

_____

How does he choose to spend his time? _____
Indoors _____
Outdoors _____
Does he do any domestic tasks? _____

_____

To what places does he go? (stores, movies, church, etc.)
Alone _____
Accompanied _____
Please answer "Yes" or "No" to the questions below. If answering
"Yes" please describe the child's difficulty on the adjoining line.
Does your child have difficulty in
Seeing? _____. _____
Hearing? _____. _____
Standing? _____. _____
Walking? _____. _____
Using hands or arms? _____. _____

Is your child often ill? _____. _____
Does he have heart trouble? _____. _____
Does he have convulsions or epileptic seizures? _____. _____
Does he have any other physical disabilities or defects not listed above?

_____. _____

To help us better understand your child and the type of program he
needs, please answer "Yes" or "No" to the following and describe
the behavior on adjacent lines:
TOILETING
Bowels controlled? __ Bladder control: In daytime __ At night__
FEEDING
Feeds self alone _____ With some help _____ No self-feeding _____
Eats most foods _____ Eats few foods _____

Foods he does not eat or drink: _____

COMMUNICATION (check)

How does he let you know his wants? Talks ____ Makes sounds ____
    Makes facial expressions _____ Gestures _____

SPEECH

Understandable _____ Uses sentences _____ Uses words _____

Can speak, but seldom does _____

How does he let you know
    his toilet needs? To have a bowel movement _____
                     To urinate _____
    his need for a drink? _____

What does he like to be called? _____

BEHAVIOR CHARACTERISTICS: (Check those which apply)

__excitable __distractible
__inactive __has temper tantrums
__overactive __destroys things
__stubborn __heedless of danger
__bored at home __has few interests
__teases others __has unusual interests
__attacks or hurts people __prolonged crying or giggling
__has no chance to play with children __is not apparently interested in people
__is timid with other children __is interested in only one or two people
__is afraid of (list fears) _____

What do you feel your child needs *now*? Check the items below that apply, and describe his need on the adjoining line.

__toilet training _____
__to learn to feed self _____
__to learn to dress self _____
__help in adjusting to other children _____
__a chance to be with other children regularly _____
__to learn better muscular control _____
__to become more relaxed _____
__to acquire manual skills _____
__to calm down _____
__to have more fun _____
__to become more cooperative _____
__to become more independent _____
__to learn to concentrate _____
__to learn to talk _____

___to improve his speech _____

___to learn how to go about community alone _____

___to learn simple work that he can do independently at home ____

What do you want the school to do for your child?

_____

_____

_____

How can your child get to such a program regularly?
1. Use public transportation: alone _____ accompanied_____
2. Be driven in car? _____ By whom? _____
3. Other means: _____

Appendix B

Here are sample plans which a teacher might make for a certain class on a particular day. Although definite time periods are listed, these actually would be quite flexible. When trips or projects are planned, the general outline would be changed considerably, with various activities and time periods being omitted and the long project substituted.

SAMPLE SCHEDULE FOR BEGINNER GROUP

Group: Seven children, chronological ages six to nine years; mental ages two years, three months to three years.

Date: A day in February—cold and snowless.

General Schedule	*Notes for the Day*
9:00 Wraps off and hung up; toilet if necessary	Free ball play until all have finished.
9:20 Educational toys; special assistance to those who need it	Sorting of colors by putting colored clothespins on plastic boxes of same color; color-matching with peg boards. Inset barrels for E. and C. (children); those who finish with the materials do inset puzzles, while teacher helps A. and B. to match colors slowly and carefully.
9:35 Self-expression (clay, painting, drawing, finger-painting), or cutting and pasting	Clay today.
9:50 Simple group table game, or pictures shown	Teacher shows large photographs of the children and they tell whose picture it is and what each child is doing; also shows photographs of group in school; then leads a finger play if attention is wandering.
10:00 Music: body rhythms; take	Photographs shown of each child again,

turns with a rhythm instrument; songs
   and child whose photograph it is walks, while all try to sing his name to the music. Sing about dog; be dogs, saying "Bow-wow." Jump, tip-toe, march, swing. Take turns beating drum to song, with piano.

10:20 Toilet if necessary
   Others look at sturdy (linen) books.

10:30 Juice and crackers
   One child passes crackers; one passes wastebasket.

10:40 Ball play with teacher
   Teacher rolls it, children seated.

10:45 Active free play
   Spring-steel horse, cardboard box to play in, inflated tube, play steps for climbing practice, and big dolls and buggy.

11:05 Toilet and wash
   While waiting for turns, use telephones; "tea party"; hammer pegs in pounding bench.

11:25 Phonograph
   Listen to "Muffin in the City," to "Put Your Finger in the Air"; march.

11:45 Lunch

12:15 Rest; toilet if necessary

12:50 Put shoes on; fold rugs; toilet and wash

1:10 Wraps on

1:30 Outdoor play
   "Mulberry Bush," "Follow the Leader"; free play with balloons; play on slide, jumping board.

2:00 Home

SAMPLE SCHEDULE FOR INTERMEDIATE GROUP

Group: Eight children, chronological ages nine to twelve years; mental ages three years to four years, three months. Length of time in school: about two years.

Date: A snowy day in January.

General Schedule	*Notes for the Day*
9:00 Wraps; jobs	Feed fish; wash out locker cupboards with sponges, soap and water. Take out name cards by lockers and give to teacher until cupboards dry. Some look at books until all are through with jobs.
9:40 Meeting ("Show and Tell")	Talk about jobs each did. Talk about name or color cards used as identification; find own card and replace it where own wraps are. Talk about color, size, and feeding of fish.
9:55 Educational toys; special individual help	Inset barrels, take-apart toys, Ben-G Boards. Teacher works with A. alone on bow-tying, then B., C. and D. together on buttoning, then E. on zipping, and F. and G. on buckling their belts.

General Schedule	*Notes for the Day*
10:20 Self-expression, or cutting and pasting	Cut out and mount pictures of people cleaning things (selected from teacher's file of pictures to be cut, or from magazines, if a child is able to cut these well enough).
10:30 Juice and crackers	Look at books while one child prepares juice and crackers.
10:40 Music	Sing about mounted pictures, about scrubbing cupboards, and about what is to be worn for snow play. Each child reads name card (larger than on locker) and then walks, while all read and sing his name. Active body rhythms.
11:00 Play	If snow is not too wet, and if it is not too cold, put on wraps to go out. Sweep and shovel snow and chase each other. (Only out a short time, because wraps will take a long time to get on and off.)
11:45 Phonograph; one at a time to washroom	Listen to "Winter Fun" and "Rhythm Band."
12:00 Lunch	
12:30 Rest	
1:00 Toilet, and wraps on	
1:15 Outdoor play	Ride on snow coaster, make snow balls.
2:00 Home	

SAMPLE SCHEDULE FOR ADVANCED GROUP

Group: Eight or nine boys and girls, chronological ages thirteen to sixteen years; mental ages four to six and a half years. Length of time in school: one to three years.

Date: A rainy day in January.

General Schedule	*Notes for the Day*
9:00 Wraps; school jobs	Look at job chart and see assignments. Water plants, dust furniture, wash piano keys, straighten books. A. and B. work on tying shoes; C. works on raincoat fastenings.
9:15 Meeting	Discuss jobs done and how to do better. Discuss each pupil's special responsibilities (e.g., keeping shoes tied, using handkerchief when necessary). Discuss calendar. Review recognition of new sign presented day before.
9:35 Craft work	Sewing cards for beginners, basting or hemming dish towels for more advanced; sewing on buttons for those who finish their towels. Practice threading needles and knotting thread.

Those pupils who finish ahead of time or who have short attention spans, work on visual perceptual materials.

10:05 Self-expression — Paint with tempera paints: Prepare to paint by having someone give out paper, another give out rags and paint brushes. Others can be donning smocks. Teacher distributes paint after boys and girls discuss the rainy day, how they feel about it and what it makes them think of. After telling about what they wear and what happens in the rain, they paint about it as they like.

10:35 Clean-up

10:45 Juice — While two pupils prepare juice and table, others tell about pictures painted.

10:55 Music — Make rain sounds with rhythm sticks. Make rain start slowly and get faster. Talk about meaning of these two words. Body rhythms: Walk, whirl, or gallop fast or slowly, depending upon the music, after telling whether music is "fast" or "slow." Be animal that moves slowly; be another kind that moves rapidly.

11:15 Active game; washroom — Bowling (while others, one at a time, go to bathroom).

11:30 Phonograph; set up for lunch — Listen to "Rainy Day" and "Let's Have an Orchestra" (pointing out parts which are fast and slow). A. and B. set lunch tables, pour milk. Teacher inspects pupils for combed hair, clean hands.

11:45 Lunch

12:15 Clean-up — C. and D. clear tables, sweep. E. washes place mats. F., G. and H. wash, wipe, and put away dishes. A. and B. make store of blocks. When others finish work, they arrange store "merchandise."

1:05 Directed games; other work indoors — Play store under teacher's direction. Use empty cans and boxes. Pay pennies, nickel, or dime for different items as marked.

1:25 Directed games outdoors if weather permits; free play if indoors — Further store play, ball play. Folk dancing if there is time.

1:50 Straighten room; wraps

2:00 Home

Appendix C

SAMPLE SCHOOL PARTIES

A PARTY FOR A BEGINNER GROUP

Duration: 60 to 90 minutes.
Occasion: The end of the school year.

Arriving with their parents, the children remove their own wraps and hang them up. Those children who are early play with a few favorite toys or with other children while the parents talk to each other and to the teacher.

When all the guests have arrived, the children have their customary music class activities (body rhythms, rhythm instruments, and songs), while the parents sit inconspicuously behind the group or to the side. Later the parents may join with the children in doing some rhythms, such as "See-Saw," and then all sit down to throw and catch a big ball.

After putting on wraps, the children and parents go outdoors and play "Mulberry Bush" or "Farmer in the Dell." Then, when all are seated in a circle on the grass, on cushions or on stools, they sing and do finger plays or action games. The teacher introduces large photographs of class activities and the children identify themselves. Those who can talk answer the teacher's questions about what they are doing in the pictures.

At refreshment time parents and children sit together at picnic tables eating ice cream from paper cups, while one child at a time passes a plate of little cookies to all the guests.

Before going home, the children may give their parents something made in school, such as a greeting card or samples of their painting or crayon drawing.

(If the weather is bad, the same activities can take place indoors.

Soft phonograph music can be played for the benefit of the children who become restless while waiting for the slower eaters.)

Duration: 60 to 90 minutes (longer if lunch is included).
Occasion: Winter holiday celebration.

Arriving with their parents, the children greet the teacher and other parents. Each child shows his parents where to put their coats, and cares for his own wraps. He tell his parents about the school plants and pets, his paintings and clay work on display, the room decorations made by the group, photographs of class activities and perhaps a scrapbook made by the group.

When all guests have gathered, the children sing songs and do some of their usual music activities. The children demonstrate a singing game or a dance and the parents then participate with them.

The parents and some of the children sit together in a large, open circle, doing finger plays or acting out a phonograph record, while the teacher or aide supervises the other children's setting of the tables.

The children sit at tables in their customary groups, taking turns in serving, while the parents sit together where they can observe the children inconspicuously. After eating, the children present their parents with gifts which they have made and wrapped. If there are presents from outsiders for the school, they may be opened at this time. Each child may then find a little present (a gingerbread boy, a picture book, a photograph of the child with his classmates in a school activity) with his name on it from the teacher or school staff. After everyone sings the "Goodby Song," it is time to go home.

A PARTY FOR AN ADVANCED GROUP

Duration: Two and a half hours.
Occasion: Spring holiday celebration.

The pupils make the following plans and preparations far in advance of the party: The boys and girls suggest games and other activities for the party. If they want a spring parade, they can make paper aprons, capes, bonnets and caps for themselves and their guests. They can practice a folk or square dance which they wish to teach their parents, and learn those games well which they will play with the guests—perhaps table games such as Bingo, Dominoes, or Parchesi.

The pupils will discuss and, through dramatization, practice greeting their guests, taking their coats, introducing them, getting their chairs, serving them refreshments, and helping them with coats.

The boys and girls may make their party tables gay by crayoning designs on paper place mats, plates and napkins. Or place mats could be cut from flowered wallpaper. Some of each pupil's art work could be selected for wall display.

Refreshments: The class might plan a very simple lunch of sandwiches and soup or a small salad; or only light refreshments could be provided, such as cookies made by the class, punch for the pupils, coffee for the parents and ice cream.

Children who need to learn table-setting, may do so in a highly motivated situation by practicing setting tables for the party. Even for light refreshments, there will need to be place mats, plates, spoons, coffee cups for the adults, glasses or cups for the pupils, napkins, cookie plates, cream, and sugar. Those who are to pour the punch and the coffee will need to learn the side from which they serve and how to refill the small pots and pitchers they use. All the group can practice passing cookies from one person to another around the table. This can be learned for daily juice-time rather than specifically for the party.

When the party day arrives, the boys and girls come an hour before the parents to arrange furniture, get refreshments partly ready, and set the tables. Each child may have been assigned certain jobs ahead of time.

The parents, upon arrival, are greeted, introduced, and shown various objects of interest in the schoolroom. All gather around the piano. The pupils sing spring songs, a few of which the parents might also sing if the song words are posted and the pupils sing them first.

After the pupils demonstrate a square dance or folk dance, they select their parents for partners and lead them in the dance. By this time all are ready to sit down for the table games. Four to six people play together, each pupil having his parents at the same table with him.

While some pupils fix the refreshments, the others, seated in a circle, play an action game with the guests, such as "Did You Ever See a Lassie?" or "Follow the Leader."

Then everyone parades in fancy hats or other spring outfits made of paper, each pupil having dressed up his own guests. When all finally march to their seats, the sons and daughters pull out chairs for their mothers. Refreshments are served as planned and eaten promptly. Everyone sings "Farewell, Ladies" and "Farewell Gentlemen." Presents made by the boys and girls are given to the parents. During the clean-up period, in which all the pupils participate as planned, the parents talk. Then the boys and girls get their parents' coats and help them on with them. If necessary, to get the enthusiastic party-goers started on their way home, a second "Good-bye" can be sung.

Appendix D

LUNCH OR JUICE-TIME BEHAVIOR

Name of Child _____   Name of Aide _____
                                      School Year _____

Date (month and day)	
Waits to eat until all are served.	
Waits to take food until passed to him.	
Takes only 1 cookie or other tidbit each time plate is passed.	
Takes serving plate from left, helps self, passes to right (or vice versa).	
Talks only when no food in mouth.	
Takes polite-sized bites.	
Chews and sips unobtrusively.	
Keeps crumbs on table.	
Breaks large pieces into smaller ones.	
Spoons food neatly, no hands in it.	
Wipes mouth and fingers effectively.	
Stays in seat until all are finished.	
Passes food without sampling.	
Passes juice or milk without spilling.	
Holds cup below edge when passing.	
Serves each child consecutively around table.	
Systematically clears table of paper trash.	

Key to Marking Chart

NC = No chance. Not being taught at present, or situation does not present itself
    at this time.

N = No.

H = Needs some adult help to complete task well.

R = Needs reminders to complete task well.

I = Independently but with adult in same room watching.

A = Completes whole task alone even when not conscious of being observed.

SAMPLE REPORT FORM:
LUNCH PREPARATION CHART

Name of Child _____   Name of Aide _____
                                   School Year _____

Date (month and day)
Washes hands.
Sets lunch boxes around tables.
Reads names.
Counts out napkins correctly.
Counts out enough cups.
Opens and closes refrigerator.
Opens milk bottles.
Fills pitchers adequately.
Carries tray from one room to another.
Napkins on left side.
Cups on right side, above place mat.
Holds cup below edge.
Gets sponge and large waste basket.
Announces that lunch is served.
Stands quietly while children sit.
Fills cups with milk—not too full.
Wipes up spilled milk with sponge.
Wipes up floor with floor rag.
Rinses rags or sponge.
Hangs rag out to dry.
Pours coffee.
Carries coffee (in cups) to adults.

Key to Marking Chart

NC = No chance. Not being taught at present, or situation does not present itself
     at this time.
N = No.
H = Needs some adult help to complete task well.
R = Needs reminders to complete task well.
I = Independently but with adult in same room watching.
A = Completes whole task alone even when not conscious of being observed.

SAMPLE REPORT FORM:
LUNCH CLEAN-UP CHART

Name of Child _____   Name of Aide _____
                                   School Year _____

Date (month and day)
Removes all dishes and papers from tables.
Moves stools against wall to aid sweeping.
Gets bowl of warm water, sponge, and
     soap.
Wipes off tables.
Rinses tables, leaving little water.
Sweeps floor systematically.
Sweeps dirt into dustpan.

Simultaneously holds dustpan and sweeps. —————|——|——|——|——|——|——|
Empties dustpan. —————|——|——|——|——|——|——|
Returns stools to places at tables. —————|——|——|——|——|——|——|
Empties trash basket. —————|——|——|——|——|——|——|
Stacks dishes in correct place. —————|——|——|——|——|——|——|
Rinses out pitchers with cold water. —————|——|——|——|——|——|——|
Fixes sink stopper. —————|——|——|——|——|——|——|
Places mat and drainer in sink. —————|——|——|——|——|——|——|
Pours detergent in dishwater. —————|——|——|——|——|——|——|
Runs enough hot water in sink. —————|——|——|——|——|——|——|
Washes dishes clean. —————|——|——|——|——|——|——|
Washes in correct order. —————|——|——|——|——|——|——|
Rinses with hot water. —————|——|——|——|——|——|——|
Wipes dishes dry. —————|——|——|——|——|——|——|
Stacks dishes in correct place. —————|——|——|——|——|——|——|
Wipes off surfaces (tables, sink). —————|——|——|——|——|——|——|
Takes mat and drainer from sink. —————|——|——|——|——|——|——|
Hangs dish towels neatly. —————|——|——|——|——|——|——|

Key to Marking Chart

NC = No chance. Not being taught at present, or situation does not present itself
    at this time.
N = No.
H = Needs some adult help to complete task well.
R = Needs reminders to complete task well.
I = Independently but with adult in same room watching.
A = Completes whole task alone even when not conscious of being observed.

SAMPLE REPORT FORM:
BATHROOM PROCEDURE CHART

Name of Child _____   Name of Aide _____
                               School Year _____

Date (month and day) —————|——|——|——|——|——|——|
Uses toilet before planning to wash. —————|——|——|——|——|——|——|
Raises seat (if boy); lowers (if girl). —————|——|——|——|——|——|——|
Stands to urinate (if boy). —————|——|——|——|——|——|——|
Wipes self (boy—when necessary). —————|——|——|——|——|——|——|
Flushes toilet. —————|——|——|——|——|——|——|
Pulls pants and overalls up straight. —————|——|——|——|——|——|——|
Zips zipper all the way and locks it. —————|——|——|——|——|——|——|
Pulls skirt down (girl). —————|——|——|——|——|——|——|
Goes to sink after toilet. —————|——|——|——|——|——|——|
Unbuttons cuffs. —————|——|——|——|——|——|——|
Pushes up sleeves. —————|——|——|——|——|——|——|
Puts stopper in. —————|——|——|——|——|——|——|
Turns on both faucets. —————|——|——|——|——|——|——|
Feels water; gets good temperature. —————|——|——|——|——|——|——|
Turns off faucets. —————|——|——|——|——|——|——|
Immerses hands in water. —————|——|——|——|——|——|——|
Rubs soap on hands. —————|——|——|——|——|——|——|
Gets hands clean before immersing. —————|——|——|——|——|——|——|
Rinses hands well. —————|——|——|——|——|——|——|

Rinses and wipes bowl.   _____|___|___|___|___|___|_____
Tears off only one or two paper towels.   _____|___|___|___|___|___|_____
Wipes both hands and backs.   _____|___|___|___|___|___|_____
Puts paper in basket.   _____|___|___|___|___|___|_____
Buttons cuffs.   _____|___|___|___|___|___|_____
Time taken (from entering to leaving
bathroom)   _____|___|___|___|___|___|_____

Key to Marking Chart

NC = No chance. Not being taught at present, or situation does not present itself
    at this time.
N = No.
H = Needs some adult help to complete task well.
R = Needs reminders to complete task well.
I = Independently but with adult in same room watching.
A = Completes whole task alone even when not conscious of being observed.

SAMPLE REPORT FORM:
MUSIC CLASS

Name: _____
Date: _____
Reported by: _____

1. Auditory Perception
   a. Tone
     _____ Sings various tones—not necessarily matching piano or teacher.
     _____ Matches tones in answer to one teacher sings.
              Sings tones pitched low _____, high _____, in medium
              range _____.
     _____ Can demonstrate or tell if tones are high or low.
     _____ Sings familiar 5-tone tune.
     _____ Sings familiar 8-tone tune.
     _____ Recognizes familiar songs and action pieces.
   b. Rhythm
     _____ Beats rhythmically (not necessarily in tempo of accompaniment).
              Own rhythm is too fast _____, too slow _____ for moderate speed
              accompaniment.
     _____ Beats instrument in time to music that has even rhythmic beats.
     _____ Beats instrument in time to music that has uneven beats (i.e. "gallop-
              ing" time).
     _____ Synchronizes body rhythm in time to music or drum beat.
              Bounces ball in time ("Bounce, Bounce, Catch") _____.
   c. Starting and Stopping
     _____ Starts and stops playing instrument or clapping when music starts and
              stops.
     _____ Starts and stops body motion when music starts and stops.
     _____ Responds to cue in music that indicates his instrument should be
              played.
   d. Volume, Quality, Tempo
     _____ Demonstrates ability to differentiate between sounds of different
              instruments.
     _____ Recognizes and responds to changes from loud to soft music.
     _____ Recognizes and responds to changes from fast to slow music.

e. Dancing
_____ Changes action when gets cue from music.
f. Follows Directions in Song or on Phonograph Record
In the music _____, words _____.
2. Attention
_____ Follows teacher's directions for starting and stopping, fast and slow, loud and soft, in hand-playing, in dancing.
_____ Stays in seat during the period, unless his turn to get up.
_____ Continues until end of piece: singing _____, beating time _____, body rhythm _____.
_____ Holds hands well in singing game.
_____ Does as well when participating with group as he does individually.
_____ Needs special help from teacher to direct his attention.
3. Orientation
_____ Learns body rhythms by watching others.
_____ In walking, stays in line.
_____ Alone, walks in a large circle around room.
_____ Walks with partner in circle behind others.
_____ In dance, faces right direction for walking after bowing to partner.
4. Language
Follows verbal instructions: stand up _____, everybody _____, behind _____, in front _____, wait _____, sit down _____.
Speech: names instruments _____, names rhythms _____, sings words of familiar songs _____.
5. Social
Participates when knows how without needing verbal encouragement in: singing _____, body rhythms _____, band _____, singing games _____, finger plays _____.
6. Emotional Tone
Appears: excited _____, enthusiastic _____, happy _____, bored _____, acts silly _____.
7. Motor Development
_____ Without reminder walks erectly, arms down, head up.
_____ Holds instruments correctly.
_____ Assumes correct position for body rhythms.
_____ Does correct motion until end of piece.

Appendix E

INSET PUZZLES

Animal Form Board. Whole shapes of four animals to be inserted (8)
Playform "Stand-up" Rubber Family. 5 pieces (8)
Playform "Stand-up" Transportation. 4 pieces (8)
Puzzles containing 6 pieces, each piece representing a whole object:
    Milkman (15)
    Policeman (15)
    Mailman (15)
    Garbage Man (15)
    Fire Engine (15)
    Service Station (15)
Pony. 8 pieces (15)
Cowboy. 12 pieces (15)
Policeman and Postman. 13 pieces (14)
Duck. 6 pieces (20)
Panda. 13 pieces (20)
Lamb. 9 pieces (20)
Airplane. 15 pieces (20)
Rudolph the Reindeer. 14 pieces (20)
Steam Shovel. 20 pieces (20)
Cow. 16 pieces (16)
Puzzles of community workers. Pieces are parts of body of each figure:
    Milkman. 8 pieces (16)
    Policeman. 10 pieces (16)
    Doctor. 10 pieces (16)

* Numbers in parentheses refer to names of manufacturers or distributors from whom these materials may be obtained. (See end of list.)

Postman. 11 pieces (16)
Susie. 12 pieces (16)
Safety Patrol. 11 pieces (16)
Fireman. 15 pieces (16)

OTHER FORM DISCRIMINATION MATERIALS

Form Peg Wagon. 4 pieces (14)
Postal Station. Holes of various shapes in large hollow mail box; "letters" (blocks) inserted in holes (20)
Coordination Board. A matching color-form board (24)
Inset Boxes. 4 small, very durable boxes of hard plastic (17)
Inset Boxes. 6 sturdy boxes of painted wood (10)
Billie and His Seven Barrels. Sturdy inset barrel halves which screw together (17)
Learning Tower. 12 inset, octagonal boxes (5)
Keys of Learning. 6 keys to insert (color- and form-matching) (5)
Fruit Plate. 3 dimensional fruits, cut in halves, thirds, quarters (20)
Playform Graded Circles, Squares, and Triangles. 12 pieces (8)
Fractional Circles. 6 circles (16)

PUT-TOGETHER AND TAKE-APART CONSTRUCTION TOYS

Interlocking Train. Only train here listed for Beginners (20)
Snap-'N'-Play. Blocks and wheels that snap together (3)
Blockraft. Pegs, blocks of various shapes, and wheels (3)
Creeper Train (14)
Tinkertoy (1)
Activity Train (14)
DeLuxe Unity Take-Apart Train (20)
Large Take-Apart Carryall Truck (20)
Minibrix. Tiny rubber bricks that fit easily together (18)
Skaneateles Train and Tracks (25)
Bolt-It. Bolts, washers, nuts, blocks, and wheels (26)

COLOR-MATCHING TOYS

Cola Carrier. 6 bottles of 6 colors, matching tops, #146 (14)
Peggy Ball Pull. 8 pegs to insert; 8 balls of same colors (20)
Color Cone. Graduated rings on a perpendicular stick (14)
Tri-Form Car (14)
Pattern Peg Tray (14)
Dolly Pull. Removable heads and colored hats to match body (20)

For Making Designs (or just for play)
Color Cubes. 2", 12 in box (20)
Landscape Peg Board, #245 (20)
Nail 'N' Peg Box (14)
Hammer-Nail Set, #511 (20)
Design Cubes, #10 (11)
Colorform. Plain geometric forms (7)
Parquetry Blocks (20)

Games
Picture Dominoes, wooden, for Beginners (10)
Picture Dominoes, velour-coated, for Beginners (9)
Picture Dominoes, large. Pictures on one side, colored domino patterns on other (4)
Hickety Pickety. Color matching (19)
Romper Room Animal Lotto (21)
Go-Together Lotto (9)
Spin and Step (19)
Picture Readiness Game (12)
Go Fish (9)
Steps to Toyland (19)
Animal Bird Fish. Card game (9)
Merry Milkman (13)
Parchesi (23)

Miscellaneous
Bingo Bed, with hammer, for pounding large pegs into bench (14)
Baby Beads, very large (14)
Bag of large wooden nuts and bolts (20)
Jumbo Beads. 1½" in diameter, 5 shapes, 6 colors (20)
½" beads. Cylinders, cubes, spheres (4)
Seequees. Going to school; trip to zoo (16)
Teach-a-Time Clock. Hour numbers fit only in their correct places (5)
Kiddiclock. Hour numbers fit only in their correct places (17)
Ben-G Reading Set. Cards 1, 2, and 3 (2)
Leather Link Belt Kits (6)

MANUFACTURERS OR DISTRIBUTORS

1. A. G. Spaulding and Brothers, Inc., 807 Greenwood Street, Evanston, Illinois.
2. Acton, H. W., 392 Hillside Avenue, Williston Park, Long Island, New York.

3. Blockraft, Inc., P.O. Box 88, Cedar Springs, Michigan.
4. Bradley, Milton, 17 Fordham Road, Allston, Boston 34, Massachusetts.
5. Child Guidance Toys (Archer Plastics, Inc.), 1125 Close Avenue, Bronx, New York.
6. Coleco Toy Products, 75 Windsor Street, Hartford, Connecticut.
7. Colorform, Walnut Street, Norwood, New Jersey.
8. Creative Playthings, 5 University Place, New York, New York.
9. Ed-U-Cards, Inc., 13-05 44th Avenue, Long Island City, New York.
10. Educational Playthings (American Crayon Company), 1706 Hayes Avenue, Sandusky, Ohio.
11. Embossing Company, 3610 Touhy Avenue, Chicago, Illinois.
12. Garrard Press, 510–522 North Hickory Street, Champaign, Illinois.
13. Hassenfeld Brothers, Inc., 1033 Broad Street, Central Falls, Rhode Island.
14. Holgate Company, 200 Fifth Avenue, New York, New York.
15. Joseph K. Strauss Products Corporation, 257 Varet Street, Brooklyn, New York.
16. Judy Company, 310 North Second Street, Minneapolis, Minnesota.
17. Kiddicraft "Sensible" Toys, Inc., 732 Third Street, Niagara Falls, New York.
18. Minibrix, 130 South Park Avenue, Buffalo, New York.
19. Parker Brothers, Inc., 190 Bridge Street, Salem, Massachusetts.
20. Playskool, 1750 North Lawndale Avenue, Chicago, Illinois.
21. Saalfield, Saalfield Square, Akron, Ohio.
22. Samuel Gabriel and Sons, Inc., 200 Fifth Avenue, New York, New York.
23. Selchow and Righter Company, 200 Fifth Avenue, New York, New York.
24. Sifo Company, 353 Rosabel Street, St. Paul, Minnesota.
25. Skaneateles Handicrafter, Skaneateles, New York.
26. Toycraft Corporation, 1139 South Wabash Avenue, Chicago, Illinois.

Appendix F

* Numbers in parentheses refer to names of books in which these songs, games, and dances may be found. (See end of list.)

The Little Gray Ponies (10)
Pony Song (4)
Cowboy (6)
Tramp, Tramp, Tramping, Tramping (10)
Turtle (6)
Giants (6)
Fall Song (7)
The Bear Went Over the Mountain (10)
Fly Away, Little Birdie (10)
Elephant (7)
Waddling Ducks (10)
Garden Gate (6)
Walking in the Sunshine (7)
Advanced:
Dance So Merrily (6)
Various rhythms for swaying, leaping, and combinations of rhythms (1)

FOR BODY RHYTHMS OR MOTIONS
EMPHASIZING AUDITORY PERCEPTION

Intermediate:
Pony Song (5)
Top (7)
Jack in the Box (4)
Jack Be Nimble (3)
Advanced:
Various rhythms in (1)

FOR SINGING GAMES

Beginner:
This Is the Way We Wash Our Hands (10)
Playing Ball—rolling ball (9)
See-Saw, Sacradown (10)
Row, Row, Row Your Boat (12)
Ring Around a Rosie (11)
Farmer in the Dell (11)
Train (4)
Intermediate:
Did You Ever See a Lassie (11)

Walking Song (2)
Tell Us What's Your Name (3)
Follow, Follow, Follow Me (1)
We're Dancing Around the Christmas Tree (4)
Walking Down the Street (7)
This Is the Way We Wash Our Hands—for Halloween words (10)
Advanced:
Looby Loo (11)
Hokie Pokie (1)

FOR PLAY-ACTING

Intermediate:
Barber (2)
Postman (6)
Traffic Man (2)
Clown (7)
Cowboy (6)
Rag Doll (2)
Let's Go Walking (5)
Coasting (10)
Resting Time (10)
Balloon Man (6)
Carpenter (9)
Indians (7)
Spring Time (5)
The Snow Is Falling Down (10)
This Is the Way My Dolly Walks (8)
Out We Go with a Hippity Hop (10)
Oh, Where Is My Little Dog Gone (2)
Hop, Little Bunny (10)
The Little Gray Ponies (10)
Animals Wake Up (4)
Sleepy Animals (4)
Skaters' Waltz (2)
Roller Skating (2)

FOR RHYTHM INSTRUMENT ACTIVITIES

Beginner:
Ding, Dong, Ding (6)

Jingle Bells (11)
Intermediate:
  How We Love to Clap Our Hands (10)
  Christmas Bells Are Ringing (7)
  Jingle Bells (11)
  Big Tall Indian (4)
  Wooden Shoes (6)
  Moon and Stars (6)
  Tambourine (4)
Advanced:
  Train Song (5)
  Theme from Haydn's Surprise Symphony (2)
  Pop Goes the Weasel (11)
  Tambourine (4)

FOR DANCING

Intermediate:
  Step, and Make a Bow (7)
  How Do You Do, My Partner (8)
  Dancing (7)
  Clap, Clap, Bow (8)
  Jump, Jump (2)
  Dance So Merrily (6)
  Bow Belinda (13)
Advanced:
  Swing Dance (6)
  Seven Steps (2)
  Jing Jang (2)
  Ach Ya (13)
  Rig a Jig Jig (11)
  Buffalo Gal (12)
  Skip to My Lou (13)
  Shoe Maker (13)

FOR SINGING

Beginner:
  Big Tall Indian (4)
  Rain Song (4)

Chickens (7)
Wind (7)
Snowflakes (4)
The Train (4)
Crow (6)
Robin (6)
The Animals Wake Up (4)
I Can Sing a Little Song (6)
Old MacDonald (11)
Going to School. Change to "Good-bye Everybody, It's Time to
  Go" (9)
Oh, I Have a Kitty (6)
Intermediate:
Farm (9)
Halloween (4)
Easter Eggs (5)
Raining (6)
Hey, Betty Martin (2)
What Shall I Wear (9)
Clock (5)
Snow, Snow (7)
Snowman (4)
Twinkle, Twinkle, Little Star (11)
Apple Tree (4)
Lollipops (6)
Colors (6)
Ding-a-Ling (2)
Ding, Dong, Ding (6)
Bow Wow Wow (6)
Advanced:
Thanksgiving (7)
Good Night, Ladies (12)
Jingle Bells (11)
Row, Row, Row Your Boat (12)
Row Your Boat, Boys (4) ·
Buffalo Gal (12)
Oh, How Lovely Is the Evening (11)
Home on the Range (12)
She'll Be Coming 'Round the Mountain (12)
Yankee Doodle (11)

Chorus only for each of the following:
Battle Hymn of the Republic (2)
Wait for the Wagon (2)
Columbia, the Gem of the Ocean (2)
I've Been Working on the Railroad (12)
Blue Tail Fly (12)
We Wish You a Merry Christmas (12)

MUSIC BOOKS

1. Andrews, Gladys. *Creative Rhythmic Movement for Children.* Englewood Cliffs, New Jersey: Prentice Hall, Inc., 1954.
2. Beattie, John W. *American Singer,* Book I. New York: American Book Co., 1954.
3. Coit, Lottie Ellsworth, and Bampton, Ruth. *Follow the Music.* Boston: C. C. Birchard and Co., 1948.
4. Coleman, Satis N. *Singing Time.* New York: John Day, 1929.
5. Coleman, Satis N., and Alice G. Thorn. *Another Singing Time.* New York: John Day, 1937.
6. Crowninshield, Ethel. *New Songs and Games.* Boston: Boston Music Co., 1938.
7. ———*The Sing and Play Book.* Boston: Boston Music Co., 1941.
8. Hamlin, A. P., and M. G. Guessford, *Singing Games for Children.* Cincinnati: Willis Music Co., 1948.
9. Le Bron, Marion, and Grace Martin Olson. *I Love to Sing.* Cincinnati: Willis Music Co., 1942.
10. MacCarteney, Laura Pendleton. *Songs for the Nursery School.* Cincinnati: Willis Music Co., 1937.
11. Wessells, Kathryn Tyler. *Golden Song Book.* New York: Simon and Schuster, 1945.
12. Wilson, Harry. *Sing Along.* New York: J. J. Robbins and Sons, 1949.
13. Tobitt, Janet E. *Promenade All.* New York: Janet E. Tobitt, 228 East 43d Street, 1947.

Appendix G

SELECTED BOOKS FOR CHILDREN

Beginners' books have one large picture per page. The text is brief and relates to the child's immediate environment:

Britcher, Phyliss (pseud. Romney Gay). *Cinder.* New York: Grosset & Dunlap, 1938.

Jackson, Kathryn, and Byron Jackson. *Busy Timmy.* New York: Simon & Schuster, 1948.

Lenski, Lois. *Davy's Day.* New York: Oxford University Press, 1943.
———— *Papa Small.* New York: Oxford University Press, 1951.

Steiner, Charlotte. *Kiki and Muffy.* Doubleday & Co., 1943.

Young, Edward W., and William Hayes. *Norman and the Nursery School.* New York: The Platt & Munk Co.

Clear pictures and simple subjects and stories are especially good for Intermediates:

Lenski, Lois. *Spring is Here.* New York: Oxford University Press, 1945.

Lindman, Marjorie. *Snipp, Snapp, Snurr and the Big Farm.* Chicago: A. Whitman & Co., 1946.
———— *Flicka, Ricka, Dicka and a Little Dog.* Chicago: A. Whitman & Co., 1946.

Large pictures are helpful for pointing out objects and for discussion:

Fletcher, Sydney. *The Big Book of Real Building and Wrecking Machines.* New York: Grosset & Dunlap, 1951.

Large, clear photographs interest most trainables:

Doisneau, Robert. *1,2,3,4,5.* Philadelphia: J. B. Lippincott Co., 1956.

Sterling, Dorothy. *Sophie and her Puppies*. New York: Doubleday & Co., 1951.

Tensen, Ruth. *Come to the City*. Chicago: Reilly & Lee Co., 1951.

—— *Come to the Pet Shop*. Chicago: Reilly & Lee Co., 1952.

Ylla (pseud. Camilla Koffler). *Duck*. New York: Harper & Brothers, 1952.

Particularly lovely illustrations give these books special appeal:

Carroll, Ruth. *Where's the Bunny?* New York: Oxford University Press, 1950.

Gay, Zhenya. *Look!* New York: The Viking Press, 1952.

Hader, Bertha, and Elmer Hader. *Home on the Range*. New York: The Macmillan Co., 1955.

—— *The Big Snow*. New York: The Macmillan Co., 1948.

Ward, Lynd. *The Biggest Bear*. Boston: Houghton Mifflin Co., 1952.

Zolotow, Charlotte. *Over and Over*. New York: Harper & Brothers, 1957.

Facts should be explained by clear pictures and simple text:

Birnbaum, A. *Green Eyes*. New York: Capitol, 1953.

Foster, Polly, and Larry Foster. *Your Parakeet*. Chicago: Melmont, 1958.

Heffelenger, Jane. *Firemen*. Chicago: Melmont, 1957.

Hull, John. *Big and Little*. New York: Grosset & Dunlap, 1957.

Lenski, Lois. *Cowboy Small*. New York: Oxford University Press, 1949.

—— *The Little Auto*. New York: Oxford University Press, 1951.

Mitchell, Lucy Sprague. *Fix it, Please*. New York: Simon & Schuster, 1947.

Podendorf, Illa. *The True Book of Seasons*. Chicago: Childrens Press, 1955.

Puner, Helen Walker. *Daddies: What they do all Day*. New York: Lothrop, Lee, & Shepard, 1946.

Radlauer, Ruth Shaw. *Fathers at Work*. Chicago: Melmont, 1958.

Rey, Harris Augusto. *Where's my Baby*. Boston: Houghton Mifflin Co., 1943.

Scarr, Grace. *The Little Red House*. New York: William R. Scott, 1955.

Schloat, G. Warren, Jr. *The Wonderful Egg*. New York: Scribner, 1952.

Udry, Janice. *A Tree Is Nice*. New York: Harper & Brothers, 1956.
Weber, Irma E. *Up Above and Down Below*. New York: William R. Scott, 1943.
Wright, Ethel. *Saturday Walk*. New York: William R. Scott, 1954.
Zion, Gene. *All Falling Down*. New York: Harper & Brothers, 1951.

Auditory perception and speech can be encouraged:
Brown, Margaret Wise. *The Noisy Book*. New York: William R. Scott, 1939.
Crampton, Gertrude. *Noises and Mr. Flibberty-Jib*. New York: Simon & Schuster, 1948.
Earle, Vana. *The Busy Man and the Night-time Noises*. New York: Lothrop, Lee, & Shepard, 1954.
Flack, Marjorie. *Angus and the Ducks*. New York: Doubleday & Co., 1930.
—— *Ask Mr. Bear*. New York: The Macmillan Co., 1958.
Kessler, Ethel, and Leonard Kessler. *Big Red Bus*. New York: Doubleday & Co., 1957.

Intermediates and Advanced can appreciate humorous books with fairly realistic stories:
Gág, Wanda. *Snippy and Snappy*. New York: Coward-McCann, 1931.
Hurd, Edith Thatcher, and Clement Hurd. *Mr. Charlie's Gas Station*. Philadelphia: J. B. Lippincott, 1956.
Krauss, Ruth. *The Carrot Seed*. New York: Harper & Brothers, 1945.
McCloskey, Robert. *Blueberries for Sal*. New York: The Viking Press, 1948.
Slobodking, Esophyr. *Caps for Sale*. New York: William R. Scott (lib. ed.).

Trainables may find it helpful to know that other children must make adjustments to new situations:
Beim, Lorraine, and Jerrold Beim. *Two Is a Team*. New York: Harcourt, Brace & Co., 1945.
Bryant, Bernice. *Let's Be Friends*. Chicago: Childrens Press, 1954.
Flack, Marjorie. *Wait for William*. Boston: Houghton Mifflin Co., 1935.
Green, Mary McBurney. *Is It Hard? Is It Easy?* New York: William R. Scott, 1948.
Kay, Helen. *One Mitten Lewis*. New York: Lothrop, Lee & Shepard, 1955.

Bibliography

Books listed here are in addition to those listed at the end of each chapter. These are of a more general nature and were used by the author primarily for reference.

Albright, M. Arline. *Not So Fast: The Retarded Child Can Be Taught Self-Management.* Milwaukee: Milwaukee Association for Retarded Children.

Amoss, Harry, et al. *Suggested Classroom Activities for Trainable Retarded Children.* Toronto: The Ryerson Press, 1954. (Distributed in the United States by the National Association for Retarded Children, Inc., 386 Park Avenue South, New York.)

Association for the Help of Retarded Children, Inc. *Specialized Rehabilitation Training for Mentally Retarded Young Adults.* New York: Association for the Help of Retarded Children, Inc., 200 Fourth Avenue, 1958.

—— *Vocational Training Center and Sheltered Workshop for Mentally Retarded Adults.* New York: Association for the Help of Retarded Children, Inc., 200 Fourth Avenue, 1957.

Baumgartner, Bernice B. *A Curriculum Guide for Teachers of Trainable Mentally Handicapped Children.* Springfield, Illinois: Office of the Superintendent, 1955. (Distributed by the Illinois Council for Retarded Children, 343 South Dearborn Avenue, Chicago.)

Bensberg, Gerard J. "Concept Learning in Mental Defectives as a Function of Appropriate and Inappropriate 'Attention Sets,' " *Dissertation Abstracts* (January, 1958), pp. 673–74.

Child Craft Advisory Service. *What Can I Do Now, Mother?* Chicago: Field Enterprise, Inc., 1954.

Clarke, Ann M., and A. D. B. Clarke. *Mental Deficiency: The Changing Outlook.* Glencoe, Illinois: The Free Press, 1958.

Davies, Stanley Powell. *The Mentally Retarded in Society.* New York: Columbia University Press, 1959.

Eisenburger, Helen, and Larry Eisenburger. *The Omnibus of Fun.* New York: Association Press, 1956.

Fils, David. *Program for Severely Retarded Children: A Pilot Study of a Public School Educational and Training Program for Children Who Are Mentally Retarded.* Los Angeles: Office of Los Angeles County Superintendent of Schools, 1955.

Graham, Ray. I Have a Conviction (mimeographed speech). Springfield, Illinois: Office of Public Instruction, 1952.

Hudson, Margaret. *Identification and Evaluation of Methods for Teaching Severely Retarded (Trainable) Children.* Nashville: George Peabody College for Teachers, 1959.

Johns, Ray, and David F. De March. *Community Organization and Agency Responsibility.* New York: Association Press, 1951.

Johns, Ray. *Executive Responsibility.* New York: Association Press, 1954.

Johnson, G. Orville. *Training Program for Severely Mentally Retarded Children.* Albany: New York State Inter-Departmental Health Resources Board, 11 North Pearl Street, 1958.

Johnson, G. Orville, and Rudolph J. Capobianco. *Research Project on Severely Retarded Children.* Albany: New York State Inter-Departmental Health Resources Board, 11 North Pearl Street, 1957.

Kolstoe, Oliver K. "Language Training of Low-Grade Mongoloid Children," *American Journal of Mental Deficiency,* LXIII (July, 1958), 17–30.

Lassman, Grace Harris. *Language for the Preschool Deaf Child.* New York: Grune and Stratton, 1950.

MacPherson, Marion White. "Learning and Mental Deficiency," *American Journal of Mental Deficiency,* LXII (March, 1958), 870–77.

Montgomery County, Maryland, Public Schools. *Guide for Teachers of Trainable Retarded Children.* Bulletin No. 140. Montgomery County, Maryland: The Public Schools, 1955.

National Association for Retarded Children, Teacher Recruitment Sub-Committee. *Opportunities for Professional Preparation in the Field of Education of Mentally Handicapped Children.* New York: National Association for Retarded Children, Inc., 386 Park Avenue South, 1957.

Plimpton, Edna. *Your Workshop.* New York: The Macmillan Co., 1932.

Rosenzweig, Louis E., and Julia Long. *Teaching the Dependent Retardate*. Darien, Connecticut: Educational Publishing Corporation, 1960.

Saenger, Gerhart. *The Adjustment of Severely Retarded Adults in the Community*. Albany: New York State Inter-Departmental Health Resources Board, 11 North Pearl Street, 1957.

St. Paul Department of Education. *A Study of School Children with Severe Mental Retardation: Research Project No. 6*. St. Paul: Department of Education, Statistical Division, 1953.

San Diego County Board of Education. *Suggested Activities for Special Training Classes*. San Diego: Office of the Superintendent of Schools, San Diego County, 209 Civic Center, 1958.

San Francisco Unified School District, Atypical Department. *Curriculum Materials for the Severely Mentally Retarded*. San Francisco: San Francisco Unified School District, 135 Van Ness Avenue, 1956.

Stevens, Harvey A. "A Curriculum for the Trainable Child," *Southern Wisconsin Colony and Training School Bulletin*. Union Grove, Wisconsin: March 1, 1953.

Williams, Harold M., and J. E. Wallace Wallin. *Education of the Severely Retarded Child: A Bibliographical Review*. Bulletin No. 12. Washington, D.C.: U.S. Government Printing Office, U.S. Department of Health, Education, and Welfare, 1959.

Wood, Donald E. *The Adjusted Curriculum for the "Trainable" or Severely Mentally Retarded*. Normal, Illinois: Illinois State Normal University, 1953.

General Index

Index to Craft Projects
and Games